Virtue, Fortune, and Faith

BORDERLINES

For more books in the series, see p. vi.

Virtue, Fortune, and Faith

A Genealogy of Finance

MARIEKE DE GOEDE

BORDERLINES, VOLUME 24

University of Minnesota Press

Minneapolis

London

Parts of chapter 2 originally appeared as "Mastering Lady Credit: Discourses of Financial Crisis in Historical Perspective," *International Feminist Journal of Politics* 2, no. 1 (2000). Reprinted by permission of Taylor and Francis, http://www.tandf.co.uk.

Parts of chapter 5 originally appeared as "Discourses of Scientific Finance and the Failure of LTCM," *New Political Economy* 6, no. 2 (2001). Reprinted by permission of Taylor and Francis, http://www.tandf.co.uk.

Published by the University of Minnesota Press
111 Third Avenue South, Suite 290
Minneapolis, MN 55401-2520
http://www.upress.umn.edu

Library of Congress Cataloging-in-Publication Data

Goede, Marieke de, 1971–
    Virtue, fortune, and faith : a genealogy of finance / Marieke de Goede.
        p.   cm. — (Borderlines ; 24)
    Includes bibliographical references and index.
    ISBN 0-8166-4414-4 (hc) — ISBN 0-8166-4415-2 (pb)
    1. Finance—History. 2. Economics—History. 3. Money—History.
4. Value—History. 5. Speculation—History. I. Title. II. Borderlines
(Minneapolis, Minn.) ; v. 24.
    HG171.G637 2005
    332'.09—dc22

                                                                2004022501

Printed in the United States of America on acid-free paper

The University of Minnesota is an equal-opportunity educator and employer.

12 11 10 09 08 07 06 05   10 9 8 7 6 5 4 3 2 1

to Marietje de Goede–de Lorijn,
in memory

BORDERLINES

Contents

Preface

The "New York Stock and Exchange Board" received its constitution in 1820; since which time it has become the scene of the most stupendous gambling operations, unchecked by public opinion, and unbridled by legislative restrictions. . . . Stock-gambling . . . is unblushingly practised by "gentlemen" in "the best society."

UNITED STATES MAGAZINE AND
DEMOCRATIC REVIEW, 1846

This book discusses how modern finance has acquired the reputation of economic necessity and scientific respectability when less than two centuries ago it stood condemned as irreputable gambling and fraud. The *United States Magazine and Democratic Review* argued that trading in stocks and credit certificates "has opened a road to the possession of great means . . . far shorter and more agreeable to the successful than the old beaten and irksome track of perseverance and industry. It is a means greatly to be deprecated. It is subject to all the chances of a game of hazard, when conducted in good faith, and susceptible of endless varieties of fraud under the guidance of persons destitute of principle" (1846, 83). Instead of being created through gambling and chance, the *Democratic Review* concluded, "all the wealth of a nation must necessarily consist of the proceeds of the industry of its inhabitants" (83).

This condemnation of stock trading practices stands in sharp contrast with the image of finance at the turn of the twenty-first

century, when financial expertise and specialist literature have proliferated and when it has become a moral imperative *not* to let one's
money "sit idle," for instance, in a savings account, but to look for
the highest investment returns. Financial speculation as a means of
income has acquired popular legitimacy, and financial theory has
acquired scientific respectability. To be sure, episodes of perceived
crisis and scandal in the financial markets can still lead to critique
and condemnation, as has occurred since the end of the so-called
dot-com boom of the 1990s. However, the fundamental morality
of investment practice, the science of financial theory, and the respectability of the financial profession are now rarely questioned.
Contemporary financial critiques concern mainly the excesses of
crisis, which simultaneously depoliticizes a presupposed domain of
"normal" finance. In this book, I aim to disturb the depoliticized
nature of finance theory and practice through a genealogical reading of the historical struggles, debates, controversies, insecurities,
and ambiguities that had to be purged from nascent credit practices
in order to produce the image of today's coherent and—largely—
rational global financial sphere. I discuss some of the moral, religious, and political transformations that have slowly constructed
the domain of finance as a legitimate, rational, and, above all, *natural* practice. These transformations concern the way in which the
virtue of financial practice was articulated in contrast to gendered
representations of *fortune,* and the *faith* that underpins the imagination of finance as a science.

These moral and political transformations should not be seen as
secondary to or separate from the emergence of material financial
networks, but are at the heart of the ways in which the institutions
of modern finance have taken shape. These debates have determined
the legal, political, and moral spaces in which modern finance operates. Moreover, the conceptual and moral struggles and debates documented here were not historical aberrations or temporary hurdles on
the path to modern finance, but remain unresolved and politically
relevant today.

This project has traveled a long way since its first insecure steps at
the Research Centre for International Political Economy (RECIPE)
at the University of Amsterdam in 1997. I am grateful, first of all,
to the funding bodies that have made it possible. These were in
1997–98, the Netherlands-America Commission for Educational

Exchange (NACEE), the Netherlands-America Foundation (NAF), and the New School Vera List Foundation; in 1998–99, the Prins Bernhard Fonds, the Stichting Doctor Catharine van Tussenbroek Fonds, and the Fundatie van de Vrijvrouwe van Renswoude; in 1999–2001, the British Council Chevening Scholarship Programme; and in 2001–2, the Economic and Social Research Council (ESRC) Postdoctoral Fellowship program. Thanks also to the British International Studies Association (BISA) and the International Federation of University Women (IFUW) in Geneva for their travel grants.

Many thanks to my editors at the University of Minnesota Press, Mike Shapiro and Carrie Mullen. For the use of the images in this book, many thanks to Eric and Liz Davis and to Chris Mullen of the University of Brighton School of Design. Special thanks to J. S. G. Boggs.

Without Marianne Marchand's enthusiastic support, this project might have never come off the ground. I wish to thank her for her continuing advice. Many thanks to the participants of the 1997–98 Culture/Knowledge Pro-Seminar at the New School University in New York. I am grateful especially to Eli Zaretsky for his enthusiasm for and contributions to this project.

I would like to thank the Department of Politics of the University of Newcastle upon Tyne for a three-year tuition waiver and for providing a pleasant working environment. Thanks to heads of department Tim Gray and Peter Jones and to Ella Ritchie for being my ESRC mentor. This manuscript has benefited enormously from debate and criticism by colleagues and friends: many thanks to Ana Clara Barbara, Alex Betancourt-Serrano, Phil Cerny, Teun van Dijk, John Hobson, Paul Langley, Mika Luoma-Aho, Christiane Miller, Katrin Mohr, Ronen Palan, Kees van der Pijl, Magnus Ryner, and Ralph. I am grateful to the participants of the 2002 workshop "Approaches to Global Finance" at the University of Warwick. Many thanks to Timothy Sinclair, who has supported my work for many years. Special thanks to Jenny Edkins, Tony Porter, and Nigel Thrift for their support during the review process and their many excellent suggestions. I wish to thank Bastiaan van Apeldoorn, who continues to challenge my thinking. I owe Martin Coward for his many critical readings of this manuscript, which have helped it take shape. Randall Germain has greatly supported my work and generously shared his academic insights and experience, for which I am grateful. Special thanks to David Campbell, whose enthusiastic commitment to this project has given it direction and drive. I am lucky to have as friend and colleague Louise Amoore, and I thank her for her contributions to my work, which knows many forms. My thanks also to Erna Rijsdijk, who is a challenging intellectual and excellent friend, and who continues to shape my thinking through our many discussions.

I am grateful to my friends Danielle Freriks, Elke Veldkamp, and Liedwien Wit, and to my brother, Jeroen de Goede, who have all supported my decision to live abroad and enthusiastically traveled to visit me during these years. I wish to thank my parents, Meu and Cyrano de Goede, who have encouraged me to pursue my curiosity. I owe my husband Gunther Irmer for his many contributions to this book. His fearless commitment to fatherhood makes my work possible. Our son Caspar, born in the middle of my writing this book, has enriched my life beyond words.

Introduction
Money and Representation

In November 1987 American artist J. S. G. Boggs was ordered to appear before London's Central Criminal Court (also known as the Old Bailey) to face charges brought against him by the Bank of England under the 1981 Forgery and Counterfeiting Act. Boggs was charged with neither forgery nor counterfeiting but with reproducing British banknotes without consent of the Bank of England. Although the artist had attempted to obtain written permission from the bank to produce artistic images freely based on the design of the British currency on two occasions, permission had been denied. This denial was affirmed even after Boggs had provided the bank's governor with slides of his work, pleading that "this was an unusual case but insisting that [it] was a serious artistic endeavor deserving of serious attention" (Boggs quoted in Wenschler 1999, 73). The bank did take the matter seriously, and just before the opening of an exhibition around the theme of money in a small gallery in London, three detectives of Scotland Yard arrested Boggs and confiscated his artworks. Boggs was questioned and released in the care of his solicitor in anticipation of the trial at the Old Bailey.

Boggs had begun his performance art around the themes of money and value about five years earlier, when a waitress in a Chicago diner accepted an impromptu drawing of a dollar bill as a payment for coffee and insisted on giving him the change he was due. "This," Boggs later recalled to *New Yorker* journalist Lawrence Wenschler (1999,

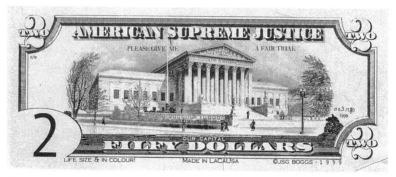

Figure 1. J. S. G. Boggs, "American Supreme Justice $2 Bill," 1999. Courtesy of J. S. G. Boggs.

17), "set me to thinking: what was it that she valued so much? Was it the way the drawing mimicked a regular dollar bill? or the fact that she'd sat and watched me do all the work?" The encounter led Boggs to do a series of experiments in which he "spent" drawings of banknotes (including British, Swiss, American, and Australian ones) and insisted on receiving both receipts and appropriate change for the transaction. For Boggs, all the different components of the economic transaction together (the drawing of the bill, change, receipt, items bought) form the artworks, which are increasingly sought after by art collectors. Boggs never sells his painted banknotes directly, although they now regularly fetch ten times their face value. Nor does Boggs mislead his accomplices in these transactions: he makes it perfectly clear that the banknote drawings are artworks and not actual banknotes and that the receiver is taking a risk or a gamble in accepting them. In spite of encountering anything from skepticism to outright hostility in attempting to spend his drawings, Boggs estimated that by the time of the trial in the Old Bailey he had spent around US$100,000 in his own currency.

This intersection of art and money that allows Boggs to (sometimes) spend his drawings but is perceived as a profound threat by the Bank of England raises a number of questions concerning money and representation that are, as I will argue, highly pertinent to the politics of international finance. Boggs's transactions provoke a moment of thought in naturalized economic practices; they are "brief, momentary tears in the ordinarily seamless fabric of taken-for-granted mundanity" (Wenschler 1999, 49). Thus Boggs disturbs the

ordinary functioning of money, which depends on the prior forgetting of the controversial and contestable nature of its value. "Money
works best," sociologists Carruthers and Babb observe in their study
of late-nineteenth-century U.S. monetary debates, "when it can be
taken for granted, when its value, negotiability, and neutrality can
be simply assumed" (1996, 1556). Boggs's performances force to
the surface these forgotten negotiations necessary for the smooth
functioning of money. They force economic participants to consider
a number of questions, beginning with what Wenschler describes as
"small perturbations" but expanding into "true tremblors": "What
is art? What is money? What is the one worth? What the other?
What is *worth* worth? How does value itself arise, and live, and gut-
ter out?" (1999, 23; emphasis in original).

This book coincides with Boggs's questions by inquiring into the
historical, cultural, and discursive constitution of modern finance.
It discusses how present financial instruments and entitlements are
legitimized through financial discourses such that they are taken as
natural reality. As Nigel Thrift argues, current debates on the world
economy are all too often founded on a "discourse of transcendental
rationality, on a notion of a single, correct, God's eye view of reason which transcends the way human beings . . . think, and which
imparts the idea of a world that is centrally organised [and] rigidly
bounded" (1996, 13). In contrast to the discourse of transcendental
rationality, I consider economic and financial discourses as historically contingent and dependent on cultural practices of valuation.
As Michael Shapiro puts it, by considering "valuing . . . [as] a radically contingent, spatio-temporally delimited practice, not a process
of discovering stable features of . . . the world, . . . we can engage in
inquiry as to how 'value' arises from historically situated human actions and involvements" (1997, 60; see also Shapiro 1993, 45–86).

I will argue that money, capital, and finance are not unmediated
economic realities that can be taken as a starting point to academic
inquiry but have been made possible through contested historical
articulations and practices of valuation. Both economics itself and
political economy as fields of inquiry often fail to address the questions raised by Boggs's performances, considering money and capital, instead, to be unproblematic material resources (Nitzan 1998,
169–74). Despite his emphasis on the importance of social relations and information for the international organization of credit,

for example, Germain still sees credit at least partly as "a material resource . . . [it] can exist in several forms: as cash, bank balances, lines of credit, or as an enforced right" (1997, 17). In this book, I will argue instead that financial instruments and practices are discursively constituted and firmly rooted in cultural, moral, political, and religious history. A closer look at money and credit makes it impossible to abstract them from practices of representation. An uncritical acceptance of the categories and containers of value offered by the financial industry, moreover, limits political economy's scope for criticism. My purpose is to criticize priorities of value that are entrenched in the modern economy and that have been depoliticized by the technical and rational appearance of financial practices. In the remainder of this introduction, I will offer a number of examples that demonstrate the inextricability of money and representation, before setting out the contours of the argument to follow.

MONEY, DISCOURSE, AUTHORITY

The mystical value of paper money has been a topic of public debate and political struggle on many occasions before the circulation of Western currencies became taken for granted, to be disturbed only by rare occurrences such as Boggs's performances. For example, in his *Structures of Everyday Life,* Fernand Braudel documents how during the siege of Tournay in 1745 lack of money made it difficult to pay the soldiers, whereupon "someone thought of borrowing 7000 florins from the canteens. It was all there was in them. By the end of the week, the seven thousand florins had returned to the canteens from which the same sum was once more borrowed. This was then repeated seven weeks until the surrender, so that the same seven thousand florins had the effect of forty-nine thousand" (1981, 468). The alchemy-like qualities of credit puzzled and mystified those who came in contact with it during the slow emergence of paper money in seventeenth- and eighteenth-century Western Europe. As Braudel argues, credit and paper money caused disruptions in the structures of everyday life, sharp variations in prices, and forced breaks with custom and tradition (436–78). This was particularly so for bills of exchange and bookkeeping money, types of "money which [were] not money at all, and this juggling of money and bookkeeping to a point where the two became confused, seemed not only complicated but diabolical" (471). As I will show, the alliance between money and the devil has appeared many times in the Western imagination (see also Shell 1995, 63–72). Braudel's point to be stressed here is that the introduction of credit, paper money, and other modern monetary instruments was not a smooth or evolutionary process but a controversial, contingent, and ambiguous transformation, firmly rooted in cultural history.

One important public debate that hinged on the question of money and representation was the U.S. greenback debate that took place between the end of the Civil War and the return to the gold standard in 1879. Greenbacks were the first paper banknotes that were not redeemable in gold or silver, and they were issued by the Union states to finance military expenses during the Civil War. By the end of the war, an estimated US$450 million was circulating in greenbacks, and a political debate ensued over the question of whether these should be made redeemable in gold or silver specie. This was a truly public debate, in contrast with present disputes around money and finance that are often technical and depoliticized. "Defining American currency," sociologist Viviana Zelizer writes, "became one of the most explosive political and social issues of the late nineteenth century" (1994, 14; see also Zelizer 1999). On one side of the debate were "gold-bugs," who argued that irredeemable paper money was socially and morally unacceptable and that gold was the natural embodiment of (monetary) value. Gold was argued to possess intrinsic value independent of authority and legislation, and "the fact that gold and silver were mined out of the ground, coming from nature itself," bolstered this argument (Carruthers and Babb 1996, 1567; see also O'Malley 1994, 380). On the other side were the "greenbackers," who argued that the creation of fiduciary money was part of the natural progress of economic civilization and therefore morally legitimate (Carruthers and Babb 1996, 1571). Although the dividing lines in the greenback debate can partly be attributed to social hierarchies, because bankers, financiers, and other creditors stood to lose most from the inflation caused by circulation of greenbacks (Frieden 1997, 218–22), the debate is not simply reducible to calculating economic interests. The very definitions of economic interests were being contested, driven by "conflicting conceptions of both money and the economy" (Carruthers and Babb 1996, 1566).

The U.S. greenback debate illustrates not just that the value of money is politically contestable, but also that cultural, moral, and social arguments are inseparable from economic ones, which is often overlooked by political and economic explanations of the gold standard (e.g., Frieden 1997; Livingston 1986, 71–125). On the occasion of the first issuance of greenbacks in 1862, Representative George Pendleton protested: "You send these notes out into the world stamped with irredeemability. You put on them the mark of Cain, and, like Cain, they will go forth to be vagabonds and fugitives of the earth" (quoted in Shell 1982, 7). U.S. resistance to paper money lamented the ghostlike and diabolical properties of it. This was exacerbated by the widespread existence not just of counterfeit notes but also of "phantom notes," issued by nonexistent banks (Shell 1982, 5–8; Gilbert 1998). One famous image supporting the gold-bugs, drawn by the political cartoonist Thomas Nast,[1] was titled "Milk-Tickets for Babies, in Place of Milk," published in 1876. The cartoon depicts a rag baby, representing inflation, being fed a piece of paper on which is written, "This is MILK by Act of Congress." On the wall behind the baby is written, "This is not a rag baby but a REAL baby by Act of Congress." On a picture of a cow, pasted to the wall behind the rag baby, Nast wrote, "This is a COW by the act of the artist," and on a picture of a house, Nast wrote, "This is a house and lot, by act of the architect" (quoted in Shell 1982, 6, 220). Nast's image captured the anxiety of gold-bugs over the fictitious creation of monetary value. Paper money, they maintained, was *real* when it could be redeemed for gold or silver at the bank and deceitful when it could not. "If we shall once get the thought fairly and fully into our minds of the difference between a thing and the representative of a thing we will be comparatively safe," said gold supporter General Garfield in a speech before the Honest Money League in 1879 (quoted in Carruthers and Babb 1996, 1568).

The issue of reality and representation—of "real" value embodied by gold versus intangible faith in paper money—was at the heart of the greenback debate and is at the heart of contemporary financial practices more generally. As Shell puts it: "A piece of paper money is almost always a representation, a symbol that claims to stand for something else or to be something else. It is not that paper depicts and represents coins, but that paper, coins, and money, generally, all stand in the place of something else" (1999, 61). To be

Figure 2. Thomas Nast, "Milk-Tickets for Babies, in Place of Milk," 1876.

sure, some early banknotes actually depicted the coins of gold or silver that they could be redeemed for (62). But more often, banknotes generate faith by depicting authority in a different way. The U.S. dollar bill, for example, arguably the most iconic monetary sign in contemporary culture, depicts what Jean-Joseph Goux calls "a richness . . . of civil symbols" (1999, 117): a portrait of George

Washington, the seals of the U.S. Treasury, the motto "In God We Trust," and the Latin inscriptions "Annuit Coeptis" ("He [God] has favored our undertakings") and "Novus Ordo Seclorum" ("A new order of the ages").[2] Goux concludes: "The State (and its Treasury), God (and our Faith in Him), the Father (founder), the dead and sacralized language (Latin): all these powerful, central signifiers converge, combine and intensify each other so as to provide the banknote with its force" (117). The imagery on paper banknotes does not just *aid* the representation of value but comes to *generate* this value itself. "Nowhere more naively than in these documents," writes Walter Benjamin, "does capitalism display itself in solemn earnest" (1978, 96; see Gilbert 1998).

What, then, of "paperless" finance? Is the problem of representation one typical for the birth of the credit economy, to be progressively resolved in subsequent centuries? On the contrary, the problem of value and representation is perhaps even more political in the age of electronic money than it was during the greenback debate. Bill Maurer (1999), for example, documents the debates around the abolishment of paper share certificates in the United States in the 1960s and 1970s. Richard Smith, commissioner of the Securities Exchange Commission (SEC) and proponent of paperless trading, wrote in 1971: "The stock certificate is not a thing-in-itself having some independent metaphysical existence, except such as man's laws have cloaked it with" (quoted in Maurer 1999, 377). This debate was partially resolved with the creation of the National Securities Clearing Corporation in the mid-1970s, which promised to replace "flocks of messengers scurry[ing] through Wall Street clutching bags of checks and securities" with "data flashing through computer networks" (quoted in Maurer 1999, 379; cf. Goux 1999). But Smith's observation remains pertinent: stocks—and other monetary instruments—have no value other than that accorded through human, and historically contingent, laws, agreements, and faith.

Nowhere is this point better illustrated than in recent debates over the so-called new economy. Even before the 2000 crash of the Nasdaq index, the leading U.S. stock market index dominated by internet and high-tech stock, the question how to value new economy stocks was widely debated. In Britain, anxiety over proper stock valuation surged in March 2000, when nine companies from the technology and communication sectors joined the FTSE 100, displacing more traditional industries such as brewing and building. "It can be a struggle to value these new companies," one Merrill Lynch analyst was quoted in the *Financial Times*, "traditional measures mean nothing for such companies" (Targett 2000). Traditional guidelines for the determination of a "stock's intrinsic value" are not applicable to internet stocks, argued another economic analyst, "because they have no assets, earnings, or dividends, and precious little management or definite prospects" (Martin 2000). The new economy debates did not just attempt to stabilize the value of the new stocks, but also provided discursive stability for the valuation of more traditional stocks, which was never as consensual and fixed as was suddenly implied.

In fact, the new economy concept came to denote a new way of measuring value and accounting for profits coupled with a romanticized image of capitalism as "an heroic adventure in innovation" (Feng et al. 2001, 468). Many of the key innovations of the new economy were financial, according to Thrift (2001b, 422–23), including the use of stock options as remuneration and the increase in initial public offerings of young technology companies. Despite its discourse of the heroic entrepreneur, "another way of understanding the new economy is as a ramp for financial markets, providing the narrative raw material to fuel a speculative asset price bubble which was also founded on an extension of the financial audience" (422). Still, we must be careful not to interpret the new economy discourse as a rhetorical way in which financial and business leaders were able to coax investors, which since the crash of 2000 has been exposed as fictive. The new economy discourse has *real* bases in and effects on financial calculations and corporate business models as well as on the ways in which money was made and distributed. These effects persist after the dot-com bubble was pronounced "burst" and have permanently transformed business and finance (Feng et al. 2001). As Thrift puts it: "Telling the new economy story worked, and worked to the extent that it began to re-describe market fundamentals. . . .Elements of the new economy will live on. *To understand it simply as a discourse is to misunderstand discourse's materiality*" (2001b, 425, 430, emphasis added).

A final example illustrating the discursive instability of financial reality is the current debate over the truth and integrity of accounting. This debate was partly triggered by the bankruptcy of energy corporation Enron in December 2001 and the subsequent failure of Enron's auditor, Arthur Andersen. Accounting's public image as apolitical number crunching, which, according to Daston (1998, 73–74) had even become a model for the sciences, collapsed under accusations of creative and aggressive accounting employed by Enron and sanctioned by its auditor and creditors. Arthur Levitt, former SEC chairman and campaigner for accounting regulation, testified before a Senate hearing on the collapse of Enron that it "did not occur in a vacuum. Its backdrop is an obsessive zeal by too many American companies to project greater earnings from year to year. . . . I [refer] to this as a 'culture of gamesmanship' . . . that says it's okay to bend the rules [and] tweak the numbers" (2002, 1). In his testimony before the U.S. Senate, Frank Partnoy (2002) similarly argued that Enron's much debated accounting techniques "actually are very common in modern financial markets." Even *The Economist* wrote: "Although Enron may have been egregious, it is not a lone offender. . . . Too many companies have got away with 'pro-forma' accounting that delivers nice numbers" (2002b, 9).

Criminal charges have been brought against Enron's executives, and the debate over whether Enron forged its accounts or used creative but legitimate accounting techniques remains unresolved. However, the Enron debate is a powerful illustration of the contested and inherently political nature of the production of financial truth and numbers. A growing body of literature that aims to scrutinize and democratize the accounting profession argues that accounting is political because it favors certain definitions of value over others.[3] As one author puts it: "Accounting systems allow only one of the many competing versions of an organization's economic reality to be legitimized" (Boland 1989, 599). As a result, alternative sources of value are delegitimized, including ecological responsibility (Power 1997, 60–66).

These illustrations—the representation of value through money iconography, debates on stock valuation, the contestability of accounting—suggest that financial truth and monetary value do not exist *prior to* discursive interpretations or explanations but are created in discourse itself. This helps clarify why the Bank of England feels so threatened by Boggs's art. Boggs's questioning of ritualized monetary practices exposes the indispensable authoritative bases and social networks that enable financial instruments to function.

Precisely because it is based on faith and confidence, the functioning of money and finance requires strong nodal points of (discursive) authority supporting and maintaining that faith. This is sometimes overlooked by sociological accounts that argue that money has been abstracted from social networks and has become a cold, calculating, and impersonal force. Such understanding of money was pioneered by Georg Simmel, who argued in his *Philosophy of Money* of 1900 that the emergence of the modern money economy objectifies social relationships, reduces kinship to calculation, and leads to "a psychically impoverished modern order" (Leyshon and Thrift 1997, 36).[4] "The money economy," Simmel writes, "enforces the necessity of continuous mathematical operations in our daily transactions. The lives of many people are absorbed by such evaluating, weighing, calculating and reducing of qualitative values to quantitative ones" (1990, 444). The depersonalizing effects of money are seen to be exacerbated by modern financial developments such as deregulation and dematerialization of finance. For instance, David Harvey establishes his influential critique of late modern capitalism partly by arguing that it reduces rich social bonds to instrumental, superficial, and impersonal profit relations. "The more flexible motion of capital," which according to Harvey characterizes the new "disorganized" capitalism, "emphasizes the new, the fleeting, the ephemeral, the fugitive and the contingent in modern life, rather than the more solid values implanted under Fordism" (1989, 171).

Although Simmel's writings offer important insights into the socioeconomic transformations of the modern money economy, his emphasis on the depersonalizing effects of money on social relations obscures the fact that modern monetary instruments are equally dependent on social networks and geographical nodal points of authority. Simmel's writings display a nostalgia for an undefined era in which economic ties were somehow more genuine and reciprocal, in contrast to the money economy that has abstracted economic exchange from its social environment. This nostalgia is shared by Harvey, who argues, following Marx, that money "dissolves the bonds and relations that make up traditional communities so that money becomes the real community" (1989, 100). Harvey laments the displacement of "a social condition in which we depend directly on those we know personally" by a social condition "in which we depend on impersonal and objective relations" (100). Thus, Simmel and Harvey insufficiently recognize that monetary practices, even modern deregulated financial practices, require in-depth social relationships, trust, interpretative communities, and authoritative underpinnings. Leyshon, Thrift, and Pratt, for example, write: "Trust is clearly of critical importance to the financial services industry. On the one hand, trust is important to the suppliers of financial services. . . . Its existence makes the granting of credit easier to sanction. On the other hand, trust is . . . important to the consumers of financial services, for they must have trust in financial institutions and the safety, reliability and general utility of their products and services" (1998, 34). By comparison, Levitt emphasized the importance of trust for finance and accounting when he argued that the collapse of Enron presented an "opportunity to repair trust in those on whom investors depend, and . . . trust in the numbers that are the backbone of our capital markets" (2002, 1).[5]

The carefully constructed but largely forgotten symbolic authority enabling monetary circulation is called into question in Boggs's performances. That the social conventions and symbolic authority required for the functioning of (paper) money are much less established than is generally believed has been discussed by Emily Gilbert and Eric Helleiner (1999). The centralization of monetary authority and the creation of exclusive national currencies were undertaken in the latter half of the nineteenth century. Although the Bank of England was founded in 1694, it did not gain exclusive rights over note issue until the Bank Act of 1844 (Helleiner 1999b, 143). In the United States, private issue of banknotes and currency of "original design" were outlawed as late as 1909 (Zelizer 1994, 16). Instead of being a natural or evolutionary process then, the creation of national currencies required elaborate and extensive state policies and coercion, ranging from the active removal of foreign currencies to the harsh sentences imposed on nineteenth-century counterfeiters. This coercive process included the persecution of late-nineteenth-century trompe d'oeil painters, whose experiments with images of money were not unlike Boggs's (Zelizer 1994, 16; Wenschler 1999, 85–91).

In short, the creation and maintenance of faith in modern currencies is a much more tenuous and unstable project than is generally conceded. If the Bank of England's authority had been natural and the use of paper pound notes had been historically inevitable, the bank would not have felt threatened by the playful imitation of its notes, being able to rely, instead, on natural propensity of humans to distinguish the "real" from the "fake." However, if we understand the maintenance of monetary authority as a carefully constructed and never completed political project, we see how Boggs's disturbances become intolerable for monetary authorities. The Bank of England's current prosecution of Boggs fits seamlessly into the late-nineteenth-century coercive establishment of exclusive national currencies.[6]

This relates to a second way in which Boggs's questions threaten monetary authority. As Carruthers and Babb (1996, 1560) point out, when the U.S. greenbackers wanted to make their new monetary form socially acceptable, they began by "remembering" the social construction of money, "thus raising the possibility of alternative monetary arrangements." If Boggs's performances similarly publicly remember the social and cultural contingency of monetary forms, they may pry open alternative monetary possibilities that create a threat to the monetary order supported by the Bank of England.

A CULTURAL HISTORY OF FINANCE

In this book I will broadly proceed from three assumptions that are further elaborated in the first chapter. First, I will consider money as a system of writing that is firmly rooted in cultural history. Attributing value to money, whether it be gold, paper, stocks, or derivatives, is only ever possible through social and historical interpretative practices. It is in this sense that Boggs's art can be considered political, as it forces us to rethink the consequences of choosing one monetary form over another. At the same time, the smooth functioning of money is conditional on a forgetting of this political contestability of the monetary form, a collective forgetting that is in the interest of some groups more than others.

Second, the current literature in the broadly defined field of political economy insufficiently considers the socially and politically constructed nature of money and finance. In fact, many authors assume finance to be an autonomous sphere or system with clearly defined boundaries and take for granted the unproblematic existence of money, banknotes, credit, financial instruments, etc., as a material starting point to their inquiries.

Third, I contend that this forgetting of the controversial history of money and finance limits potential for political criticism. In other words, it is difficult for political economy as a field of economic criticism to expose and question the political consequences of current financial discourses that have taken shape instead of and at the expense of alternative financial possibilities and representations. Instead, I will argue that a "genealogy of finance" considers these foreclosed possibilities and decisive moments in financial history and thus contributes to imagining alternative economic futures.

Chapters 2 to 5 each focus on a "moment of openness" in the development of financial practices, during which the meanings and boundaries of *the financial* and the character and behavior of *financial man* were subject to political and cultural struggles (Edkins 1999, 8). According to Jenny Edkins, moments of openness occur when changing social practices are not yet naturalized in discourse and fixed in institutional structures. I reread these moments of openness and historical struggle, then, attentive to the arguments and questions their discursive resolutions sought to exclude. The chapters discuss, subsequently, the controversial birth of public credit in seventeenth-century England and its associated gendered discourses of financial crisis; the slow imagination of a conceptual separation between gambling and finance and the articulation of risk as a calculable entity; the development of financial statistics in general and the Dow Jones Industrial Average in particular as representative measures of the market; and the politics of regulation and risk in contemporary markets, seen through the lens of debates surrounding the failed U.S. hedge fund Long-Term Capital Management. While proceeding broadly in chronological order, each chapter will discuss the continuities and contrasts with current financial understandings when relevant. Despite the political force of contemporary arguments concerning the logic of the market and the objectivity of numbers, my rereading of these moments of openness demonstrates that there is nothing natural or obvious about these arguments.

The historical episodes of political struggle and controversy that are reread in this book concern primarily the British and U.S. financial centers (London, New York, and Chicago). This choice does not deny that financial debate and controversy took place in other financial centers as well, most notably in Paris during the Mississippi bubble in the first half of the eighteenth century and in Berlin in the late nineteenth century. For example, in 1896, the German government passed an act to prohibit financial speculation, which outlawed futures trading and severely restricted the operations on the Berlin exchange. This case was closely followed in the United States, which was considering similar legal action at the time, as will be discussed in chapter 3 (see Emery 1895, 1908).

But my choice to focus on London and New York is underpinned by their particular place in financial history. As Langley (2002) demonstrates, London emerged as a "world financial centre" during the nineteenth century, to be succeeded by New York during the twentieth century (see also Germain 1997). Financial centers are defined by their functions of information gathering, interpretation, and dissemination, and consequently the ways in which financial instruments and responsibilities are defined in these localities are of particular importance to the development of modern practices. Moreover, the twenty-first century importance of U.S. firms and institutions for globalizing financial practices means that *their* concepts and legitimations, which were formulated through the nineteenth-century controversies, are of particular current importance. However, it is important to observe that there is a historical continuity rather than a disjunction between the London and New York financial centers, and even after the American War of Independence a high degree of cooperation and integration existed between London and New York's financial establishments. As I will show in chapters 3 and 4, British voices were part of U.S. debates on speculation, and British economists played an important role in the abstraction of financial practices from their political and moral contestations.

Throughout the book, it will become clear that the exclusions from financial discourses, the objections and arguments that have been consigned to the aborted histories of irrationality, gambling, madness, or miscalculation, continue to haunt financial practices today. Chapter 6, finally, will consider how this genealogy of finance, this rereading of the weaknesses and insecurities in the present financial order, opens up possibilities for political disturbance and dissent as well as alternatively imagined financial futures.

1

A Genealogy of Finance

It is really against the effects of the power of a discourse that is considered to be scientific that the genealogy must wage its struggle.

MICHEL FOUCAULT, *TWO LECTURES*

DEPOLITICIZED FINANCIAL PRACTICES

In the same week in May/June 2000, two international reports statistically assessing Western societies, including Britain, were published. The first report was published by the United Nation's children's fund, UNICEF, and presents a comprehensive study of children's health, wealth, opportunities, and education in twenty-three industrialized countries (all belonging to the Organization for Economic Cooperation and Development [OECD]). UNICEF's conclusions for Britain are devastating: Britain is among four industrialized countries in which child poverty is most common, with 19.9 percent of British children currently living below the poverty line, suffering poor education, insufficient housing, and bad health. Almost half of British children live in households that are unable to afford one week's holiday per year. UNICEF concludes that the material, cultural, and social resources of almost one-fifth of British children "are so limited as to exclude them from the minimum acceptable way of life" in Britain (UNICEF 2000, 6; also Ahmed 2000).

The second report appearing in June 2000 was delivered by OECD and reports a very favorable view of the British economy.

According to the OECD, Britain compares very well with other Western countries including the United States, France, and Germany on key economic indicators such as growth, inflation, and macroeconomic stability. British economic growth is praised and is expected to last. Although the report does note that "poverty, including among children, is unacceptably high" (OECD 2000, 17), it does so only to address ways in which Britain can improve its productivity levels and employability, which are lagging behind the rest of Europe.[1]

The almost simultaneous publication of these reports begs the question how the OECD can value the British economy so highly when child poverty is widespread in Britain. How can U.K. economic performance be praised for its global competitiveness when one in five British children lack access to adequate housing and education? How have economic indicators been formulated that exclude measures of equality and poverty? How has such an exclusive definition of the economic domain been historically legitimized? How can it be challenged? I contend that historically constructed discourses of the economy have made possible this separation between the domain of the economic and the domain of the political, in which child poverty has been assigned to the latter. It is therefore legitimized for the OECD to praise the U.K. economy while assuming that concerns over child poverty belong to a different, less important, sphere of thought and action. Moreover, these discourses that valorize (a certain definition of) economic performance while devaluing child welfare channel money and investment. Although it would take no more than an estimated 6.45 percent of the British gross national product to eradicate child poverty (UNICEF 2000, 9), and despite the Blair government's awareness of the issue of child poverty,[2] current priorities of value prohibit channeling public money toward large-scale improvement of housing, education, and health in the United Kingdom's poorest areas.

Finance and economics are among modern society's most depoliticized areas of activity. Edkins (1999) makes a distinction between "politics" and "the political," in which politics, paradoxically, refers to practices that are depoliticized or "technologized" in modern Western societies. The political, in contrast, "has to do with the establishment of that very social order which sets out a particular, historically specific account of what counts as politics and defines other areas of social life as *not* politics" (2, emphasis in original). My aim here is to inquire into the historical processes that have depoliticized financial practices, not "through some sort or lapse of mistake but [as] an express operation of . . . technologization: a reduction to calculability" (1). In other words, modern finance, perhaps more than any other area of politics, has acquired a logic of calculability and an appearance of scientific objectivity that places its fundamental assumptions—such as its indicators of performance—beyond discussion and debate. In contrast, to repoliticize (financial) practices "would be to interrupt discourse, to challenge what have, through discursive practices, been constituted as normal, natural, and accepted ways of carrying on" (12). My purpose in this book, then, is to disrupt financial discourses through questioning that which is considered to be normal, natural, and, most importantly, *scientific*. As Foucault puts it in this chapter's heading: the task of a genealogy is to struggle against the power of the "discourse that is considered to be scientific" (1980, 84). This chapter sets out the purpose and method for a genealogy of finance but starts by considering the depoliticizing effects of representing global finance as a coherent, clearly bounded system with its own dynamics.

GLOBAL FINANCE AS SYSTEM

Current understandings of global finance as a system need to be challenged in order to question the discursive and ideological constitution of economic reality. Much of the academic literature on the politics of global finance depicts finance as a coherent, powerful and clearly bounded system (or agent)—on which questions of discourse and representation have little bearing.

"Like a Phoenix risen from the ashes," as one widely accepted metaphor goes, "global finance took flight and soared to new heights of power and influence in the affairs of nations" (Cohen 1996, 268; see also Cohen 2000). Benjamin Cohen's metaphor attributes a large capacity of agency to an abstracted image of global finance. The mythological phoenix bird symbolizes immortality and resurrection, and the image of finance as an immortal being, preying on the capacities of nation-states, has become a common theme in academic literature on international finance. Such conceptualizations see international finance as a "mastering force" undermining national sovereignty and scope for domestic policy intervention, in contrast to the postwar Bretton Woods order when finance was the "servant" of economic production and financial flows were subjected to capital controls.[3] For instance, Philip Cerny (1994, 320) has argued that "the evolution of the international financial system . . . characterized by the acceleration of international capital movements" has "challenged the capacity of the state to provide effective governance not only of financial markets themselves, but also of economic affairs generally." This financial evolution, according to Cerny, is mainly driven by inventions in information and communications technology, creating a situation in which financial trading can take place through "a computer screen which can be linked into almost any market in the world at any time of the day or night" (1994, 332). Cerny not only offers an understanding of international finance that implies a trade-off between market and state authority, but he also assumes the unproblematic existence of financial markets as self-regulating and self-contained entities. Even if Cerny's work criticizes the emergence of self-regulating markets on a global scale, he bases his arguments on a profoundly uncritical image of the financial market as an efficient and transparent mechanism, allocating capital on the basis of price information. It is only thus that Cerny's political agenda can prioritize the promotion of a stable international financial order based on undistorted financial markets (Cerny 1993, 6–7; also Cerny 1995).

Another way in which finance is reified as a homogenous and clearly defined structure is through the increasingly common metaphor of the "global financial architecture." For example, Louis Pauly's *Who Elected the Bankers?* (1997) proposes to understand global financial markets as a building for which international political institutions have provided the foundations and the plumbing. In this international financial architecture, "constructively interacting national macroeconomic policies are the foundations and a modicum of convergence in national regulatory standards is the plumbing" (142). Pauly's preoccupation is with the promotion of a stable international financial order, but his metaphor depoliticizes financial governance, reducing it to a technical problem.

Especially since the Asian financial crisis, calls for a new international financial architecture (NIFA) have multiplied. In this, political economy literature shares its discursive representation of finance with the language of policy makers. Tony Blair, for example, said in a 1998 speech to the New York Stock Exchange: "Together, we must design a new international financial architecture for a new international financial age" (quoted in Langley 2004, 69). By comparison, political economists, while critical of policy proposals, uncritically accept the architecture metaphor. Kahler writes, for instance, "The current official design . . . resemble[s] a modest home improvement rather than a fundamentally new architecture" (2000, 235). Soederberg, while highly critical of the NIFA, follows through its metaphor: "In view of the NIFA's potential for generalizing and enforcing the rules governing the international financial system . . . it is important to investigate this project critically. Why was new architecture required? Whose building is it? What shape is it taking?" (2002, 176; see also Bond 2000; Noble and Ravenhill 2000; Soros 2001).

Similar to the metaphor that casts finance as an autonomous powerful agency, the metaphor that casts finance as an architectural structure—while acknowledging a more important role of politics in its construction—presents finance as a coherent and homogenous sphere of thought and action with clearly defined walls, thus constricting scope for critique (Langley 2004). This representation of finance as an autonomous and clearly bounded structure obscures all historical ambiguity, political struggle, and cultural confusion over what may be legitimate preoccupations within "the financial sphere." It assumes the incontestable economic reality of globalizing capital flows and powerful markets and leaves questions concerning the representation of financial and economic reality unanswered.

PERFORMANCE AND PERFORMATIVITY

Instead of assuming that finance is a system defined by undeniable economic realities, it can be argued that it is a particularly interpretative and *textual* practice. Money, credit, and capital are, quite literally, systems of writing. This goes for the earliest forms of credit and bookkeeping money as much as for early twenty-first century definitions of capital. For instance, Mary Poovey argues that early modern bookkeeping, which forms the basis of current accountancy practices, was a rule-governed kind of writing that "tended to *create* what it purported to describe" (1998, 56; emphasis in original). Poovey demonstrates that the systems of writing and numbering that made up bookkeeping not just actualized the categories it assumed to exist as prior economic reality but also disciplined and regulated economic agency and credibility. By comparison, modern credit and accounting practices have necessitated international negotiations over the definition of "capital," and the political effects of adopting one definition over another have made these negotiations anything but consensual (e.g., Kapstein 1989).

In fact, credit, from the Latin *credere*, signifies belief, faith, and trust—a person being worthy of trust or having the reputation to be believed. To be a creditor was originally possible as a function of social and moral standing: "Extending credit . . . meant that you were willing to trust someone to pay you in the future. . . . To have credit in a community meant that you could be trusted to pay back your debts" (Muldrew 1998, 3). Further, Nigel Thrift has documented the historical importance of the "narrative of the gentleman" to London's financial district. This was one way in which the worth of people and practices was assessed; it was "a widespread narrative based on values of honour, integrity, courtesy, and so on, and mani-fested in ideas of how to act, ways to talk [and] suitable clothing" (Thrift 1994, 342; see also Tickell 1996). Historically, then, credit carries a gendered dimension: the reputation and authority that underlies credibility distinctly belong to the gentle*man*.

If anything, current practices have increased finance's textual na-ture rather than resolved its interpretative struggles. The importance of information for financial participants is well documented. In his ethnographic study of financial markets, for example, Abolafia quotes one bond trader as saying: "Everybody is inundated with information. Every machine in the world is spewing out technical information, fundamental information, news releases, everything. You have to be very agile, very focused" (1996, 232). "International finance," Leyshon and Thrift write similarly, "is awash with printed and screen based information, ranging from specialist financial and economic analysis, which circulates only among a few subscribers, to the daily financial news, which appears on television, radio, news-papers, the internet, much of which originates with specialist finan-cial 'wire' services like Reuters, Dow Jones and Bloomberg" (1999b, 165). Because of the avalanche of information available to financial participants, they are engaged in constant processes of selection and interpretation—trying to determine the meaning of news and the ways in which "the market" will react to news. As one journalist put it, "True, I've got information coming out of my ears. But what it all *means* I haven't got a clue about" (quoted in Leyshon and Thrift 1997, 300, emphasis in original). Thrift concludes: "International financial centres are centres of representation. They are . . . centres of discursive *authority*, able to describe what constitutes 'news' and how that 'news' is interpreted" (1994, 335, emphasis in original).[4]

In contrast to understanding finance as a system, then, I will understand finance as a discursive domain made possible through performative practices, which have to be articulated and rearticulated on a daily basis.[5] In discourse theory, a performative is that which enacts or brings about what it names—the quintessential example being the priest whose words "hereby I thee wed" enact the marriage (Butler 1993, 13; Austin 1962, 4–7). Understanding finance as a performative practice suggests that processes of knowledge and interpretation do not exist in addition to, or of secondary importance to, "real" material financial structures, but are precisely *the way in which "finance" materializes.* Judith Butler proposes to replace the notion of discourse *constructing* reality with studying the "process of materialisation that stabilises over time to produce the effect of boundary, fixity, and surface we call matter" (1993, 9). According to Butler, this process of materialization "is neither a single act nor a causal process initiated by a subject and culminating in a set of fixed effects" but an ongoing, citational practice "which operates through the reiteration of norms" (10). It is not just the case then that financial knowledge is socially constructed, but the very *material structures* of the financial markets—including prices, costs, and capital—are discursively constituted and historically contingent.

This understanding avoids the theoretical limits of what I have elsewhere (de Goede 2003) called economism—or the assumption that in economics and finance there exists a prepolitical domain of material economic reality—and shifts attention to the historical and discursive processes through which a domain we now call finance has materialized.[6] In addition, it provides a contrast to notions of *performance* in conventional economic and financial analysis. The work of financial analysts professes to measure and comment on economic performance. While acknowledging the importance of information for their profession, financial analysts assume economic performance to be an objective and measurable reality, which may, to be sure, lead to different interpretations of what profitable investments are, but which exists prior to and independently from their scrutiny and recommendations. In contrast, a notion of finance as made possible through performative practices rejects the existence of an objective and measurable prior reality in favor of considering the "manifest political consequences of adopting one mode of representation over another" (Campbell 1993, 8).

Anna Tsing provides an interesting example of this mutual constitution of discourse and investment, thus illustrating finance's performativity. Tsing documents the story of the Canadian gold mining company Bre-X, which attracted speculative investment after claiming to have discovered gold in the forests of Indonesia—a claim that was later disputed, after which investors lost their money. The point of the story, for Tsing, is not that the investors were misled with false claims of gold discovery, but that investment *always* requires stories of discovery and opportunity to coax monetary flows and that this is the way in which finance operates. "Bre-X was always a performance, a drama, a conjuring trick, an illusion, *regardless* of whether real gold or only dreams of gold ever existed at Busang" (Tsing 2001, 158, emphasis added). In fact, in "speculative enterprises, profit must be imagined before it can be extracted; the possibility of economic performance must be conjured like a spirit to draw an audience of potential investors" (159). It is thus that performance and performativity are linked: the magical storytelling of investment opportunities (in Bre-X as well as in the new economy and countless other instances) performatively constitutes "real" economic performance, in the form of measured international capital flows, investments, stock prices, etc. (see Tickell 2003, 124–25).

POWER AND AGENCY IN FINANCIAL PRACTICES

Understanding finance as made possible through performative practices has consequences for the way in which power and agency are conceptualized. It breaks with what David Campbell has called an "economistic conception of power" that can be found in much of the existing literature in political economy and that regards power as "a commodity to be wielded by agents" (1996, 18). Instead, it entails a Foucauldian understanding of power as "employed and exercised through a net-like organisation. . . . Individuals circulate between its threads; they are always in the position of simultaneously undergoing and exercising this power. They are not only its inert or consenting target; they are always also the elements of its articulation" (Foucault 1980, 98; see Campbell 1996, 18).

In Foucault's work, the power of ideology is no longer seen as a more or less conscious distortion of the truth in order to further particular (class) interests, but rather as bound up with complex and historically grounded technologies of truth production. Foucault proposes to reject the concept of ideology in favor of the study of historically constituted "apparatuses of knowledge" (1980, 102). In this manner, knowledge, ideas, and ideology no longer *follow* material production and institutions, but are *a requirement for* material and institutional possibilities: "Indeed, we must produce truth *in order* to produce wealth in the first place" (93, emphasis added). The power of financial ideas exists in the spaces in which "production of effective instruments for the formation and accumulation of knowledge" takes place, including "methods of observation, techniques of registration, procedures of investigation and research" (102). Before events and phenomena can be discussed in policy forums or be the subject of international negotiations—thus *before* they come into focus within political economy—they must be "rendered into information," in the form of, for instance, "written reports, drawings, pictures, numbers, charts, graphs, statistics" (Miller and Rose 1990, 7). "Information in this sense is not the outcome of a neutral recording function," Miller and Rose conclude, "it is itself a way of acting upon the real" (1990, 7).[7]

Foucault's analysis suggests that there are general regulative practices that govern "the limits and forms of the *sayable*" within a constituted domain of discourse (1991a, 59, emphasis in original). They determine what it is possible to speak of within the historically constituted financial sphere, which events are recorded as evidence and which utterances are recognized as valid (59–60). These same limits govern which statements are considered futile and irrelevant to the financial domain, which evidence is inadmissible, which utterances are invalid. Indeed, is it not precisely through its *exclusions* that a more or less coherent financial domain becomes thinkable at all? Most importantly, then, understanding finance as a performative practice focuses debate on the exclusions made for financial discourse to emerge as a rational, normal, scientific, and respectable practice.

The regulative practices that govern the limits of the financial domain act on the ways participants in this sphere understand their roles, interests, and possibilities. In Austin's example of the priest enacting marriage, the priest's power is not a totalizing sovereign power, nor is it solely a mechanic derivative of prior structures. The power of the priest is dependent on but not exhaustively determined by prior institutions of power and ritualized formulas for enacting marriage. As Butler puts it, "The subject is neither a sovereign agent with a purely instrumental relation to language nor a mere effect whose agency is pure complicity with prior operations of power" (1997, 26). Similarly, we can think of financial agents as neither sovereign subjects nor reducible to the mechanics of financial power structures. Instead, they are regulated through historically constituted financial discourses but also acquire the authority to perform, affirm, and amend these discourses. "A general theory of the performativity of political discourse," Butler writes, understands "performativity as a renewable action without clear origin or end [which] suggests that speech is finally constrained neither by its specific speaker nor its originating context" (40). In other words, financial participants articulate and execute financial decisions or strategies but are not sovereign originators of their actions.

Thinking through Butler's formulation in a more concrete way, the importance of financial education and examination as sites that produce and constrain financial agents becomes clear. Stephen Gill (1995, 1997b) has taken a first step toward the problematization of economic agency with his concept of "economic citizenship." Modern capitalism, Gill argues, prepares its members for economic citizenship from an early age, by including in the education curriculum lessons on financial rectitude. Teenagers are targeted with programs explaining how to develop a personal credit-rating record, which has become increasingly important in order to obtain employment and accommodation (Gill 1995, 20–27). One banker has even suggested that a "personal finance money management course [is] introduced into the school curriculum, as an *examination subject*" (quoted in Leyshon, Thrift, and Pratt 1998, 51, emphasis in original). That pedagogical programs are not just targeted at teenagers is discussed by Adam Harmes, who documents that investment companies are increasingly teaching financial skills to their members and have set up "investment clubs for children" (1998, 112–14).

Targeting children is done through marketing strategies such as special children's mutual funds, for instance, the "Rupert the Bear Fund" in the United Kingdom and the "FUNds for Kids" program in Canada. The latter includes "a package for children under nine, with a stuffed 'Henry the Hedgehog' (as in 'hedge your investments'), a mock mutual-fund certificate and a storybook, *Henry's Mysterious Present: A Story about Mutual Funds*" (Harmes 2001, 113–14).

It is important to note that education in financial rectitude and responsibility is not a *new* phenomenon. Zelizer documents how the development of American consumer society in the 1920s and 1930s went hand in hand with popular education in "spending well": "to spend money is easy," as one economist put it in 1912, "but to spend well is hard" (1994, 31). Education in spending well consisted of magazine articles, essays, and pamphlets targeted mainly at poor and middle-class housewives. American immigrants received instructions on financial responsibility, shopping, banking, and budgeting during programs in citizenship training upon arrival in the United States (30–35). Often, these educational programs were a way of governing the behavior of the poor, who were considered to be financially incompetent with a tendency to spend "recklessly or foolishly" (151). It is not simply the case that (preexisting) citizens are disciplined in particular modes of financial responsibility with these rules of economic citizenship, but it is more precisely the case that responsible and respectable subjects *emerge through* these rules (see Edkins 2002).

Another important example through which financially correct behavior is articulated, taught, and incited is provided by technologies of credit rating. These technologies define and patrol the boundaries between "good" and "bad," or financially responsible and financially irresponsible, economic citizens. In retail finance, Leyshon and Thrift argue, "Potential customers are required to demonstrate to the bank that they are suitable and appropriate persons to do business with" (1999a, 440). Procedures for consumer credit rating are increasingly standardized and computerized, reducing the determination of creditworthiness to a few variables on a scorecard, such as age and employment. Increasingly, financial decisions are being made on the basis of geographical information such as postcodes, leading to geographies of financial inclusion and exclusion (Leyshon and Thrift 1999a; 1997, 225–59). These articulations of creditworthiness demonstrate a clear continuity with older definitions of credit as moral standing, trustworthiness, and social responsibility. At the same time, what is *new* about late modern computerized credit rating is the speed and intensity with which it operates. As Leyshon and Thrift put it, "In the world of business information, it is always census time" (1999a, 435).

That it is not just consumers and citizens whose identities are shaped and regulated through criteria of financial rectitude and responsibility is demonstrated by Timothy Sinclair's studies on bond-rating agencies, who assess the creditworthiness of states. These agencies "disavow any ideological content to their rating judgements" by claiming that their rating processes are "technical rather than judgmental in nature" (Sinclair 1994, 454). However, bond-rating agencies have acquired authoritative positions in international credit networks, offering particular visions of financial truth and particular criteria of financial responsibility that shape and regulate the behavior of states and financial institutions. Rating agencies, Sinclair argues,

> vet and judge practices, opportunities, forms of organisation, whole fields of human enterprise. They adjust the ground rules inside capital markets and thereby shape the international organisation and behaviour of those institutions seeking funds. . . . Thus the agencies do not just constrain capital markets . . . but actually provide significant pressures on market participants themselves, contributing importantly to their *internal constitution as agents*. (1999a, 161, emphasis added)

Finally, at the level of financial experts—those participating in financial decision making, being employed by banks and other financial institutions—a proliferation of financial education can also be observed. Business managers, as Thrift puts it, "are being locked down by regimes of perpetual training, which also, at the same time, demand an opening up of their imaginative powers" (2002, 206). Expensive and prestigious master of business administration courses can be considered to govern not just abstract or expert knowledge of financial participants but also behavior, dress, self-understanding, and sense of community for those who participate in them (see also Amoore 2004; Thrift 1998). In this sense, financial education is part of the constitution of agents and their interests. Financial agents do not deliberately and consciously delude subordinate classes, but emerge within a domain of explicit and implicit norms that regulate the limits of the sayable for legitimate participation in the financial sphere (see Butler 1997, 133). It is thus *not* the case that a focus on identity "supersede[s] political economy" or "displace[s] its central problematic" (Gills 2001, 238), but it is on the contrary the case that identity is *at the heart* of motivation, behavior, and possibilities in political economy.

Indeed, it is precisely their initiation and education that makes it possible for financial professionals to articulate, reaffirm, reformulate, but sometimes also resist discourses of financial rationality. Butler emphasizes the instability of power and the multiplicity of possible resistances by placing emphasis on the continued necessity of performance and enunciation of (financial) governance. In Butler's formulation, the fact that social institutions are not static entities but instead dependent on the continued performance and rehearsal of conventional formulae, is precisely what makes them vulnerable: "If . . . a structure is dependent upon its enunciation for its continuation," Butler writes, "then *it is at the site of enunciation that the question of its continuity is to be posed*" (1997, 19, emphasis added). In other words, despite the rigorous training and education financial agents are initiated by, their performances do not flawlessly reproduce previous formulations, but may reformulate, rearticulate, transform, and even fundamentally question financial orthodoxies.

In conclusion, then, understanding finance as rendered possible through performative practices serves a triple purpose. First, it prioritizes investigation into how understandings of economic reality and rationality *in themselves* exercise a particular power. Second, it places identity—the way in which financial participants understand their interests, roles, responsibilities, and possibilities at the heart of an understanding of financial power. Third, it moves debate away from images of finance as a rational and coherent whole to demonstrate the weaknesses, contingencies, and contradictions within existing practices.

A GENEALOGY AS A PRACTICE OF CRITICISM

A genealogy, for Foucault, is not a search for origins but an account of the contingent, piecemeal, and unsteady emergence of the conditions of possibility for a particular discursive domain. According to

Foucault, historians are all too often on a quest for origins, search-ing for "that which was already there . . . a primordial truth fully adequate to its nature" (1984a, 78). Conventional historical enquiry thus risks communicating that present orders are inevitably and evo-lutionary the way they are as a result of a teleological unfolding of history. This happens, according to Edkins, "when events are 'read' backward or retroactively: at that point it is easy to explain 'objec-tively' why certain forces were effective and how particular tenden-cies 'won'" (1999, 8). In contrast, a genealogy argues that no logical or evolutionary trajectory for the development of contemporary (financial) practices was implicit in history or human nature. To defy retrospective readings, a genealogy "will never neglect as inac-cessible the vicissitudes of history. On the contrary, it will cultivate the details and accidents that accompany every beginning; it will be scrupulously attentive to their petty malice" (Foucault 1984a, 80).

A genealogy, in short, is a practice of criticism that is motivated by finding insecurities and uncertainties in that which is represented as stable, coherent, and self-perpetuating. The politics of freedom and "possible transformation," according to Foucault, start with "following lines of fragility in the present": "History serves to show how that-which-is has not always been; i.e., that the things which seem most evident to us are always formed in the confluence of en-counters and chances, during the course of a precarious and fragile history" (1988a, 36–37). Demonstrating the contingency of history, Foucault argues, enables political criticism and the imagination of alternative futures: "It is fruitful in a certain way to describe that-which-is by making it appear as something that might not be, or that might not be as it is" (36). In this book, I show that the history of finance is ambiguously located in religious symbolism, colonial con-quest, sexual imaginations, gambling, superstition, and discourses of moral obligation, which still underpin the ways we make sense of money, credit, and investment today. However, these aspects have largely been written out of financial history to maintain the carefully protected identity of modern rational finance (Foucault 1984, 78).

Much literature in political economy has eliminated all ambi-guity and disturbances from its understandings of financial history. As Maurer puts it: "Scholars of finance almost without exception write stories of inevitability: capital needed to get faster or more mobile, and so it did, and the manner in which it did so logically followed from what went before" (2001b, 470). This literature thus presents the emergence of money and finance as what Shapiro (1993), quoting Erich Auerbach, calls a legend. A legend can be recognized because it "runs far too smoothly. All cross-currents, all friction that is casual, secondary to the main events or themes, everything unresolved, truncated and uncertain, which confuses the clear progress of the action and simple orientation of the actors, has disappeared" (Auerbach quoted in Shapiro 1993, 56). Accordingly, Shapiro argues, a legend consciously or unconsciously aims at "silencing all tendencies subversive to the main, naturalizing and legitimating story" (56).

For instance, in her account of the emergence of the present monetary order, Strange presents financial history as a legend. After Strange rightly asserts that in order to criticize "the mix of values" prevalent in the current financial order it is helpful look at past financial orders, she presents the trajectory from a primitive to a developed monetary system far too smoothly (1988, 93). Strange's money legend can be demonstrated by a lengthy quotation:

> A primitive economy, to begin with, makes very little use of money. . . . The money economy is only a small part of the real economy. . . . Money moreover tends to be in a form that can be seen and touched— asset money as the economists would say—not fiat or credit money. So it is apt to be some reasonably portable but scarce commodity—metal or shells or beads—over whose supply the ruler has little control.
>
> At intermediate stages in semi-developed monetary systems, the money economy begins to penetrate more of the real economy. Physical asset money becomes more sophisticated. Money is made into coins. . . .
>
> Next, banks appear. To begin with, they accept money or valuables for safe-keeping, give the depositor a receipt and allow him to draw on his deposit and settle accounts with third parties through the bank. Finding from experience that all the depositors will not want to draw money out at the same time, the banks lend, at a price, to others. The borrowers draw on their bank loans. Credit has been created. Pretty soon, the banks start printing "promises to pay" beyond their liabilities to depositors and borrowers. . . . As the number of banks and other specialized financial enterprises grow, the variety of forms of credit-money—what the bankers call "credit instruments"—multiplies. Financial markets proliferate. (94)

In Strange's legend, there is no mention of the confusions and disruptions to everyday life caused by money and credit as discussed by Braudel. Nor is there acknowledgment of the intense political controversies the appearance of credit produced in seventeenth-century England and the gendered metaphors through which credit slowly became legitimized. Even when Strange does discuss periods of financial instability, these are made to appear like small regressions on the way to the modern international financial order (98).

Similarly, Cohen presents the historical emergence of money and finance as a legend. "The development of money," writes Cohen,

> was one of the most important steps in the evolution of human society. . . . Before money there was only barter, the archetypical economic transaction, which required an inverse double coincidence of wants in order for exchange to occur. The two parties to any transaction each had to desire what the other was prepared to offer. This was an obviously inefficient system of exchange, since large amounts of time had to be devoted to the necessary process of search and bargaining. . . .
>
> The introduction of generalized exchange intermediaries cut the Gordian knot of barter by decomposing the single transaction of barter into separate transactions of sale and purchase. . . . This served to facilitate multilateral exchange; with costs of transactions reduced, exchange ratios could more efficiently equate the demand and supply of goods and services. Consequently, specialization in production was promoted and the advantages of economic division of labour became attainable—all because of the development of money. (1977, 16–17)

Cohen's story races without glitches, doubts, or confusions from primitive times to the emergence of Adam Smith's liberal trading order, thus naturalizing and legitimizing the latter. Cohen's more recent work uses these same phrases to describe the emergence of monetary economies, but places more emphasis on the social bonds enabling the functioning of money (1998, 10–13). However, he still casts monetary exchange as a natural and evolutionary human practice, which evolves from primitive forms and understandings to modern ones without encountering much resistance.[8]

Ron Martin provides a third example of the representation of financial history as a legend that naturalizes present conditions by assuming a linear historical progression of financial innovation.

Martin identifies three phases "in the historical evolution of the financial system of advanced capitalist countries" and presents these in tabular form (1994, 255–56). "The earliest stage, associated with industrialization," Martin explains,

> was essentially a "regional" and "bank-oriented" system, based on a network of regional banks using local resources of capital and saving to channel into private industry. . . . To the extent that international movements of money took place, they were mainly associated with financing overseas trade. As the advanced capitalist countries moved into the mature stage of industrial development, so their financial system became much more spatially and organizationally centralized. In this second, "national" or "market-oriented," phase, national capital markets largely replaced regional banks as sources of funds. . . . The latest, contemporary, phase, associated with the passage to a late- or post-industrial era, marks the onset of a further shift in the nature of the financial system toward a "transnational" and "securitized" form. Capital and money markets are separating from industry, money has been commodified, and as national financial centers become increasingly globalized and globally integrated, it is now national monetary autonomy that is being challenged. (255)

Martin presents a linear progressive history that dismisses all political debate, confusion, contingencies, and reversals from the history of financial networks. His term "historical evolution" accords to the financial sphere a self-propelling ability, which only ever proceeds in one direction and cannot be reversed. Martin leaves no possibility for aspects of the different historical phases to exist simultaneously, except for a certain transition period in which, he notes, the phases may overlap (see also Hutchinson, Mellor, and Olsen 2002, 67–69).

Legends of monetary history, Jean-Christophe Agnew points out, arise partly because what we now call market exchange took place within a web of social actions that cannot be disentangled and partly because of the lack of historical records of early motives for exchange. "The absence of documentation," Agnew observes, "is scarcely a deterrent for those who prefer to think of markets as the institutional expression of a natural human propensity to truck and barter. If anything, the seemingly magical appearance of markets in the landscape of antiquity tends to confirm this view of trade as a kind of sociobiological tropism, suggesting, as it does, a spontaneous gravitational pull toward commodity exchange encoded deep within the cellular structure of primitive societies" (1986, 17). In such a view, Agnew asserts, "an event such as the establishment of the Royal Exchange in London in 1658 is . . . but a more complex and sophisticated variation of transactions carried out elsewhere with yams, shells and salt" (2; see also Foucault 1994, 166–68).

In contrast to such retrospective readings of market exchange, Agnew documents the cultural webs of meaning within which concepts of the modern market emerged, demonstrating a close historical connection between the ways in which meanings of the market and the theatre evolved in sixteenth- and seventeenth-century England. The theatre did *more* than reflect the "disruptive and transformative powers of market exchange," according to Agnew (1986, 7). The theatre was pivotal in making sense of new social relations and the questions of "authenticity, accountability and intentionality" that surrounded the credit economy; "it modelled and in important respects materialized those relations" (11, xi). Thus Agnew shows that Boggs's performances are not as alien to the financial sphere as the Bank of England argues. Late medieval fairs, which are now regarded as the earliest incarnations of the modern market, were carnivalesque marketplace festivals during which money was ridiculed with "mock coinage passed from hand to hand" (Agnew 1986, 35).

Similarly, Braudel's work documents the nonlinear histories of monetary networks, showing that various forms of money, barter networks, silver and gold coin, paper money, and credit existed side-by-side instead of as subsequent stages of monetary evolution. Barter and "primitive" currencies, Braudel argues, were perpetuated in many countries long after the emergence of monetary economies: "Under the thin surface of monetary economies, primitive activities continued and blended into the others in the regular meetings at town markets, or in the more concentrated atmosphere of trade fairs. Rudimentary economies survived in the heart of Europe, encircled by monetary life which did not destroy them but kept them as so many internal colonies within easy reach" (1981, 444–45; see Shapiro 1993, 57).[9] Even in the modern globalized economy, it is not difficult to distinguish networks of barter and informal exchange existing alongside sophisticated financial networks.

In contrast to an evolutionary history of modern credit practices, a genealogy is attentive to the insecurities, confusions, and contingencies of history. It aims to "bring to light both the contingency of the institutionalized frameworks of society within which everyday social practice take place and the existence of other possible resolutions" (Edkins 1999, 5). Is it then possible to discern, through genealogy, a number of founding acts that gave meaning (and value) to our current financial concepts? Does this imply that we can identify historical alternatives and choose a different path? Ernesto Laclau points out why this is not the case, for the passing of time has modified systems of possibilities. Moreover, we can never exactly reconstruct the alternatives of the past, nor can we clearly identify historical "moments" of decision, nor are historically discarded options the only weaknesses in present discourses (1990, 34–35). In other words, present orders of discourse cannot simply be "wished away" because they regulate, shape, and constrain current actions, possibilities, and identities. In Judith Butler's formulation, discourses should not be understood as "merely cultural," but have become part of material life in the sense that they define legal "personhood" and operate the "gendered distribution of legal and economic entitlements" (1998, 40–41).

We can, however, reread the historical controversies and political struggles that slowly and contingently produced the meanings that are in many instances unquestioned today. Some of the ways in which these discourses were stabilized may even be discernible as "moments," for instance, when legal decisions succeeded in fixing the meaning of contested concepts, after which controversies slowly refocused. This happened, for example, when the U.S. Supreme Court in 1905 formalized a certain demarcation between gambling and finance that had been contested and resisted for decades previously. Still, we must be careful not to portray the court's decision as a solitary and definitive act in history, but understand it within the historical constellation of discourses that made it possible and attributed authority to it.

Finally, and most importantly then, a genealogy is an inquiry into financial history that is "a history of the present" (Foucault 1989a). It looks for and emphasizes the weaknesses in present (financial) practices, which are "not systemic contradictions, but rather, effects of fragmented histories, colliding discourses, forces that prevailed without triumphing, arguments insecure about themselves" (Brown

1998, 45). The genealogy of finance that follows, then, will demonstrate that financial practice is less sure of itself and its discursive groundings than linear histories allow. If the distinction between gambling and finance, for instance, remains tenuous and insecure, we may imagine consciously in law determining the boundaries after which legitimate finance becomes illegitimate gambling. If the definition of financial indicators can be shown to be arbitrary and unfounded in historical necessity, a redefinition of such indicators may be thought possible that includes, for instance, measures of child poverty. If the boundaries of the sphere of finance are shown to be less fixed and rigid, moreover, the legitimacy of broad public debates on financial issues may be restored. In this manner, the social and gendered effects of financial practices may be addressed. "If everything about us is the effect of accident rather than will or design," Brown says, "then we are, paradoxically, both more severely historical and also more malleable than we would otherwise seem. We are more sedimented by history, but also more capable of intervening in our histories" (1998, 36).

2

Mastering Lady Credit

With what rimes and what verses shall I sing of the kingdom of Fortune and of her chances favorable and adverse? . . .

She often keeps the good beneath her feet; the wicked she raises up; and if ever she promises you anything, never does she keep her promise . . .

This unstable goddess and fickle deity often sets the undeserving on a throne to which the deserving never attains.

She times events as suits her; she raises up, she puts us down without pity, without law or right . . .

Usury and fraud enjoy themselves with their crew, powerful and rich.

    NICCOLÒ MACHIAVELLI, *TERCETS ON FORTUNE*

THE VIOLENT HISTORY OF EARLY MODERN CREDIT

I have argued that the representation of financial history as a legend, in which the use of shells, the minting of coin, the invention of paper money, and the creation of credit are seen as logical subsequent steps in monetary evolution, abstracts modern financial instruments from their political, and often violent, histories. Instead, it has to be recognized that the history of modern credit practices is inextricably bound up with the violent histories of European state formation, colonial conquest, and slave trading. Susan Strange has argued that the international economy as we now understand it consists of the unique combination of "a political system based on territorial states" and an "economic system based on markets and

21

profit" (1999, 347; see also Germain 1999, 76–77; Langley 2002, 41–42). So defined, the invention of national debt in seventeenth-century Britain can be regarded as monetary transformations that inaugurated modern finance. "The big breakthrough for states," Strange argues, "came at the turn of the [seventeenth] century with the introduction of a new kind of money—state promises-to-pay. Two Scots, John Law and William Paterson, both saw that by this means money could be created with which to replenish the resources of the state by issuing pieces of paper carrying the 'guarantee' of the monarch" (1999, 347).[1]

The historical importance of the connection between state formation and modern money is expressed in one of the most enduring tropes for money, that of *currency*. Today's official definition of national money supplies in terms of different liquidities, referring to the ease with which one monetary form or instrument can be interchanged with another, is based on the historical imagination of money and credit as the *blood* of the national economy. One of the earliest articulations can be found in Thomas Hobbes's *Leviathan*, who made it clear that the blood flowing through his envisioned "Body Politic" was money. "Money [is] the blood of a commonwealth," Hobbes wrote, money "passeth from man to man, within the commonwealth; and goes round about, nourishing, as it passeth, every part thereof; in so much as this concoction, is as it were the sanguification of the commonwealth: for natural blood is in like manner made of the fruits of the earth; and circulating, nourisheth by the way every member of the body of man" (1962 [1651], 188–89; see Foucault 1994, 179). According to Hobbes, this nutritive and vital role of gold and silver originated from their intrinsic value ("their value from the matter itself"), rather from value produced in exchange (189). Still, Hobbes offered a powerful and enduring trope by arguing that money passing through the heart of the body politic, "the public coffers," enabled the survival of the state (189). "And in this also, the artificial man [the commonwealth] maintains his resemblance with the natural," Hobbes concludes, "whose veins receiving the blood from the several parts of the body, carry it to the heart; where being made vital, the heart by the arteries sends it out again, to enliven, and enable for motion all the members of the same" (1962, 189–90). In conjunction with Hobbes's articulation of the sovereign state through the body politic discourse (Campbell 1992, 61–68), then, we find here one of the first imaginations of a *national financial system.*

What was *new* about the credit money that emerged in Western Europe from the sixteenth century onward, Ingham argues, was that it was a form of "depersonalised debt," that departed from commodity money and "laid bare the essential property of money in general as constituted by *social relations*" (2001, 305, emphasis in original; see also Ingham 1999). When in the early seventeenth century the Dutch East India Company (the Verenigde Oost-Indische Compagnie [VOC]) stipulated that subscribers to its shares could not demand their capital back but instead could retrieve their funds by selling the shares to third parties, the credit certificates, shares, and tickets used to finance expeditions became marketable in themselves (Neal 1990, 45). The Amsterdam Beurs (stock market) emerged as a secondary market for the shares of the VOC. Similarly, in seventeenth- and eighteenth-century England, secondary markets in credit certificates grew up around the ventures of joint-stock companies such as the Royal Africa Company and the South Sea Company. The birth of secondary markets in the shares, tickets, and certificates of the national debt and joint-stock companies was anything but smooth or uncontroversial, however. Trading in stock of the South Sea Company soared in 1719–20, and the ensuing confusion generated the still-current metaphor of a "bubble" to make sense of financial trading. Much has been written about the nature, origins, and causes of the so-called South Sea Bubble.[2] The point to be stressed here is that the South Sea scheme was not a self-fulfilling financial crisis, the puncturing of which was inevitable (as the bubble metaphor implies), but a political struggle over the proper meanings, legitimacy, and possibilities of the new secondary markets in shares and credit. Depersonalized credit certificates were highly controversial and created legal as well as moral problems. Rotman (1987) documents how the invention of anonymous and transferable paper money and promissory notes broke English law, which stipulated that a contract had to be between (two) named individuals. Legal turmoil centered on "whether or not, in other words, the practice of making bills (payable to bearer) transferable without a slow and expensive assignation, or even any endorsement, should be permitted" (Rotman 1987, 49; see also Maurer 1999).

It is important to note that in joint-stock companies, politics and economics, or state and finance, were inextricable. "National rulers," Burch points out, "solicited, promoted, and often created large (joint-stock) companies in order to address the chronically destitute, nearly insolvent character of crown/national finances. The crown extended property rights and granted privileges (grants, charters, exemptions) primarily to induce companies to act on behalf of foreign policy interests" (1994, 50). Or as Carswell puts it, "Politically speaking the South Sea Company was a marvellous synthesis of finance, commerce and foreign policy" (1960, 53). Joint-stock companies received monopoly concessions to conduct trade and conquest in the name of a state, and it was not rare for these monopolies to concern the slave trade. The Royal Africa Company (RAC) was chartered in 1672 with a thousand-year monopoly on African trade, with the specific purpose to impede Spanish and Portuguese trade in Africa and to open the way for British slavers. The RAC was empowered to "deal in slaves, gold and silver, and to establish forts and factories at appropriate places on the African coast" (Palmer 1981, 5; Burch 1998, 121). The monopoly charter meant that the RAC could seize foreign (mostly Spanish and Portuguese) ships in the name of the English crown.

The South Sea Company was also a slaving enterprise. At the settlement of Utrecht in 1713, the British Crown was granted an *Asiento* contract, the right to supply the Spanish Caribbean islands with slaves for thirty years. Queen Anne sold the Asiento contract to the South Sea Company, which had been chartered in 1711 with a monopoly on trade with South America "forever" (Palmer 1981, 10). The South Sea Company chartered private ships or fitted out its own ships for the slave trade, and in 1714 at least seven of its own ships sailed, "among them the *Hope* and the *Liberty* . . . with commissions for no less than 2,680 slaves. To finance them the company raised £200,000 in bonds" (Carswell 1960, 66). Between 1714 and 1738, at least 134 slave ships of the South Sea Company sailed to the West African coast (Palmer 1981, 31). It was the long-term time horizons and unprecedented costs and uncertainties involved in colonial voyages that underpinned financial innovations such as shares and insurance (Burch 1998, 107–35; see also Leyshon and Thrift 1997, 294; Neal 1990, 9–10). The triangular trade, in which English ships sailed from the African coast to deliver slaves to the West Indies for Spanish and British plantations and brought back bullion, spices, sugar, and slaves to the ports of London, Bristol, and Liverpool, was made possible by innovations in long-term credit and fostered banking and financial trading networks in the home ports. Well-known British banking houses such as Barclay and Baring have their origins in the triangular trade (see Williams 1944). However, the violence of its institution is largely written out of contemporary histories of finance.

These historical developments—the invention of credit money, the birth of the national debt, the emergence of secondary markets in shares and credit certificates, the invention of insurance—have been summarized as constituting a veritable Financial Revolution that entailed a rapid and critical transformation of English society, upsetting existing social orders (Dickson 1967). However, Dickson's influential work is mostly preoccupied with reconstructing "how the market actually worked" and mentions the moral and religious history that were part and parcel of these developments only in passing (33). In fact, Dickson expresses incredulity at the contemporary controversies, when he thinks it "worth noting that while few aspects of the Financial Revolution were of greater political and economic utility than the development of a market in securities in London, none united contemporary opinion more against it" (32). Thus, Dickson assumes the proven utility of securities trading and considers the critiques of financial practices mainly as archaic remnants. Instead, I argue that no logical or evolutionary trajectory for the development of financial thought or rationality was implicit in these monetary innovations. Even more than the invention of financial instruments, the Financial Revolution must be thought of as the articulation of moral and political spaces in which these instruments became possible and condoned. Such an approach places the political and literary debates surrounding credit at the heart of the development of financial institutions, instead of being secondary to "objective" economic or financial transformations.

CREDIT AND FORTUNA

At the time of their invention, paper money and credit were regarded as morally conspicuous instead of naturally beneficial. The concepts of promise and pledge underlying credit were seen to deliver England to the whims and fancies of its emerging financial class. Thus credit became a focus of political struggle and satirical debate in this period. Pocock documents a peak in these "paper wars" between 1698 and 1734 (1975, 423–505). The paper wars were conducted by a number of legendary British authors, including Daniel Defoe, Jonathan Swift, and Alexander Pope. These debates have generally been understood as expressing the political confusions around the transition from feudal society, in which wealth was visibly embodied in land, to a commercial and trading society, in which wealth was more intangibly located in the mechanisms of credit-creation (Pocock 1975, 1985; Nicholson 1994; Sherman 1996). However, it is important to note that literary representations do more than reflect on emerging credit structures: they *produce and manage* new (financial) knowledge and subjectivities. As Osteen and Woodmansee put it: "Literary texts, and particularly novels . . . both produce and respond to reformulations of the nature of representation and credit" (1999, 6).

Catherine Ingrassia has documented how public discussion and literary representations of the new credit structures and the South Sea Bubble centered around sexual metaphors and female allegorical "figures of disorder" (1998, 24). According to Ingrassia, the new financial activities unsettled the entrenched gender orders, exemplified by the many women who invested in stocks, shares, lottery tickets, and other paper instruments of wealth. The desirable and seductive wealth of speculation became represented by images of women and goddesses, frequently of loose sexual morals. Descriptions of credit, Ingrassia argues, embodied "many associations of negative and stereotypically female qualities [such as] avaricious sexuality, emotional instability [and] hysteria" (26). With this rhetoric, the paper wars fought in the pages of *The Spectator* and *The Tatler* adhered to a tradition of sexualized public discourse. For instance, in the early seventeenth century Francis Bacon had constructed Nature as a female that had to be subdued and mastered by the male scientific mind. "I am come in very truth," Bacon instructed the scientific observer, "leading you to Nature with all her children to bind her to your service and make her your slave" (quoted in Lloyd 1984, 12). Evelyn Fox Keller has argued moreover that Bacon's projection of Nature as a female to be mastered and controlled underlies modern conceptions of science and scientific facts (1985, 33–42).

The representation of credit as an "inconstant, often a self-willed but persuadable woman," was used by both the opponents and defenders of the new credit structures (Nicholson 1994, xi). In 1698, political economist Charles Davenant was one of the first to project credit as an autonomous and inconstant agency. "Of all beings that have existence only in the minds of men," wrote Davenant, "nothing is more fantastical and nice than Credit; it is never forced; it hangs upon opinion, it depends upon our passions of hope and fear; it comes many times unsought for, and often goes away without reason, and when once lost, is hardly to be quite recovered" (quoted in Pocock 1975, 439). Similarly, in 1711 Joseph Addison wrote in *The Spectator:*

> [When] I returned to the Great Hall [of the Bank of England]. . . . to my Surprize, instead of the Company that I left there, I saw towards the upper end of the Hall, a beautiful Virgin seated on a Throne of Gold. Her Name (as they told me) was *Publick Credit.* . . . Both Sides of the Hall were covered with such Acts of Parliament as had been made for the Establishment of Publick Funds. . . . Behind the Throne was a prodigious Heap of Bags of Money. . . . The Floor, on her right Hand and on her left, was covered with vast Sums of Gold that rose up in Pyramids on either side of her. (quoted in Dickson 1967, xxi, emphasis in original)

By comparison, Jonathan Swift's *Voyage to Laputa* (the third book of *Gulliver's Travels*) is reputed to be inspired by the Spanish word for whore. Swift was a fierce opponent of public credit, and *Voyage to Laputa* represents Gulliver's trip to a land driven to madness by the desire for constant enrichment, jeopardizing all value systems. Laputa thus symbolizes a form of compromised morality for the sake of instant wealth (Nicholson 1994, 102).

Within the sexualized public discourse on credit, Daniel Defoe's imagination of Lady Credit was of particular importance, because Defoe used these sexual metaphors to articulate a new conception of morality in which the nascent credit structures would be able to flourish. He denied that there was any need to return to a "precommercial morality," as many of the paper war participants including Swift desired (Pocock 1975, 435). In the place of the visibility and sturdiness of wealth embodied in land, Defoe conceded the possibility of wealth based on circulation and credit. Money-as-pledge could provide a basis for sturdy financial structures, Defoe argued, on the precondition of a gentlemanly ethic. Thus, Defoe provided a uniquely modern defense of investing society preceding the work of Adam Smith that is often taken as a starting point for modern economic rationality (e.g., Williams 1999). As such, Defoe's work is well positioned to give us insight into the discursive foundations of the modern financial economy as defined by Strange (1999).

Defoe's personification of credit embodies all the irrational, fantastical, passionate, and irresponsible elements that Swift and other participants in the paper wars attributed to the new credit-based economy. Defoe's introduction of *Lady Credit* in a 1706 issue of his *Review of the State of the English Nation* is worth quoting at length to consider her ambiguous character:

> Money has a younger Sister, a very useful and officious Servant in Trade, which . . . is very assistant to her; . . . Her name in our Language is call'd CREDIT, in some countries Honour, and in others, I know not what.
>
> This is a coy Lass, and wonderful chary of her Self; yet a most necessary, useful, industrious creature: she has some Qualification so particular, and is so very nice in her Conduct, that a World of Good People lose her Favour, before they well know her Name; others are courting her all their days to no purpose, and can never come into her Books.
>
> If once she be disoblig'd, she's the most difficult to be Friends again with us, of any thing in the World; and yet she will court those most, that have no occasion for her; and will stand at their Doors neglected and ill-us'd, scorn'd and rejected like a Beggar, and never leave them. (Defoe 1706a, 17–18; quoted in Pocock 1975, 452–53)

In this introduction, Lady Credit displays a whole range of potentially unpleasant feminized characteristics. Although she is fundamentally good-natured, nice, and useful, she is also stubborn and sulky. She is a "coy Lass," meaning that she is shy and quiet in a tempting way; she is attractive and innocent, but mature enough to know how to use her attractiveness, coquettishly inviting the public men to play. In typical female fashion, she desires those who "have no occasion for her," while ignoring the men who court her "all days."

By drawing out the ambiguous and fickle character of Lady Credit, it can be made clear not only how Defoe and his contemporaries perceived the problematic nature of institutionalized credit, but also how a moral justification for credit, based on a long lineage of political thought concerning public virtue, was constructed. In the enormous amounts of Defoe's writings, Lady Credit appears alternately as a innocent lady, a virtuous virgin or a gentlewoman on one hand and a spoiled flirt, a demanding mistress, and a prostitute on the other. The image of credit as a spoiled mistress returns in various issues of the *Review,* for instance in Defoe's discussion of her behavior during the reign of Queen Anne, when the Lord Treasurer "made her the compliment . . . effectually to convince her, that her Majesty *had no Occasion for her*—This is one of the best ways to get full Possession of her; for as once to want her, is entirely to lose her; so once to be free from Need of her, is absolutely to possess her" (1709b, 126, emphasis in original; see also Defoe 1709a). Credit displays various degrees of (sexual) activity, from being an "absolute and despotick" governess (Defoe 1706a, 18) to being a passive victim of the concoctions of various political fractions (see also Backscheider 1981).

Similarly, in the work of other participants in the paper wars, credit appears as both a stately lady and as prostitute. Ingrassia documents how in 1720 James Milner represented the two most important financial institutions of the time, the Bank of England and the South Sea Company, as women (and in fact, the Bank of England is still known as "the old lady of Threadneedle Street"). After a decision favoring the South Sea Company for the management of the public debt, Milner depicted the Lady of the South Sea sitting "on her throne in a most magnificent manner" with "at her Feet . . . the poor Annuitants in mourning, petitioning to be admitted Sharers in the glorious Harvest" (quoted in Ingrassia 1998, 25). By comparison, when Chancellor of the Exchequer John Aislabie was called before the House of Lords in 1721 to answer accusations that he had given the South Sea Company preferential treatment, he characterized the company as a seductive prostitute, thereby, as Ingrassia (1998, 19) points out, displacing responsibility for his actions.

Eighteenth-century sexualized representations of credit—not just Defoe's Lady Credit, but also the images of Swift, Davenant, Milner, Aislabie, and others—can be understood as new political incarnations of the ancient goddess Fortuna (Pocock 1975, 453; Ingrassia 1998, 24). Fortuna, the mistress of chance and luck, has a long historical lineage in political theory; Aristotle attributed to her the task of doling out earthly goods such as wealth, health, and beauty. Her main characteristics were capriciousness and fickleness, and although man could attempt to please and honor her, he was never guaranteed success. Thus, she was at once impartial and unfair: all were equal before Fortuna, but she gave no special rewards to those who worked hard or were of good moral standing (Daston 1988, 151–52). Her unfair, willful, and untrustworthy character is described in Machiavelli's *Tercets on Fortune* quoted at the beginning of this chapter. Machiavelli does not only sing of her unpredictability and her control of time, giving her the power to "[time] events as suits her; she raises up, she puts us down without pity, without law or right," but he also alludes to her association with the moneylenders, and "usury and fraud enjoy themselves with their crew, powerful and rich" (Gilbert 1965, 746–47). Machiavelli's poem goes on to say: "Above the gates [of Fortune's palace] that never, they say, are locked, sit Luck and Chance, without eyes and without ears. Power, honor, riches and health are ready as rewards; as punishment and affliction there are servitude, infamy, sickness, and poverty. Fortune displays her mad fury with these distresses; the gifts she offers to those she loves" (747).

Fortuna's historical lineage has resulted in contrasting images of her, tied to different conceptions of human agency or, more specifically, to different degrees of human autonomy in face of her powers. For instance, in the *Divine Comedy*, Dante portrays Fortuna as a true goddess, who carries out her task of handing out external goods with "disinterested tranquillity," thus leaving no possibility for human defense against, or even human understanding of, her actions (Cioffari 1947, 3). Later, in Boccaccio's *Decameron*, Fortuna not only takes on a cunning and mischievous streak, but she also becomes associated with the developing financial sphere, favoring "the business of lending at usury" (Cioffari 1947, 3). Eventually, in Machiavelli, she ceases to be an instrument of Divine Will (6). More precisely, as Hanna Pitkin has pointed out, Fortuna loses many of her medieval god-like dignities and becomes more amenable to human intervention. What remains from the medieval tradition of Fortuna's image, Pitkin argues, "is the image of fortune as a woman, mostly in juxtaposition to autonomous human effort, often explicitly to *virtù*. Although still a superhuman figure of mythical proportions, fortune can no longer be regarded as a goddess in any ordinary sense. She is not to be worshipped, supplicated, treated with reverence, nor does she represent any transcendent order. Rather, she acts on the basis of familiar human motives, impulses and desires, by no means always admirable" (1984, 153).

There are distinct similarities between eighteenth-century representations of public credit and Fortuna, these two despotic female rulers over men's affairs. Both are unreliable, malleable, and fickle, both are seductive and tyrannizing, both are represented as stately ladies who need to be treated with respect on one hand and as unreliable loose women who cause destruction on the other. Both are, in Pitkin's words "fickle and inconstant . . . changeable, capricious, unreliable, not to be trusted, sometimes downright perverse in [their] desire to violate expectations and alter established patterns" (1984, 154).

MASTERING LADY CREDIT

As a direct result of Fortuna's more humane demeanor in Machiavelli's writings, man and the goddess became engaged in a sexual conflict in which *virtù* becomes the means by which he can control and dominate her. Particularly in the work of Defoe, the possibility is opened for the new credit practices to become respectable—in contrast to Swift's *Laputa,* where all morality was irredeemably lost. In spite of Lady Credit's complexity and her potentially dangerous nature, Defoe asserts that she is indispensable to the well-being of English nation. "What has this invisible Phantom done for this Nation[?]" Defoe asks, and goes on to answer, "She cuts all the Notches in your Tallies . . . ; your Exchequer Bills have her Seal to them . . . ; 't is by her you raise Armies, fit out Fleets, cloth your Soldiers, establish Banks, sell Annuities, pay Equivalents, and in short by Her . . . by this Invisible, *Je ne Seay Quoi,* this Non-natural, this Emblem of a something, tho' in itself nothing, all our War and all our Trade is supported" (1709a, 122). Thus, Defoe suggests that Lady Credit not be abolished or banned, but rather be actively mastered and controlled. She is neither essentially a virgin nor a whore, but it becomes the responsibility of financial man to make an honest woman out of her.

A short consideration of Machiavelli's recommendations to man in his struggle with Fortune illustrates how his conceptions of virtue foreshadow Defoe's. Machiavelli's *Tercets on Fortune* contemplate the ways in which man can counteract Fortune's mad fury and violent reign. "Within her palace," Machiavelli writes, "as many

wheels are turning as there are varied ways of climbing to those
things which every living man strives to attain" (Gilbert 1965, 746).
In the Middle Ages, Fortune was often depicted with a wheel or
standing on a ball, which signified her instability and unpredictability (Patch 1967, 147–77). Machiavelli's depiction of many wheels
opens the possibility for man's cunning and intelligence to foresee
Fortune's changing moods, which cause her to "reverse [the wheel's]
course in midcircle," so that "a man who could leap from wheel to
wheel would always be happy and fortunate" (Gilbert 1965, 747).
Moreover, Machiavelli's poem asserts that the fate of great historical
figures teaches "how much he pleases Fortune and how acceptable
he is who pushes her, who shoves her, who jostles her" (748–49).
Thus, man must not be complacent in his struggle with Fortuna but
must actively attempt to master and control her, pushing and shoving her.

This is also the advice Machiavelli gives to *The Prince* [1532],
where he pits the virtues of foresight and prudence against the potentially ruinous and always unpredictable ways of Fortune. "When
times are calm," writes Machiavelli men must "make provisions,
with both dikes and levees" (1997, 91). Man must show virtuosity,
not so much to passively follow Fortuna's cues as to preempt and
cunningly foresee her actions. As Brown (1988, 80) has argued,
Fortuna represents man's inadequate grasp of his circumstances.
Thus, Machiavelli emphasizes knowledge and expertise as virtues
through which Fortuna can be mastered. The Prince must plan for
war in time of peace and never be lazy and complacent in his position; he must know and explore his own lands, "learn the nature
of sites and come to know how the mountains rise, how the valleys
open, how the plains lie, and to perceive the nature of the rivers
and the swamps, and to put the greatest care into this" (Machiavelli
1997, 55). The solid and historical knowledge required of a successful Prince can be attained, according to Brown, by clearing the mind
of "all that makes it 'soft' or 'effeminate'" (1988, 85). Machiavelli's
confrontation of Fortune and virtue led him to value the virile qualities of "skill, courage . . . and virtuosity" (Walker 1989, 36), while
abhorring weakness, passivity, and indecisiveness (Pitkin 1984, 50;
Brown 1988, 85).

In Defoe's sexualized warfare between Lady Credit and her suit-
ors, the Machiavellian virtues of foresight, knowledge, and strength

emerge as means through which credit can be mastered. As mentioned, Lady Credit will be possessed and conquered only by those who pretend to "have no occasion" for her. Most importantly, Defoe argues that the construction of foundations and "regular structures," such as honor and mutual trust, must underpin the new credit practices. "If you will entertain this Virgin," writes Defoe, "you must Act upon the nice Principles of Honour and Justice; you must preserve Sacred all the Foundations, and build regular structures upon them; you must answer all Demands, with a respect to the Solemnity, and Value of the Engagement; with respect to Justice; and honour and without any respect to Parties—If this is not observed, credit will not come" (1710b, 463; see Pocock 1975, 455). An honorable marriage will be able to guarantee the respectability of Lady Credit. If she marries, according to Defoe, "a Young Man full of Application, sober, sensible, and honest, that lays his Bones to his Work, and his Head to his Business," she will reward him well: "She'll support him, she'll carry him through the World upon her Shoulders—When he walks, she leads him; when he sleeps, she awakens for him, and when he swims, she holds him by the Chin" (1710a, 222).

The virtues of strength and activity required of financial man to master credit must be read as the strength to *resist her temptations.* Financial man must never forget that Lady Credit is a cunning temptress, that disaster looms in her wake. Defoe emphasizes caution and the strength of moderation and advises the young tradesman thus: "Caution, therefore, is the best advice can be given to a young Tradesman; and Moderation is a useful Vertue in Trade . . . the Tradesman has the most need of that Petition in the Lord's Prayer, of any Man living, *Lead me not into Temptation*" (1706c, 25, original emphasis). Defoe denounces those who sink deeper and deeper into debt because they desire "luxurious Extravagancies in eating and drinking . . . ; or in Magnificent Equipages . . . ; or in Drunkenness and Play" and asserts that ruin will be the effect of "Luxury, Gaming, Lewdness, and all sorts of Vices" (1706c, 26–27). Not only does Lady Credit threaten financial man's self-control and his mastery of his passions, so also does the desire for luxury and wealth threaten to infect him with feminine softness and complacency regarding his business (Pitkin 1984, 117).

The emphasis on moderation and (sexual) restraint in matters of money was not just typical in the work of Defoe, but more generally significant within the political arguments supporting the new capitalist practices and the formulation of a discursive distinction between the (harmful) "passions" and the (beneficial) "interests" of economic man (Hirschman 1997 [1977]). Hirschman's discussion of the ways in which "money-making pursuits [became] honorable at some point in the modern age after having stood condemned or despised as greed, love of lucre, and avarice for centuries past" points to the slow articulation of money making as a calm virtuous pursuit, which remains occasionally threatened by excess and passion (1997, 9). For example, Shaftesbury's *Characteristicks* praises the pursuit of wealth as "compatible with virtue," but "if it grows at length into a real passion" it can cause "injury and mischief" (quoted in Hirschman 1997, 64). Hirschman concludes that, in the new discourses of political economy, money making "when pursued in *moderation* . . . is promoted all the way to a 'natural affection,' which achieves both private and public good, while it is demoted to an 'unnatural affection,' which achieves neither, when it is indulged to *excess*" (65, emphases added).

Indeed, in Defoe's work, the confrontation of Lady Credit with financial man's *unrestrained* lust and desires proves disastrous. To Defoe, stockbrokers who sold credit certificates for gambling purposes were evil incarnate:

> a Vermin never heard of before, Creatures not of GOD's creating, nor form'd in the World by usual generation, but sprung from the Corruptions of the National Honesty, and vivify'd by the contagious Fermentation of the publick Distempers . . . they [are] called stockjobbers.
>
> The first Violence they committed was a downright Rape . . . — [Lady Credit] was no sooner come over [to England], but these new-fashion'd Thieves seiz'd upon her, took her Prisoner, toss'd her in a Blanket, ravish'd her, and in short us'd her barbarously, and had almost murther'd her. (1709a, 124)

Defoe portrays stockjobbers, which is how brokers and middlemen in the London City were then commonly called, as the rapists of Lady Credit. They take advantage of her flirtatious behavior, spoil and tempt her, with the disastrous consequences of nearly killing her. It is through this sexual violence that credit is made a whore and her innocence is violently, if not permanently, lost, according to Defoe: "To recover Credit to any place, where she has been ill Treated, and perswade her to return, is almost as Difficult to restore virginity, or to make a W—re an honest Woman" (1706a, 19).

ACCOUNTING AS A TECHNOLOGY OF THE SELF

Because it is not only the woman but man's *own lust* that undermines his self-mastery (Brown 1988, 90), mastering and submitting Lady Credit requires first and foremost a mastering and submitting of the self. The authority and autonomy required to govern others, as Foucault (1991b) has argued, is fostered by requirements of how to govern oneself. This is a specifically masculine practice in Defoe's writings, or what Lois McNay has called a "virile self-mastery . . . which involved a struggle against the immoderate and womanly side of one's character" (1994, 151). In the *Compleat English Gentleman*, Defoe stresses that man needs to learn to govern himself before he is able to govern his subordinates: his wife, children, and household. "If the gentleman we are treating of can not govern himself," Defoe asks, "how should we expect any good oeconomy in his household? how shall he direct his family or mannage his fortune?" (1890 [1729], 232). Defoe stresses that the gentleman is not fully autonomous when given over to desires of luxury and wealth: "It is a great mistake to say that a vicious life is consistent with a *compleat* gentleman" (234, emphasis added).

The way to self-mastery and good government, Defoe and others propose, is through meticulous bookkeeping. The combination of calculation and foresight will foster an ethical relation with the self that makes possible the mastering of Lady Credit. It should never be below the "gentleman of fortune," Defoe points out, "to meddle with learning and books . . . also to audit their own accounts, let their own lands, mannage their own revenues" (244). Defoe's insistence on the punctual payment of commercial commitments can be read as a way of keeping Lady Credit and all her temptations in check. "The great Injury to Trade," Defoe argues, "is the little Regard the Tradesmen in England have to the Punctual Compliance with their Times of Payment. . . . I shall make the Essay, at Reducing Credit to proper Periods, Payments to punctual Compliance; and so make the Laws of Trade, as sacred as those of the Nation" (1706b, 22–23). The mathematization of one's commitments makes possible an active and anticipating relationship to the world. Through calculated foresight man no longer needs to resign himself to the decrees of providence and the blows of fate, but gains active responsibility over one's affairs, even in times of misfortune (Ewald 1991, 207). Because Fortuna's irrationality also signifies the unpredictability of secular time (Pocock 1985, 99), the careful keeping of books becomes a way of mastering credit, mastering the self, and eventually, mastering time.

It is important to understand how this ethical relation to the self required for the mastering of credit subsequently holds out the promise of undistorted access to economic truth. Foucault has argued in his later work that self-government has a particular relationship to truth and truth telling (1988b, 16–19). If one has to govern oneself to acquire the moral authority to govern others, Foucault and Sennett have shown that this is achieved by a kind of courageous truth telling or a Christian duty to truth: "Self technology implies a set of truth obligations: learning what is truth, discovering the truth, being enlightened by the truth, telling the truth. . . . Everyone in Christianity has the duty to explore who he is, what is happening with himself, the faults he may have committed, the *temptations* to which he is exposed" (1982, 10–11, emphasis added). This duty to truth, then, becomes a way in which the temptations of Lady Credit can be resisted: owning up to one's desires, truthfully exposing them, is a first step in renouncing them.

Truthful exposure of oneself and one's desires is precisely how Defoe conceptualizes accounting and bookkeeping. Defoe discusses bookkeeping as a mechanism through which an undistorted truth will be revealed to the tradesman about himself and his business. If the tradesman does not keep his books, Defoe (1987 [1726], 188) warns, "then he knows nothing of himself, or of his circumstances in the world; the books can tell him at any time what his condition is." Moreover, to Defoe accounting and the "casting up of books" are moral technologies that will not only reveal the truth of the tradesman's circumstance, but that will also guarantee the cleanliness of the tradesman's conscience. "A tradesman's books, like a Christian's conscience, should always be kept clean and clear," writes Defoe, "and he that is not careful with both will give but a sad account of himself either to God or man" (188). To Defoe, honesty and precise bookkeeping are signs of strength and courage—they are virtues through which the tradesman can resist credit's temptations. "As a profligate never looks into his conscience, because he can see nothing there but what terrifies and affrights him," writes Defoe, "so a sinking tradesman cares not to look into his books, because the prospect there is dark and melancholy. 'What signify the accounts to me?' says he, 'I can see nothing in the books but debts that I cannot pay'. . . . Whereas, in truth, the man understood his books well enough, but had no heart to look in them, *no courage to balance them*" (197, emphasis added).

It was not just Defoe's texts that effected this critical link between accounting, truth, and virtue. Defoe's work can be seen in the context of the consolidation of double-entry bookkeeping as an economic technology in eighteenth-century England (e.g., Poovey 1998; Sherman 1996; Winjum 1972). Because it enters each transaction into the books twice (on the debit and on the credit side) double-entry bookkeeping became constructed as the epitome of reliable calculation and the undistorted access to external commercial reality. The appeal to truth and reality forms a consistent theme in accounting manuals of the time. It was by this scientific mechanism that the tradesman would find his way through trade networks and dispel confusion, as poetically advised in Colinson's accounting manual of 1683: "This is the kind Ariadne's silken thread; Conducts them through the Labyrinths of trade; While *Colinson* like *Theseus doth* devour; CONFUSION that monstrous minotaur" (Robert Colinson's *Idea Rationara, or the perfect accomptant,* 1683, quoted in Winjum 1972, 58).

However, despite the accountancy manuals' emphasis on accessing a prior economic reality, Poovey argues that early modern bookkeeping, which forms the basis of current accountancy practices, was a rule-governed kind of writing that actualized and objectified its discursive constructions. Bookkeeping stipulated fictional categories, including "stock," "profit," and "money," that did not directly correspond to actual events or sums and that were transcribed from one ledger to another in a reifying and abstracting manner. This "fiction of total disclosure," Poovey writes, "underwrote the creditworthiness [of the merchant] by proclaiming his credibility" (1998, 59). Double-entry bookkeeping had both a disciplining and a credentialing effect: it disciplined those writing in the books while according them credibility. In this manner, credit and virtue were joined.

Similarly, Steven Shapin has argued that in seventeenth-century England, the *gentleman* was a "paradigm of the type of individual one could trust to speak the truth" (1994, xxvi). And there "was no truer gentleman," Shapin goes on to argue, "than one who was sovereign over his own passions, and who displayed his calm indifference to attempted injury and insult" (64). In contrast to women, servants, and "the vulgar," who were assumed prone to "undisciplined and inaccurate perceptions," the gentleman was assumed to have outstanding "perceptual competence" (75–77). Gentlemanly selfmastery was fostered by the rules and abstractions of bookkeeping as well as by solitude and serious demeanor. Poovey recounts how "privacy" emerged as a class-specific concept that promised to facilitate the husband's administration and governance of the household, embodied in architectural innovations such as the closet and the study (1998, 34). Roger North's *The Gentleman Accomptant* (1712) connects these requirements of solitude, truth, and governance when he describes the process of accounting as "an Act of the Mind, intent upon the Nature and the Truth of Things" requiring "the solitude of a Compting-House, or the Retirement from all Manner of Interruption" (quoted in Sherman 1996, 131). In double-entry bookkeeping, thus, undistorted access to financial truth became possible as a function of a masculine demeanor that included austerity, selfmastery, and the disciplining of the inner enemy of desire for luxury and wealth.

In conclusion, then, the articulation of Fortuna on one hand and the virtuous gentleman on the other effects a division in which irrationality and fantasy are split off from truth and rationality, and in which the former are defined as external to the financial sphere. Defoe and other contemporary writers on the subject of doubleentry bookkeeping set up two distinct spheres, in which capricious, unpredictable, irrational, and inconsistent Fortuna or Credit is articulated in opposition to virtuous, honest, reliable, and rational financial man. Fortuna's irrationality also signified the unpredictability of secular time, and according to Pocock she embodies the "random and the recurrent, the lunar and the cyclical . . . and the contingent with which virtue . . . contends" (1985, 99). Mastering Fortuna was thus a way of mastering the future, by reducing it to orderly slots of "punctual payment." Finally, mastering Fortuna holds out the promise of undistorted access to economic reality and truth. As

Pocock concludes in his study of the eighteenth-century paper wars: "Virtue must involve the cognition of things as they really were; the power of Credit was irredeemably subjective and it would take all authority of society to prevent her from breaking loose to submerge the world in a flood of fantasy" (1975, 457).

HYSTERIA, DELUSION, AND EXUBERANCE: THE GENDERED DISCOURSES OF FINANCIAL CRISIS

While sexualized representations of credit may seem very specific to eighteenth-century political discourse, I contend they are at the heart of the way we understand finance today. The gendered representation of financial crises as instances of madness, delusion, hysteria, and irrationality has had particular historical durability, which simultaneously constructs the sphere of financial normality or rationality. For example, retrospectively the dot-com boom has been largely attributed to the investing public's "irrational exuberance," words coined in a now famous speech by Alan Greenspan, who suggested that "irrational exuberance has unduly escalated asset values" (1996). The term has gained prominence through Robert Shiller's book *Irrational Exuberance,* which argued that "deep down, people know that the market is highly priced, and are uncomfortable about this fact. . . . We are unsure whether the market levels . . . are indeed the result of some human tendency that might be called irrational exuberance" (2000, 14). Earlier, Kindleberger famously argued that, despite modern assumptions that financial markets behave rationally, they are time and again disturbed by manias, including "a loss of touch with reality or rationality, even something close to mass hysteria or insanity" (1978, 25).

Compare further the work of Charles Mackay, whose 1841 *Extraordinary Popular Delusions and the Madness of Crowds* describes stock speculation as a popular delusion likened to alchemy, fortune telling, witch hunts, crusades, and haunted houses. "During the progress of this famous bubble," writes Mackay of the South Sea speculation:

> England presented a singular spectacle. The public mind was in a state of unwholesome fermentation. Men were no longer satisfied with the slow but sure profits of cautious industry. The hope of boundless wealth for the morrow made them heedless and extravagant for

to-day. A luxury, till then unheard of, was introduced, bringing in its train a corresponding laxity of morals. The overbearing insolence of ignorant men, who had arisen to sudden wealth by successful gambling, made men of true gentility of mind and manners blush. (1995, 71)

Mackay's image of men driven to madness by luxury and sudden wealth reminds of Defoe's representation of man's vulnerability to the cunning temptations of Credit. Similarly, when after the 1869 gold panic on Wall Street a government committee was appointed to investigate, it made sense of the panic in these same terms of fortune's temptations and man's madness. "The foundations of business morality were rudely shaken," the report stated, "and the numerous defalcations that shortly followed were clearly traceable to the mad spirit engendered by speculation. . . . Hundreds of active, ambitious men were lured from the honest pursuit of wealth by the delusive vision of sudden fortune" (Committee on Banking and Currency 1974 [1870], 19).

In finance, delusion and hysteria are the most salient and durable metaphors of crisis. After the 1929 stock market crash, the then vice president of the New York Stock Exchange Richard Whitney lamented the "distinctive emotional aspects" and the "public hysteria" that caused the crash (1930, 4, 9). Hysteria, of course, is historically constructed as a women's affliction, being derived from *hystera*, the Greek word for uterus. Elaine Showalter discusses how classical healers "described a female disorder characterized by convulsive attacks, random pains and sensations of choking" (1997, 15), supposedly caused by the uterus wandering around the female body. In the nineteenth century, hysteria became cast as a mental disease, producing symptoms such as attacks, fainting, spasms, emotional outbursts, and excessive sexual desire. For example, in 1866 one doctor enumerated the possible symptoms of hysteria, including "strange thoughts, extraordinary feelings, unseasonable appetites [and] criminal impulses," which may all "haunt a mind at other times innocent and pure" (quoted in Poovey 1988, 37). Foucault documents how hysteria was understood as a "pathology of the imagination" and quotes one doctor who wrote, "This disease in which women invent, exaggerate, and repeat all the various absurdities of which a disordered imagination is capable, has sometimes become epidemic and contagious" (1999, 138–39).

It becomes clear that medical discourses of hysteria and financial discourses of crisis have been linked. Although in the case of financial crises it is mostly men who are affected by hysteria, symptoms similarly are assumed to include strange thoughts (including bad investment decisions), extraordinary feelings, and excessive appetites and desires (most notably for excessive credit and speculation). The model of the human body underpinning the medical identification of hysteria, Poovey points out, "is that of a closed system containing a fixed quantity of energy" (1988, 36). Crises in the system, Poovey continues, were associated with female "biological periodicity," and doctors developed elaborate models charting and predicting periodical disturbances in the female body (36–37). Models of the financial system resemble Poovey's description of the model of the female body in medical discourse: finance is regarded as a delicate and closed system, vulnerable to distortions and disturbances. Walter Bagehot, financial journalist and editor of *The Economist,* for example, offered the following image of finance as a vulnerable but autonomous structure in 1873: "Our credit system [is] much more delicate at some times than at others; and that it is the recurrence of these periodical seasons of delicacy which has given rise to the notion that panics come according to a fixed rule, that every ten years or so we must have one of them" (1991 [1873], 61). Financial panic, moreover, is assumed to be contagious—contagion has become a durable metaphor used to understand the spread of financial crisis and has to some extent become a technical term (see, e.g., Eichengreen 1996, 35; cf. Ling 2002, 125).

Fortuna's instability can be recognized in this new identification of periodic financial crisis, and Figure 3 shows the business cycle as portrayed on the cover of the first issue of *Fortune Magazine* in 1930. Thomas Cleland's image shows Fortuna and her wheel, with labor, industry, and shipping symbolized on the left behind her, while fruits and parcels of goods are piled up on her right. Fortuna's periodicity and instability are represented by her wheel and by the ball on which her left foot rests—a poignant image in the wake of the 1929 stock market crash and at the beginning of the Great Depression. Inside this first issue, the editors stated *Fortune's* purpose to be "to reflect Industrial Life in ink and paper and word and picture as the finest skyscraper reflects it in stone and steel and architecture."[3]

Figure 3. Fortuna and the Business Cycle, cover of Fortune Magazine *1, no. 1 (February 1930), design by Thomas Cleland.*

What is the political significance of the sexualized struggle informing contemporary understandings of financial crisis? Why is it important to understand how seemingly disinterested financial language is firmly rooted in gendered cultural practices? First, the argument that situates financial crises in the realm of delusion and madness simultaneously produces a domain of "normal" market operations. As Campbell points out: "Reason and rationalism are not simply modes of thought that are desirable; they are dispositions that are produced through differentiation from their opposites" (1992, 67). Thus, it is precisely through the identification of moments of irrationality and madness that the financial sphere can be thought rational *at all*. This is why contemporary debates on rational versus irrational markets are still committed to the same—restrictive—discursive framework: rationality and irrationality produce each other.[4] If irrationality and excess are seen to disturb the financial system from time to time, they are still seen as essentially external to it, outside the "temporal window defining the period of 'crisis'" (Kelly 2001, 720).

Second, the subject of rational economic man is produced through discourses of crisis as hysteria and delusion. In the work of Defoe, financial participants are called upon to demonstrate masculine virtues in the face of Fortuna's temptations and dazzling promises. This argument can also be found, for example, in Whitney's speech about the 1929 stock market crash. "No one, I am sure, likes panics," Whitney concluded, "but if we must face such periods of adversity, we must do so boldly and like men" (1930, 29). Paradoxically, then, the discourse that identifies irrationality and hysteria in the financial markets at the same time produces the norm of masculine agency in modern credit practices.[5]

The masculine agent who is called on to resist Credit's temptations is part of a wider discourse that casts capitalist investment as masculine conquest of virgin territories. For example, in her analysis of representative practices in *The Economist*, Charlotte Hooper found that a 1994 article on Myanmar portrayed the country as "Ripe for Rape" because, in the words of *The Economist*, "It still has teak forests to be felled and its gem deposits are barely exploited. Its natural beauties and its astonishing Buddhist architecture make it potentially irresistible to tourists" (2001, 139). Similarly, Tsing argues in her analysis of gold mining company Bre-X that the "frontier story" of capitalist investment and exploitation requires that the explorers "wander alone on an empty landscape" (2001, 173). The natural resources of, in these cases, Indonesia and Myanmar, need to be represented as undiscovered and waiting to be explored, abstracted from all evidence of indigenous people, local politics, and environmental damage. It is these gendered stories of masculine explorers and virgin territories that bring about *real* capital flows, according to Tsing: "The story of lonely prospectors making independent discoveries in a remote jungle moved North American investors and stimulated the capital flow that made Bre-X rich" (2001, 173). Thrift argues that the discourses of the new economy similarly depended on a "certain kind of male role model," which entailed a combination of "the open frontier consisting of limitless possibilities, the self-made person [and] the elemental force of entre-preneurialism" (2001b, 422, 419; see also McDowell 1997).

The Asian financial crisis of the late 1990s can be read through this lens of sexualized investment and crisis.[6] In media and policy papers, the crisis was understood through the historically durable discourse of delusion and madness. For example, Harvard econo-mist Jeffrey Sachs argued in the *Financial Times* that the crisis was caused by "two optical illusions" that had "channelled money into the wrong investments" and that has made investors "reckless" (1997, 26). By comparison, MIT economist Paul Krugman, although in disagreement with Sachs on the appropriate role of the IMF in the wake of the crisis, argued that the Asian crisis is best seen as "brought on by financial excess and then financial collapse. . . . The Asian story is really about a bubble in and subsequent collapse of asset values in general" (1998). Western investors, in other words, were influenced by illusions and driven to excess and recklessness.

It can be argued that in the case of the Asian crisis the Western investor was confronted by the *dual* temptation of Asia's (finan-cially) virgin territories and Lady Credit's promises of wealth and quick profit. Historically, Asia has been represented as "an exotic, sensual and feminised world" (Hooper 1999, 482). The imagination of Asia's otherness included, according to Edward Said, "the motif of the Orient as insinuating danger. Rationality is undermined by Eastern excesses, those mysteriously attractive opposites to what seem to be normal values" (1994, 57). More recently, according to Jongwoo Han and Lily Ling, Asian countries such as Korea have been feminized in globalization discourses for lacking industrial "manhood" (1998, 61). Economic discourses have portrayed Asia as "dormant, isolated and backward" and in need of economic pene-tration by Western technology and industry (Han and Ling 1998, 60). It can be argued, then, that the weaknesses of Asia's banking system and the promises of quick profit posed a dual temptation to Western money managers. In retrospect, the transition from Asian miracle to Asian crisis was blamed on cronyism, overvalued currencies, over-hasty liberalization, and the absence of proper banking regulation (Strange 1998, 81). However, as Tsing asks, "If the same economic policies can produce both in quick succession, might *deregulation* and *cronyism* sometimes name the same thing—but from different moments of investor confidence?" (2001, 155, emphases in original). The gendered discourses of the Asian crisis, then, have effected a representation through which the Asian countries are portrayed as "wrong about the fundamentals for a healthy, modern economy . . . [and] morally unfit to lead the global economy," while the responsibility of Western investors is displaced through emphasis on temptation and temporary delusion (Ling 2002, 125; see also de Goede 2000; Truong 1999). This representation has made possible an international policy response that prioritized for Western-style regulation, accountancy, and transparency and that will allow "international banks to make major inroads into the region's banking sectors" (Higgot 1998, 346).

CONCLUSION

In this chapter I have illustrated the historical contingencies in the formulation of financial concepts that are at the basis of our understanding of financial crises today. Rather than the result of a natural economic evolution, the invention of paper instruments of credit took shape through historical struggle and political discussion. I have suggested that Daniel Defoe's writings start articulating a new moral space in which credit certificates, stocks, shares, and other paper instruments could become virtuous and legally acceptable. However, the discursive split between irrationality and rationality, or between fortune and virtue, can never be completely secured or stabilized. In other words, the mastery of Lady Credit is never complete and financial man is never safe from her temptations and the internal desires and weaknesses she generates in him. This discursive tension becomes most apparent in times of "crisis" when the integrity of the system needs to be reaffirmed by the retroactive identification of financial irregularities, as I have argued with respect to the Asian crisis.

The next chapters will continue to interrogate the problematic boundaries between virtue and fortune that underpin the possibility of financial rationality. The core moral problematic of financial practices was displaced from credit to more complex financial instruments, such as futures and options. While, as I have argued, there is a continuity between Defoe's articulations and contemporary understandings of financial crisis, there is not a linear and unproblematic progression from Defoe's writings to current practices. Defoe's passionate defense of public credit and his sophisticated formulation of financial virtue did not extend to many of the financial instruments that we now regard as natural and unproblematic. The next chapter will document how gambling and speculation came to form the core problematic of emerging financial networks, and how moral, legal, and political spaces for share and futures trading were slowly pried open.

3

Finance, Gambling, and Speculation

Muse rise! With satire cloath'd in verse so glib
assist to lash the speculating tribe;
To them in honest verity declare
What common sense and reason say they are . . .
A set of chaps, that Fortune's goods engross,
And draw their happiness from other's woes.

THE GLASS, OR, SPECULATION: A POEM, 1791

He who sells what isn't his'n
Must dig it up or go to prison.

NINETEENTH-CENTURY U.S. SAYING

CASINO CAPITALISM

In April 1998 a Moscow Court declared certain financial instruments in breach of Russian antigambling laws. The court argued that a certain type of derivative, called a "nondeliverable forward contract," was best viewed as a betting contract as it did not lead to any exchange of underlying assets and was therefore not enforceable under the Russian Civil Code. Afraid that this court decision would deter foreign investors, the Russian Central Bank hurried to defend derivatives trading to Russia's supreme arbitration court. The Central Bank argued that forward contracts were a legitimate part of the banking system and made it known that a breach of this kind of contract could lead to the revocation of banking licenses.

Still, the exact basis for the legitimacy of nondeliverable forwards remained unclear in the bank's argument. A Western lawyer working in Moscow admitted, "You can see the court's decision that forward contracts are a . . . gamble. But they are done all over the world and they should be done in Russia. The central bank is absolutely right" (Thornhill 1998, 2).

The ambiguity between credit practices and gambling is not unique to the Moscow court's decision but is a recurrent historical debate that has shaped the laws and institutions of modern finance. In the eighteenth and nineteenth centuries, the lack of a conceptual distinction between "finance," "gambling," and "speculation" increasingly became an obstacle to the respectability of trading in stocks, shares, and credit certificates. A separation between gambling and finance became thinkable only through a prolonged political, cultural, and legal struggle surrounding the meanings and boundaries of "the financial sphere" and the character and behavior of "financial man." This chapter presents a detailed account of these debates, in which, I argue, the increasing denunciation and demonization of gambling served to accord legitimacy to its discursive double: speculation.

Of particular importance in this regard is the U.S. "bucketshop debate," which took place in the second half of the nineteenth century. This was a public debate over the legitimacy of the trading on financial exchanges in general, and futures and options in particular, fought in the pages of newspapers and popular magazines. The existence of so-called bucketshops, small-scale betting shops in which the public could bet on the movement of stock prices without actually purchasing stock, complicated the articulation of a dividing line between gambling and speculation. The bucketshop debate was also a legal debate, and numerous court cases on state and federal levels were decided on the enforceability of futures contracts between, roughly, 1850 and 1930. These cases are important because they legally inscribed, objectified, and reinscribed the boundaries between gambling and finance. In some cases, the courts thus enshrined financial concepts as they are still used today.

The separation between gambling and finance, then—with speculation as uneasy middle ground—is directly related to social and moral questions concerning the legitimate bases for making profit. To some extent, financial globalization and liberalization have revived these questions. In Japan, for instance, recent financial liberalization has meant relaxation of its strict gambling laws as well as financial deregulation. Until Japan's "Big Bang" program of financial deregulation, over-the-counter options as well as some sophisticated financial derivatives were prohibited by the country's criminal code for breaking gambling laws (Robinson 1997b, 34; Robinson 1997a, IV). Although there have been no actual lawsuits with regard to the breach of gambling laws by derivatives trading in Japan, the *Financial Times* has argued that these "regulatory irritants" have forced Japan to remain in the "derivatives second league" and have moved Japanese derivative trading offshore, particularly to Singapore (Tett 1998, 6).

In Britain, derivatives contracts entered into by the London borough Hammersmith and Fulham were declared null and void by a ruling of the High Court in January 1991 on the grounds that trading for speculative purposes was beyond the powers invested in local governments (Tickell 1998). Hammersmith and Fulham had been investing council money in complex financial instruments, including swaps, since 1983. At the height of its trading activity, Hammersmith and Fulham accounted for half a percent of all the swaps trading globally. In 1988, the Audit Commission, which is responsible for overseeing the expenditures of local governments in Britain, questioned whether the Hammersmith and Fulham derivatives trading was lawful and decided to seek a legal ruling in the matter. As a result, the 1991 High Court ruling declared swaps dealing *ultra vires* for local government. Although the Hammersmith and Fulham swaps affair did not actually evoke notions of gambling, it did establish a dividing line between trading derivatives for "formal risk management" and "trading for profit." The High Court ruling effectively argued that speculative profit making is inappropriate for local authorities trading with public money (Tickell 1998, 872–73).

Within the political economy literature, attention to the problematic nature of the distinction between gambling and finance has been drawn most notably by Strange's (1986, 1998) critical accounts of financial globalization. Strange argues that the newly deregulated financial markets resemble a giant casino, in which financial institutions such as banks and pension funds gamble with public money. The collapse of the Bretton Woods system of fixed exchange rates in the 1970s has increased uncertainty in international financial practice. The response to this increased uncertainty, according to

Strange, has been increasingly complex strategies of risk management, insurance, hedging, and speculation. Paradoxically, these increasingly complex financial strategies have fueled financial uncertainty and volatility rather than dispelled them, Strange (1986, 119) concludes. Despite its importance, Strange's argument obscures the fact that the association between gambling and finance is not specific to the late twentieth-century financial sphere and that no "natural" distinction between the concepts can be assumed. Indeed, the distinction between gambling and finance was not stabilized until the early twentieth century, when risk was codified as a calculable entity.

THE MORAL PROBLEMATIZATION OF GAMBLING

Finance and gambling are both strategies of confronting chance and uncertainty, and as such had no conceptual difference in early modern Europe (see also de Goede 2004). A number of practices that we would now consider to be firmly in the realm of finance, including government borrowing, insurance and stock trading, emerged in a network of activity that also boosted what we would now call gambling practices. Over time, the attack on gambling became a means though which finance distinguished itself as a morally responsible sphere of thought and action. In other words, it was only through creating a contrast with gambling that finance was able to emerge as a respectable element out of early modern networks of monetary activity.

In medieval and early modern Europe, lotteries were used regularly for the financing of public works and colonial settlement (Brenner and Brenner 1990, 8–11). Lotteries were more suitable for the raising of public moneys than loans because, as Ian Hacking (1975, 111) points out, "Usury was suspect and not a proper business for the state." In the cities of Holland and Flanders, for example, lotteries were organized as early as the fifteenth century for the raise of specific expenditures. The Dutch town of Middelburg financed its fortifications by lottery in 1615, and Amsterdam raised money for the building of a hospital in 1592. In England, Queen Elizabeth chartered a lottery in 1569 for financing public works, including the improvement of harbors. This lottery could render the lucky winner free from arrest for seven days (except for major crimes) as well as offering monetary prizes. In the early seventeenth century, James I authorized a number of lotteries to finance settlements in colonial

Virginia, but in 1621 Parliament temporarily halted national lotteries to address the "inconveniences and evils" caused by these events (Brenner and Brenner 1990, 10).

When English governmental lotteries were resumed through an act of Parliament in 1694, they were transformed from incidental fund-raising for specific projects to a solid basis for the creation and the management of a national debt in the absence of large-scale taxation. R. D. Richards (1934, 58) points to three purposes of the eighteenth-century English state lotteries: they were used to raise state loans, they were used to raise state revenue (including revenue to pay the obligations of previous lotteries), and they were used for the financing of special projects. The creation of regular lotteries, then, should be considered *part of* the financial revolution instead of as a perpetuation of archaic monetary practices. In contrast, while the National Lottery in Britain, reintroduced in 1993, again fulfills the function of financing special projects such as museums, lotteries are now not regarded as a regular and legitimate part of modern financial practices. For example, when in 1998 municipal governments in Colombia organized lotteries to raise revenue to pay their staff, the *Financial Times* wrote: "It was clear something was wrong when municipal governments in southern Colombia began organising impromptu lotteries to cover their payroll obligations. . . . Throughout Colombia, regional governments are having to adopt radical—and sometimes unconventional—measures to avoid declaring bankruptcy" (Thomson 1998, 4).

However, between 1694 and 1826, around 170 state lotteries were launched in London. Initially, these took the form of so-called lottery-annuities, in which *all* ticket holders were entitled to a periodic payment, but in which special money prizes were awarded to a small number of ticket holders. The first large-scale state lottery-annuity was the Million Adventure of 1694, which formed part of an overall plan by the Chancellor of the Exchequer to finance the war against France (Richards 1934, 58–59). From 1710 onward, the English state lotteries were managed by the Bank of England, which introduced "pure" lotteries because the annuity schemes were proving far too costly for the state. In 1719 the George I lottery was authorized, in which there was a number of blank tickets not entitled to any prize or periodic payment. Only fortunate tickets earned a yearly income and a chance of an additional prize. The transfer of the responsibility for lotteries from the Government Lottery Office to the Bank of England marks the emergence of the bank as the manager of the national debt. The bank would play an increasingly important role in the management of government lotteries and annuities, and by the 1760s the bank was managing around 70 percent of the national debt (Bowen 1995, 10; Richards 1934, 60–73).

Despite the introduction of blank tickets in the lotteries, the popularity of lotteries increased considerably during the eighteenth century. If the Elizabethan lottery of 1569 had to be extended to sell more tickets, the lottery "Adventures" of 1711 and 1712 were very popular and oversubscribed (Daston 1988, 143; Richards 1934, 60). During the second half of the eighteenth century, the drawing of the national lottery was a very popular annual event that took several days. A lively secondary market in lottery tickets emerged, and it became possible to make side bets on the outcome of the draw, which were known as insurance (Munting 1996, 56). Moreover, as the usual £10 tickets of the state lotteries were too expensive for the general public, smaller unofficial lotteries were organized, which were drawn more often than the state lotteries. The state suppressed these and other private lotteries, albeit not very successfully.

State lotteries were not the only eighteenth-century practice in which no conceptual difference between finance and gambling existed. Early insurance incorporated elements that we would now consider to be gambling practices, and insurance offices were a mix of communal provision societies and gambling houses. For instance, Lloyd's of London, the best known contemporary insurer, started out as a so-called coffee house where well-off citizens gathered to do business. Lloyd's was a meeting point for sailors and shipowners who contractually agreed to support each other financially in case a ship of one of the signatories was lost or damaged. Lloyd's moreover sold protection against floods, storms, and fires. However, no conceptual difference existed between these contracts and other strategies of wagering on uncertain outcomes. For instance, at Lloyd's and similar offices it was possible to buy insurance against lying and losing at the lottery. It was moreover possible to place bets on the outcome of battles, the longevity of celebrities, the succession of Louis XV's mistresses, and the outcome of trials (Daston 1988, 163–82). In 1771, bets placed at Lloyd's and other underwriters on the true sex of Charles de Beaumont, a French diplomat, approximated £60,000. Although de Beaumont declined to provide the proof necessary to resolve speculations concerning his gender, in 1777 a court ordered an underwriter to pay out to a bettor who had gambled that the diplomat was, in fact, a woman. The court did however express "grave reservations about the propriety of such bets" (Clark 1999, 48).

Early life insurance frequently took the form of a policy on the life of a third party, sometimes a person who owed the insurer money, but often a stranger—a prince, king, or pope. Traveling merchants gambled with their own lives by placing bets on their safe return, bets were placed on the survival of generals in battle, and in 1765 bets were placed on the survival of eight hundred German immigrants who had arrived in Britain and were abandoned without food or shelter (Daston 1988, 165). But also insuring one's own life and the lives of loved ones incorporated gambling elements. Mutual aid societies offered a combined attraction of safety and wagering. An early form of mutual aid was a "tontine," a pool to which members contributed a small amount periodically. The last surviving member of the tontine was entitled to the total amount of all contributions, and members thus effectively gambled on each other's deaths (Zelizer 1983, 67–73).

Clearly then, eighteenth-century monetary networks incorporated a wealth of practices for the wagering on uncertain events, whether it be death, fire, lottery draws, marriages, or births, in which no distinction between finance and gambling was made. How, then, did finance and gambling become assigned to different moral and legal spheres by the early twentieth century? How was it possible for gambling to become condemned as immoral, idle, and blasphemous, while its kindred practices, such as insurance and speculation, became praised for inculcating prudence and foresight?

What we see during the course of the eighteenth century is the moral problematization of gambling in a Foucauldian sense. In *The History of Sexuality,* Foucault suggests that it was precisely in the absence of legal interdictions or absolute prohibitions that moral discourses were formed around certain sexual practices. "It is often the case that the moral solicitude is strong precisely where there is neither obligation nor prohibition. In other words, interdiction is one thing, moral problematization another," writes Foucault. "It seemed to me therefore, that the question that ought to guide my inquiry was the following: how, why, and in what forms was sexuality constituted as a moral domain. . . . Why this 'problematization'?" (Foucault 1984b, 10). A similar argument can be made with respect to gambling: the moral problematization of gambling took place in the absence of strict obligations and interdictions with respect to gaming practices and sought to moderate, regulate, and condition these practices. The problematization of gambling established at the same time a "pattern of normalization," which made possible, as I will argue, the emergence of speculation as a legitimate practice (12).

During the course of the eighteenth and nineteenth centuries, then, there was a proliferation of moral discourse on the subject of gambling. Gambling had not always been condemned in Christian teachings, and the Bible records passages in which the drawing of lots was used to discover God's will when appointing functionaries or determining guilt (Brenner and Brenner 1990, 1–7). The church itself regularly used lotteries for financing special projects, and the Archbishop of Canterbury was among the commissioners of the Westminster Bridge in London, which was financed by a series of lotteries between 1737 and 1741 (Richards 1934, 65–66). But increasing religious condemnation of gambling can be observed during the period of the state lotteries, and the reliance on chance came to be seen as an attempt to escape or overturn divine providence (Daston 1988, 150–63).

For instance, in 1790, Charles Moore, a vicar in Kent, published a *Full Inquiry into the Subject of Suicide,* to which he added, "as being closely connected with the subject," a *Treatise on Gaming.* Concerning the lotteries Moore wrote:

> If it should also be a principal view in every good government, to bestow its favours and rewards on industry, and to discourage idleness, to promote virtue and to discountenance vice, then do lotteries seem purposely contrived to confound and frustrate these ends. The profit or reward is indiscriminately held out to the industrious citizen and to the drone, to the foolish and the wise, the worthless and the valuable, the virtuous and the vicious; and perhaps he alone is crowned with success, who is on every account least deserving of his good fortune. (1790, 359)

Moore's argument illustrates what became the core of the moral problematization of gambling in the eighteenth and nineteenth centuries. As Daston argues, by asserting that the lotteries and other gambling practices were "severing the link between merit, skill, . . .

hard work and temporal rewards," the unproblematic existence of such link was constructed and propagated by gambling reformers (1988, 148). Lottery critics claimed that their concerns were for the poor, wishing to protect them from false hopes and financial ruin caused by lotteries, but at the same time they decried the potential subversion of the rigid class order of eighteenth-century England (149). As a popular song of 1790 went:

> The Name of a Lott'ry the Nature bewitches,
> And City and Country run Mad after Riches: . . .
> The Footman resolves, if he meets no Disaster,
> To mount his gilt Chariot, and vie with his Master.
> The Cook Maid determines, by one lucky Hit,
> To free her fair Hands from the pot-hooks and Spit:
> The Chamber-maid struts in her Ladies Cast Gown,
> And hopes to be dub'd the Top Toast of Town.
>
> (146–47)

The evil of gambling was inserted into a web of meaning that linked gambling to other vices, including drunkenness, crime, and prostitution. Lottery critics complained that the prolonged lottery draws and the side betting were distracting Londoners from their proper labors and were accompanied by loudness, drunkenness, riots, and pickpocketing in the area of Guildhall where the draws took place (Munting 1996, 57). As Moore put it: "Whoever wishes to know what are the 'blessings' of a lottery, should often visit Guildhall during the time of its drawing; when he will see thousands of workmen, servants, clerks, apprentices, passing and repassing with looks full of suspense and anxiety, and who are stealing at least from their master's time, if they have not also robbed him of his property, in order to enable them to become adventurers" (1790, 359). Another antigambling author asserted: " 'tis easy to infer that Gaming brings People into ill Company. 'Tis an Inlet to Drinking and Debauchery . . . your gamesters are commonly finish'd Rakes, and their Morals are as bad as their Mystery" (Collier and Goldsmid 1885, 33). It was argued that gambling men lost all sight of their familial and professional responsibilities, were consumed by their gaming passions, and wasted their time. When engrossed in gambling activities, Collier and Goldsmid wrote, "a Man can't manage with that Steadiness and Force he would do otherwise. For when the

Head runs Muddy, the Sight grows dim, and the Judgement is pro-
portionately Disabled . . . when he is sunk at Play, there's no emerging, no Physick will reach his Distemper . . . the Evil is irrevocable
and past Redemption" (1885, 28–35).

Particular concern was expressed over gambling by women; it was
said that women gambled with the household money and forsook the
running of the house and the care of their children (Munting 1996,
26). Moore devoted an entire chapter of his *Treatise on Gaming* to
"Gambling among Females," and wrote, "For tell me, ye daughters
of eager play, does not its desire increase with its gratification? Does
not every domestic employment in consequence pall and tire? . . . Is
there music any longer in the prattle of your babes? . . . or do you . . .
count the tedious moments till the hour of play arrives, and fly from
home?" (1790, 369). Sometimes, gambling women were blamed
for the proliferation of gaming in society, by failing to set a good
example. "Have we not heard of Ladies losing hundreds of Guineas
at a Sitting?" wrote Collier and Goldsmid, "And when the Women
are thus Courageous, the Men conclude their own Sex calls for a
bolder Liberty: That they ought to go farther in Danger, and appear
more Brave in the Methods of Ruin" (1885, 19). Like the practice of
stockjobbing, the excesses of gambling were associated with female
unruliness and prostitution. "How can due respect await the characters of those women, who make no scruple of thus spending whole
nights with men over the gaming-table?" asked Moore, "the 'man'
that plays beyond his income pawns his estate; the 'woman' must find
something else to mortgage, when her pinmoney is gone. The husband
has his lands to dispose of, the wife her person" (1790, 369–70).

In response to the increased opposition to lotteries and gambling, the government appointed a Select Committee of Parliament
in 1808 with the mandate to "inquire how far the evils attending
Lotteries have been remedied by the laws passed" (Richards 1934,
75–76). The committee was unambiguous in its findings and re-
ported in that same year that "the foundation of the Lottery is so
radically vicious. . . . that under no system of regulations that can
be devised will it be possible for Parliament to adopt it as an efficient source of Revenue, and at the same time divest it of all the evils
and calamities of which it has hitherto been so baneful a source"
(quoted in Richards 1934, 76). Despite the report, the government
was reluctant to give up this very profitable source of income, and

it took another fifteen years before the lotteries were outlawed. In 1823 the Lottery Act was passed, which provided for the outlaw of state lotteries after the last draw in 1826. The following "memoriam" was written for the occasion:

> In Memory of
> THE STATE OF LOTTERY
> the last of a long line
> whose origin in England commenced
> in the year 1569 . . .
> As they increased, it was found that their
> continuance corrupted the morals,
> and encouraged a spirit
> of Speculation and Gambling among the lower
> classes of the people.
> (quoted in Brenner and Brenner 1990, 12)

Life insurance had already been restricted and regulated some fifty years earlier, when the Gaming Act of 1774 stipulated that the policyholder had to demonstrate a legitimate interest in the life of the insured. Betting on the lives of third parties thus became outlawed, although, as Clark (1999) demonstrates in his history of British life insurance, legal ambiguity over what this insurable interest constituted persisted for some decades. But "with this legal rationale in place," Clark argues, "both the state and insurance companies acquired the statutory authority as well as the categorical means to segregate existing life insurance practices into 'licit' and 'illicit' behaviors as defined by the emerging moral and rational calculus for economic action" (2002, 93).

The point here, then, is that the moral problematization of gambling and the proliferation of discourse on the subject, defined, classified, and distinguished the licit and illicit in emerging monetary practices. Rather than understanding the Gaming Act, for instance, as a pure prohibition in the sphere of gambling, it can be interpreted as a code that regulated, modified, and normalized certain practices hitherto indistinguishable from gambling (Daston 1988, 175–76). However, the end of the state lotteries did not end the political controversies over the gambling elements in monetary transactions. On the contrary, the nineteenth century saw a proliferation of texts concerning the immorality of "gambling in the forms of trade" (Dewey 1905).

SPECULATION DEBATES IN THE NINETEENTH-CENTURY
UNITED STATES

In the nineteenth-century United States, there was an explosion of public debate on the moral and legal ambiguities between gambling, speculation, and the practices of financial exchanges. This debate is not just a rhetorical addition to changing economic structures, but the very means through which the financial sphere was defined, shaped, and legitimized. In other words, the institutional, legal, and moral framework of the twentieth-century financial sphere can be traced back to these debates.

For example, the 1791 anonymous poem cited at the beginning of this chapter, which was published in New York, accuses speculators of unjustly acquiring more than their deserved share of "Fortune's goods" (*Glass* 1791, 3). The poem goes on to say:

> You sons of earth, did God alone for you
> Bid countries rise and spac'ous rivers flow? . . .
> In Virtue's cause have thousands labour'd hard,
> That you should run away with the reward? . . .
> Have you no bowels for th' unfortunate?
> Does not soft pity reach your stoick state?
> Can you see thousands ruin'd by your means,
> And yet in perfect ease enjoy your gains? (7, 10)

The poem clearly contrasts speculation and virtue, assuming that virtue and hard work ("thousands have laboured hard") are not only speculation's opposites, but are exploited by the speculators who get easy rewards ("run away with the reward"). Given such damning critiques, how was it possible that by the early twentieth century, speculation had been rearticulated as a virtuous business practice while speculators had become masculine and responsible managers of the future?

The bulk of the debate concerning the legitimacy of speculation in the United States took place after the Civil War (1861–65), which had given a boost to the emerging monetary networks. The uncertainties and volatility of war had created unprecedented opportunities for investment and speculation, and the republican army was one of the major purchasers of grain futures contracts as a way of securing food supplies to its soldiers (Dunbar 2000, 27). According to Cronon, it was no accident that that the Chicago Board of Trade

(CBoT) adopted the first formal rules governing futures contracts just after the war in 1865 (1991, 124). The CBoT had been founded in 1848 to facilitate and centralize long-distance grain trading between the agricultural Midwest and Eastern cities. After the Civil War, it became one of the largest and most hotly debated futures markets in the United States.

Futures, or "to-arrive" contracts, allowed future delivery of batches of produce at a fixed price—they were not new and had been used, for example, for gambling and speculation in Amsterdam in the seventeenth century (De Marchi and Harrison 1994). What was *new* about the CBoT's grain futures markets, however, was that they were governed by strict market rules, which facilitated an unprecedented increase in their use.[1] The new futures trading rules depended on processes of produce standardization and contract formalization. As Witold Kula (1986) has shown, units of measurements for grain and other agricultural commodities displayed extensive spatial and temporal variation until well into the nineteenth century. For example, many measures were defined by body parts such as foot, pace, and elbow (ell) and therefore displayed large variations. Moreover, ill-defined measures could be tampered with: a wagonload of grain could be flat or heaped, of greater or lesser quality, while grain poured from a greater height packs more densely. Because of this, trading in to-arrive contracts would habitually involve personal inspection of the product upon delivery or would at least require a high degree of personal trust between buyer and seller to guarantee the measure and quality of grain.

During the second half of the nineteenth century, however, produce exchanges, led by the CBoT, introduced uniform measures and quality categories of grain, thus making personal inspection of deliveries of grain superfluous (Cronon 1991, 97–147). Most importantly, standardization made possible the introduction of margin trading—the requirement of a 10 percent deposit when entering into futures contracts. Margin trading allowed market participants to make profits on price differences without owning or intending to own the actual produce and allowed positions far in excess of the cash paid for them. It quickly became custom to settle price differences between contracts when the delivery day arrived instead of making the actual delivery. From 1872 onward, the amounts of produce traded on the exchanges far exceeded annual crop production, and the amount of futures contracts that led to delivery of the produce or commodity stipulated was estimated to be anywhere between 10 percent to a fraction of 1 percent of all futures trading (Cowing 1965, 5). By the late 1800s, then, traders on the Chicago Exchange did not even need to know what grain looked like in order to buy, sell, and make a profit on it. "A successful trader of wheat," writes Theodore Porter, "no longer had to spend his time at farms, ports, and rail terminals judging the quality of each farmer's produce. . . . The knowledge needed to trade wheat . . . now consisted of price data and production data, which were to be found in printed documents produced minute by minute" (1995a, 48). Increasingly, professional speculators rather than farmers and merchants operated on the futures markets. As one historian put it, the futures markets were a place where "men who don't own something are selling that something to men who don't really want it" (quoted in Cronon 1991, 125).

Speculators were accused of the same vices as gamblers: it was argued that they were rewarded without effort or hard work and that they profited from the labor of others, particularly farmers. In fact, farmers and agricultural organizations were among the most powerful sources of critique of speculation and futures trading in produce.[2] They argued that futures trading had caused enormous price volatility in produce since the end of the Civil War and that speculating for a price decline, or short selling,[3] induced financial operators to deliberately drive the prices down. Farmers attacked futures trading as gambling in food and produce and accused professional speculators of trading in "fictitious commodities" or "wind wheat." "While a few men really buy and sell wheat [on the exchanges]," a New England preacher wrote in 1888, "the majority of speculators buy and sell promises" (Hubbard 1888, 6). Reverend George Hubbard blamed speculation for the inequality of income in the United States and went on to say:

> The paper contracts of the various Exchanges already mentioned, involving billions of dollars, imply an actual loss on one side and gain on the other of hundreds of millions. This enormous sum of money does not represent any benefit conferred upon the community, but is absorbed by the fortunate speculators without any return whatever, leaving the country at large so much poorer. . . . Thousands of poor people may be starving for want of bread while millions of bushels of wheat lie stored away in the elevators held to compel a rise in prices. (7–8)

Similarly, a satirical poem of 1840 lamented the influence of speculators on prices and produce markets in the following verses:

But [in 1838] Speculators *swarm'd again*
And bought up all our *meat* and *grain*
While av'rice and its kindred *vices*
Near *starv'd* us with their famine prices
For *Bread*, the hapless widow sighed
And *orphans* of starvation died!
(Citizen of Saratoga Springs
1840, 7, original emphases)

In 1892, in a letter to the Committee on Agriculture in support of a bill designed to tax futures trading in produce,[4] a Minnesota wheat farmer compared speculators to the devil. "The gambling in food products," this farmer wrote, "utterly destroys anything that could be called a market. What business has a man (or devil) selling or pretending to sell, a food product which he does not possess? . . . These men who 'operate' on the boards of trade (more appropriately called gambling hells) have no right to the consideration of honest men than the devil has to a seat in heaven" (quoted in Fabian 1999, 153). The argument that speculating was the work of the devil was voiced also by Charles William Smith, a former Liverpool broker who had become a fierce opponent of financial trading. In support of the farmers Smith wrote: "All raw materials, say, the land and all its actual products, were not made by man, but created by God, for the use and sustenance of the human race. And this dealing in 'fictitious' commodities, I maintain, is directly antagonistic to the spirit of Christianity, and consequently must be forbidden in all Christian countries" (Smith 1906, 6).[5]

Indeed, as Hilton (1988) demonstrates, the new monetary practices and religious values stood in a profoundly uneasy relation with each other. Religious condemnation of speculation, or "over-trading," was common in nineteenth-century Britain. "Over-trading is *fast* trading," one British opponent of speculation wrote in 1866, "[it] is, in fact, the criminal folly against which the Word of God so clearly warns us—the *making haste to be rich*, which is never innocent, but always culpable and baneful" (quoted in Hilton 1988, 123, original emphases). This argument was made also by the Scottish reverend and theology professor Thomas Chalmers, who rallied against the sins of excess associated with speculative practices. "We feel no dread anticipation of national loss, either from profuse expenditure or from excessive speculation," Chalmers wrote in his treatise on political economy, "but both habits are much to be deprecated, as being alike unfavourable to private virtue and happiness. And both these excesses may in fact be realised by the same individual—in whom the appetite for gain and the appetite for indulgence, may meet together in hurtful and vicious combination" (1832, 123–24; see Hilton 1988, 115–20). Chalmers regarded speculation to be excessive and indulgent and praised the "plodding and painstaking" virtues of hard work over the "gambling artifices" of financial practices (1832, 124, 168).

In sum, like gamblers, speculators were accused of making money from nothing and of being "idlers who made profit even while they slept; [they] had money that reproduced itself without labour" (Fabian 1999, 159). The popular financial journalist Garet Garrett described New Street in the New York financial district as "the Hall of Delusions" and lamented that "in New Street all men are equally under the delusion that the ticker is a source of wealth—that wealth is made and unmade by the going up and down of prices" (1911, 2–3). Another critic of financial trading, James Hamilton Howe, published a popular tract against speculation and futures trading in 1882, "written especially for the education and protection of our young men and women, about to enter the business or professional world." Howe, a lecturer at Boston University, took aim at the CBoT, which he called "the Dragon and Juggernaut of Speculation." "Dragon takes advantage of Drought, Hail, Wind, Rain, Frost, Floods and Fire," wrote Howe, "the Devilish Tricks that He Daily Frames Up, in order to Deceive the Poor Fish, are Many and Subtle. . . . Dragon is the most powerful and dangerous robber of the present time; disturbing, as he does, the normal prices of the food products of the world, even to far-away Zanzibar" (1916, 38). Howe flamboyantly argued that the CBoT was a giant casino that received the support of the government and the most powerful business interests in the United States.

The asserted parallels between speculating and gambling resulted in a bleak portrait of financial traders. Speculating was seen as leading to financial ruin at best and madness and suicide at worst. We have already seen that the Englishman Moore devoted a whole section of his investigation into suicide to gambling, which he believed to lead to "despair, rage and madness," and, eventually, suicide (1790, 362). Moore strongly opposed stockjobbing and lotteries and concluded: "Did ever extravagance and gambling in all its varied forms reign more triumphant in the bosom of trade? Did ever consequent fraud and forgery so fearfully pervade the whole system of commerce?—The career begins in idleness . . . and terminates in the chambers of infamy and death" (363–65). Similarly, the American author of a tract on the *Ethics of Gambling* argued that gambling and suicide were closely related and wrote in 1896, "If we could but obtain accurate statistics, we should find that gambling was of all vicious habits, not even excluding hard drinking, the one which most predisposed its victims to suicide" (MacKenzie 1896, 44). Suicide, argued MacKenzie, was the logical outcome of the gambling process, which induced the gambler to "step outside the conditions of rational, human action, [and] to resign the use of your own manhood" (30). Howe also argued that insanity took hold of those who gambled on the CBoT. "The usual person whom Dragon induces to enter these gambling halls soon becomes hypnotized and sadly influenced to his personal ruin and dismantlement of his household goods," Howe asserted, "His few short hours of gain are filled with excitement and fidgety dreams, rather than happiness. His feelings are more like the ecstatic musings of [a] maniac . . . a sanatorium would be the proper place for him" (1916, 38).

THE LEGAL AMBIGUITY OVER SPECULATION

In addition to growing popular resistance against their practices, stock and produce exchanges faced considerable legal restrictions. During the nineteenth century, most U.S. states passed laws against speculation, futures trading, and commercial wagering. Opposition against futures trading was strongest in Midwestern states, where agricultural organizations hostile to speculation had the most political clout. As late as 1927, the *Harvard Law Review* lamented the existence of antifutures laws that affected the stock and produce exchanges. While antifutures laws were "clearly desirable when applied to transactions not conducted through the medium of stock and produce exchanges, as, for example, bucketshop operations, considerable difficulties arise from [their] application to futures contracts on exchanges" (*Harvard Law Review* 1927, 638).

The legal discussion over speculation in the United States was more public and more controversial than the one in Britain and offers unique insight into the arguments and objections that had to be muted in order for speculation to become considered a legitimate and socially beneficial practice in the mid-twentieth century. Still, it is important to point out that speculation was contested in Britain in similar terms as in the United States. Britain passed an anti-speculation law in the aftermath of the South Sea Bubble in 1734. In addition, there was some discussion in Britain over whether stock exchange transactions and "time-contracts" were affected by the Gaming Act of 1845 (Morgan and Thomas 1962, 148). In 1877, a Royal Commission was appointed to inquire into the legitimacy of the activities of the London Stock Exchange, particularly speculation. One of the problems, a member of the House of Commons asserted, was that the Stock Exchange "encouraged speculation by admitting a low class of members with small security" (quoted in Kynaston 1994, 277). One ruined speculator testified before the Commission that "the Committee of the Stock Exchange is in one word corrupt. . . . How can it be otherwise? The Committee is an irresponsible body. They frame their own laws to suit their own objects. Such of their laws as are framed with a view to protect the public, and these are few, they disregard when challenged to do so . . . as I have proved to my cost" (283). The secretary of the London Exchange, on the other hand, testified that in order to prohibit fraud, "The best restriction is to take all the means in one's power to see that the applicant is a person of good character and credit" (278). In 1878, the Royal Commission delivered a report that recommended the incorporation of the exchange and the public visibility of the trading floor, but that denied the need for any fundamental transformation of the London Stock Exchange. In addition, British courts often "refused to interfere with the exchanges' own rules or their relations with their own members" (May 1939, 489).

In contrast, in the United States the courts and other legislative bodies were more sympathetic to the cases of ruined speculators and more willing to restrain speculative practices. New York State was one of the first to pass an antispeculation statute as early as 1812, by prohibiting sales for future delivery when the seller did not own the stock to be delivered (short selling). The "Act to Regulate Sales at Public Auction and to Prevent Stock Jobbing" declared void all future sales of stocks or shares, "unless the party contracting to sell . . . shall at the time of making such contract be in actual possession of the certificate" (Fayant 1913, 54–55). The New York statute was controversial in the state legislature, demonstrated by the fact that the law was contested but reenacted in 1830. The statute was eventually repealed in 1858 by an act that held that no contract shall be void or voidable "because the vendor at the time of making such contract is not the owner or possessor of the certificate . . . or other evidence of such debt, share, or interest" (Dewey 1886, 18–19).

In contrast to the New York State legislature, most U.S. states formulated laws against stock gambling, bucketshops, and futures trading after the Civil War. For example, the criminal code of the 1880 Revised Statutes of the State of Illinois includes a section on "Gambling in Grain," which stipulates: "Whoever contracts to have or give himself or another the option to sell or buy, at a future time, any grain, or other commodity, stock . . . or gold . . . shall be fined not less than $10 nor more than $1,000, or confined in the county jail not exceeding one year, or both; and all contracts made in violation of this section shall be considered gambling contracts and shall be void" (Cothran 1880, 471). Similarly, the "Georgia Statute against Short Sales" held that "a contract for the sale of goods to be delivered at a future day where both parties are aware that the seller expects to purchase himself to fulfil his contract, and no skill and labor or expense enters into the consideration . . . is a pure speculation upon chances, is contrary to the policy of the law and can be enforced by neither party" (Dewey 1886, 21).

Texas enacted an antifutures law as late as 1907. Section 14 of the Texas law emphasized the urgency of its enactment and stated: "The fact that there is now no adequate law to prevent dealing in futures and the further fact that the prices of agricultural and farm products are greatly depressed by such gambling transactions and that such transactions are against good morals and contrary to public policy . . . creates an imperative public necessity . . . that this bill takes effect" (*General Laws of the State of Texas* 1907, 174). However, the controversial nature of the Texas law is demonstrated by the fact that one of the most important supporters of the law, president of the Texas Farmers' Union, E. A. Calvin, made a public announcement withdrawing his support for the antifutures law in 1909. Calvin argued that the law, while intending to eradicate bucketshops, had damaged exchange trading, and concluded: "Speculation, as commonly known, is a venture based on calculation containing elements of reason, while gambling is without calculation and simply blind chance. One is an evil, the other a necessity. The law condemns gambling, but should sustain speculation" (quoted in *Functions of the Legitimate Exchanges* 1910, 187).

It was frequently left to the courts to decide whether exchange transactions were affected by the various statutes against futures trading and bucketshops. Numerous court cases were fought on state and federal levels concerning the legality of futures, usually brought by unfortunate speculators who hoped to avoid paying their losses by arguing that the contracts entered into were gambling contracts and should be declared void.[6] It was not unusual for judges to find in favor of these ruined traders. For example, in the Illinois case *Cothran v. Ellis*, which was decided in the late 1800s, Judge Mulky found futures trading to be unambiguously within the jurisdiction of the antigambling laws. "Dealing in futures or options, as they are commonly called, to be settled according to the fluctuations of the market, is void by the common law"; this judge held:

> It is not only contrary to public policy, but it is a crime—a crime against the state, a crime against the general welfare and happiness of the people, a crime against religion and morality, and a crime against all legitimate trade and business. This species of gambling has become emphatically and pre-eminently the national sin. . . . In its pernicious and ruinous consequences, it is simply appalling. Clothed with respectability and entrenched behind wealth and power, it submits to no restraint, and defies alike the laws of God and man. (quoted in Howe 1916, 123)

Other courts delivered similar decisions. For instance, a Court of Appeals in Tennessee annulled a number of futures contracts in 1896 and argued "that stock speculation of this kind, where the party trading neither has nor expects to get and to pay for the actual stock, is merely gambling, and illegal, and contracts founded thereon are void and unenforceable, is beyond dispute" (quoted in MacDougall 1936, 72).

During the course of these legal controversies, a number of themes emerged that became decisive in the question whether futures contracts could be declared void. The large number of court cases fought

on the topic produced confused and contradictory evidence and varying definitions of futures trading, wagering, and speculation. However, the "intent of the parties to deliver" became a validity test for
futures contracts that was formulated as early as the 1852 federal case
Grizewood v. Blane. If parties to a contract do not intend to deliver
the underlying stocks or commodities, this reasoning held, and if "the
real intent be merely to speculate in the rise and fall of prices," then
the contract would be void (Taylor 1933, 66–67).

Dewey presents an overview of "facts and circumstances that
have been considered by the courts as indicating an intention to
wager," which he admits to be "unsatisfactory and contradictory"
(1886, 76). First, notes Dewey, intention to wager has sometimes
been considered proven when the seller of the futures contract did
not actually own or posses the articles sold (95–106). The court
cases that annulled futures contracts on this basis thus had the
same effects as the statutes against short selling mentioned above.
Dewey demonstrates that this line of reasoning was subject to much
debate, as in a series of Illinois cases that formulated, questioned,
and eventually overruled the annulment of contracts on this basis.
Other factors indicating the intention to wager included evidence
that a purchaser of futures contracts intended to resell the contract
before the stipulated time of delivery; evidence that the party dealing in futures contracts would not be able to pay for the actual delivery of the underlying stock or produce, and thus merely intended
to settle the price differences; and evidence that the parties to the
contract were engaged in a large number of transactions at the same
time (115–35). For example, the argument that engagement in a
large number of speculative transactions indicated intention to wager
was voiced by a Pennsylvania court that said: "If besides this contract it should be shown that many others of a similar kind were
entered into by the same man, and at about the same time, certainly
it would strengthen the conviction that the plaintiff was not a bona
fide contractor in a legitimate business" (133).

As late as 1933, the U.S. Supreme Court considered the professions and financial capacity of parties to futures contracts among
the decisive factors for annulment of the contracts. In *Dickson v.
Uhlmann Grain Company*, the court held Uhlmann to have conducted a gambling establishment in the Missouri town of Carrollton,

which enabled local residents to gamble on the fluctuations in grain prices. The court said:

> The accounts of the defendants were carried on margin; and the extent of their purported obligations exceeded their financial capacity. . . . Between 40 and 50 local residents from widely divergent walks of life in no way connected with purchasing or selling grain became customers of the branch. Of the five defendants . . . who were the plaintiff's largest customers at Carrollton, two were farmers, two were clothing merchants, and one was an ice dealer. These defendants, who were not in the grain business, who had never traded on a grain exchange, and who had no facilities for handling grain, purported to buy and sell in amounts up to 50,000 bushels in a single transaction. In a period of nine months the total number of bushels involved in the transactions of four of the defendants, according to one of the plaintiff's witnesses, was 2,360,000.[7]

THE WAR AGAINST BUCKETSHOPS

The debate over the legitimacy of speculation and futures trading was fueled by the emergence of so-called bucketshops in the 1870s. Bucketshops were small betting shops where it was possible to bet on the movements of stock prices without actually purchasing stock. Bucketshops used all the paraphernalia associated with established exchanges, such as stock quotes and ticker tape, and established themselves in financial districts, not just in New York and Chicago, but in all major cities in central and western United States. They were reputed to have derived their name from saloons in London where the urban poor drank beer that had been spilled and collected in buckets from larger pubs (Fabian 1999, 189). Bucketshops accepted small bets on the movements of stock prices (much smaller than the minimum investments required by the exchanges), but most of them did not actually execute their client's orders on the exchanges. They simply took the opposite position to their customer's bets, sometimes hedging their positions on the exchanges. By their appearances and practices, bucketshops publicly associated financial trading with gambling (Hieronymus 1971, 89–93). According to one critic of the CBoT, for example, the exchange was nothing but a giant bucketshop: "A certain Board of Trade . . . is little more than a mammoth bucketshop . . . in which trickery of the most unscrupulous kind is exalted into a science. Futures are not so fair a game as cards" (Howe 1916, 53).

Faced with growing popular and legal opposition to their practices, the established exchanges in Chicago and New York realized
that explicitly dissociating themselves from gambling had become
crucial to the legitimacy of their profession. One of the ways in
which they attempted to do so was by waging a legal war against
bucketshops. If they managed to portray bucketshops as the *real*
gambling houses, they would be able to acquire respectability as
legitimate places of business. Instead of passing various antifutures
and antispeculation laws, one author asserted in a collection on *The
Functions of Legitimate Exchanges,* published in 1910, "The efforts
of law makers . . . should be directed toward the elimination of the
bucketshop evil, and not toward prohibiting the meritorious system
of marketing our cereal crops by the buying and selling of grain for
future delivery. . . . The bucketshop is the racetrack of the speculative game. . . . It is this kind of gambling that has wrought widespread ruin, sorrow and disgrace" (Brown 1910, 131–32). In spite
of Brown's assertion to be acting in the interest of the speculating
public, the exchanges were not in the last place acting in their own
financial interest when waging the war on bucketshops, which had
appropriated much of the business in stock and produce speculation.

The problem with the discursive strategy that sought to legitimate exchange activity by arguing that bucketshops were the real
gambling houses was that it was hitherto impossible to make a
consistent and fundamental distinction between the practices of
bucketshops and the financial instruments traded on the exchanges.
This is exemplified by the ambiguous formulation of the various
antifutures statutes and the legal struggle over the definition of the
intention to wager. As Fabian puts it: "For twenty years the Board
of Trade tried to close the bucketshops, but the directors and their
lawyers kept stumbling on their own troublesome similarity to
bucketshops. How could the Board rid itself of its diabolical double
without crippling itself and limiting the very practices that made
modern markets possible?" (1999, 198).

The practical and legal way in which the exchanges attempted to
close down the bucketshops was by withholding price quotations for
stocks and produce, meaning that the bucketshops had nothing to
bet on. After the first bucketshops opened in Chicago in the 1870s,
the CBoT began prohibiting the dissemination of price quotations
in 1882. Between 1882 and 1892, the struggle over price quotations

intensified, and CBoT withheld the quotations from the bucket-shops and from the Western Union Telegraph Company that distributed the quotes to other states. Many CBoT members, however, continued to communicate the quotes to interested parties for a fee, and bucketshops reputedly hired agents to look into the windows of the exchange. In 1892, the CBoT resumed sending continuous quotations over the telegraph wires, and by 1895 there were an estimated eighty bucketshops in Chicago alone. In the late 1890s, legal action against the bucketshops was resumed, and the CBoT managed to have a number of them condemned for being illegal gambling operations. This legal action culminated in a prolonged battle between the CBoT and a large Kansas City bucketshop operation called Christie-Street Commission Company, popularly known as the "bucketshop king" (Boyle 1920, 89–97; Ferris 1988, 117–30).

Between 1900 and 1905, eight court cases between the CBoT and Christie were decided, five of which found in favor of the bucket-shop (*Harvard Law Review* 1932, 914–15). In 1900, Judge Tuley of Cook County, Illinois, affirmed the right of the CBoT to withhold its price quotations from Christie and ruled:

> So prevalent has this [bucketshop] evil become that the betting upon the price of grain without the intention of delivery may be said to have become the national mode of gambling. . . . The evidence shows that Christie-Street Commission Company never purchased or sold a bushel of grain, although it made trades amounting to 157 million bushels in a year. The evidence shows that bucketshopping or gambling in prices on the Chicago Board of Trade of grain and other products was the main business of complainants . . . the quotations being used as dice are used, to determine the results of the bet. (quoted in Ferris 1988, 123)

However, in 1901 Christie reopened under the name of Christie Grain and Stock Company, and when the CBoT resumed legal action against the bucketshop, Christie won a significant victory. In 1903, the Circuit Court of St. Louis accepted Christie's defense that there was no essential difference between its practices and those of the CBoT. The St. Louis court held:

> It is thus proven beyond all reasonable question that the Chicago Board of Trade . . . members . . . engage in making and carrying through deals in grains and provisions, in which it is not intended to

make a future delivery of the article dealt in, but which are to be settled by payment of money only according to the fluctuations of the
market and which are in all essentials gambling transactions. . . . *In
seeking the aid of the Court . . . the Board of Trade does not come
with clean hands, nor for a lawful purpose.* (126, emphasis added)

The CBoT appealed against this decision, and in 1905 the case
was referred to the U.S. Supreme Court. In its defense, Christie
Grain argued not just that the activities of the CBoT were indistinguishable from its own, but moreover that price quotations were
public property and that the board had no right to limit their distribution. Attorney Charles D. Fullen, representing the bucketshop,
pointed out to the court that 95 percent of the transactions of the
CBoT did not result in delivery but merely settled price differences.
Fullen concluded: "There is no limit which can be placed upon the
trading in the pits of the Board of Trade . . . it is all wind trading
and the volume of the trading is not dependent upon any condition
of . . . the quantity of produce in the country (quoted in Howe 1916,
117–18). However, the Supreme Court delivered an opinion in favor
of the CBoT, which sought to legitimate futures trading regardless
of actual delivery of the underlying stocks and produce. Justice
Holmes, who delivered the opinion of the court, said:

> People will endeavor to forecast the future, and to make agreements
> according to their prophecy. Speculation of this kind by competent
> men is the self-adjustment of society to the probable. Its value is well
> known as a means of avoiding or mitigating catastrophes, equalizing
> prices, and providing for periods of want. It is true that the success
> of the strong induces imitation by the weak, and that incompetent
> persons bring themselves to ruin by undertaking to speculate in
> their turn. But legislatures and courts generally have recognized that
> the natural evolutions of a complex society are to be touched only
> with a very cautious hand.[8]

The court moreover stipulated: "In the view which we take, the
proportion of the dealings in the pit which are settled in this way
[through price differences] throws no light on the question of the
proportion of serious dealings for legitimate business purposes to
those which fairly can be classed as wagers, or pretended contracts."
Holmes provided the exchanges with the legal ammunition required
to close down the bucketshops by stipulating that price quotations

are a "trade secret" and thus private property of the Board. It is important to note however that despite its ruling in favor of the CBoT, the Supreme Court did not, and could not, make a clear and consistent distinction between CBoT trading and bucketshop practices.

Although the 1905 decision was a landmark victory for the CBoT and affirmed the legitimacy of futures trading at the highest possible legal level, it did not immediately eradicate the existence of bucketshops. Bucketshops had become more sophisticated and continued to imitate exchange practices. For instance, by the late nineteenth century most exchanges stated explicitly in their rules that all transactions seriously contemplated delivery, as a way to circumvent accusations of gambling and nondelivery. By the 1930s this had become a decisive legal argument. As one lawyer put it in the *Yale Law Journal:* "Clearly speculation in commodity futures does not usually involve the purchase and sale of physical property. Just as clearly it does not consist in mere betting on fluctuations in the price of the subject-matter. The former is manifest from the insignificant percentage of contracts consummated by delivery; the latter perhaps needs explanation. Speculation is not betting because delivery of actual goods *can be required* on future contracts" (Taylor 1933, 89, emphasis added). The bucketshops that continued to operate after the Christie decision similarly claimed to contemplate delivery, and most now executed their orders on the exchanges. In effect, bucketshops had become small brokerage firms (*Harvard Law Review* 1932, 915).

A few more cases involving charges of bucketshopping reached the Supreme Court after the 1905 Christie decision. In the 1907 case of a small Memphis broker, Clarence Hunt, versus the New York Cotton Exchange, Hunt challenged the right of the exchange to withhold the price quotations that were vital to his business. Hunt's defense argued that his was a legitimate brokerage business, in which all contracts *contemplated* delivery: "He [Hunt] has transacted no business except as a broker, as stated, and is duly licensed under the laws of Tennessee. Every transaction made by him as evidenced by a report made to his customers . . . has upon it the following: 'All orders for the purchase or sale of any article are received and executed with the distinct understanding that actual delivery is contemplated.'"[9] The Supreme Court, however, dismissed Hunt's argument and upheld the Christie decision, ruling that the Cotton

Exchange had the right to sell or withhold the price quotations to whomever it pleased.

A final important Supreme Court case that involved charges of bucketshopping, decided as late as 1933, was that of *Dickson v. Uhlmann Grain Company*, which ruled a number of futures contracts entered into by citizens of the small Missouri town of Carrollton to be gambling contracts and thus void. Uhlmann Grain was a "member in good standing" of a number of stock and produce exchanges, including the CBoT, and executed the orders from its Carrollton office on those exchanges. When a number of Carrollton citizens, including Mr. Dickson, suffered large losses as a result of their transactions with Uhlmann and refused to pay, Uhlmann started legal proceedings against its clients. The case was appealed all the way to the Supreme Court, which found in favor of Dickson and the other Carrollton citizens who had been financially ruined by the grain speculation and accepted the argument that Uhlmann conducted a bucketshop. Although there was little difference in the appearance of bucketshops and that of small brokerage firms, one of the factors that influenced the Supreme Court's ruling was the following stereotypical description of a bucketshop office:

> This office was in the basement of the Florence Hotel. It consisted of a roll-top desk, some chairs where the prospective victims might rest, a blackboard where they might study figures which they could not understand, a desk for telegraph instruments, a typewriter and some other paraphernalia that added a touch of mystery to the situation. . . . Here sat throughout the day some of the citizens of Carrollton and vicinity who expected to grow rich rapidly by gambling in the purchase and sale of imaginary commodities. (quoted in MacDougall 1936, 81)

This description led the Supreme Court to conclude that "the Carrollton office was equipped in a manner common to bucketshops" (see Figure 4). The court held that Uhlmann knowingly enticed the Carrollton citizens to gamble and declared Uhlmann's contracts to be illegal and void under Missouri law.

A lawyer who disputed the findings of the Supreme Court in the Uhlmann case wrote in the *Yale Law Journal* that the Court's bucketshop description was merely "argument by creation of atmosphere" and objected to the ruling that the Carrollton office was

Figure 4. Bucketshop in New Castle, Pennsylvania, ca. 1908. Photograph by George Elmer Fisher (1864–1953). From the archives of Eric and Elizabeth Fisher Davis.

a bucketshop on the grounds that it executed all its contracts on the legitimate exchanges (Taylor 1933, 82). Taylor concluded that Uhlmann's actions "include nothing which suggests anything out of the ordinary course of speculation" (1933, 84). However, it was precisely the meaning and content of the *ordinary course of speculation* that was disputed in the various court cases mentioned, and that remained ambiguous in the 1930s. The argumentation in the Uhlmann case suggests that the sinister stereotype of the bucketshop had become the discursive basis on which its opposite, ordinary speculation, could be articulated. At the same time, however, the case demonstrates that the dividing line between gambling and speculation, as well as that between bucketshop and broker, remained disputed well into the twentieth century.

THE MORAL JUSTIFICATION OF SPECULATION

All parties involved in the bucketshop debate, including the courts, assumed that the dividing line between gambling and speculation was a moral problem, rather than an objective economic distinction. Outside the courts discourse on the moral distinction between gambling and speculation proliferated. Exchanges tried to cast speculation as a normal business practice, in opposition to the excessive vices of gambling. A number of arguments was put forward by exchange supporters, who sought to articulate the moral superiority and economic productivity of speculators.

First, it was argued that futures trading and professional speculation enabled the existence of modern produce markets that were a source of national greatness and prosperity. As Brown put it: "Dealing in grain and pork products is essential to the national prosperity. If it were done away with the farmer would suffer and consumers would not benefit. The market for those commodities would be disorganised and prices over the country would not be uniform" (1910, 130). Similarly, in a memorial in protest of the Hatch bill, which had been proposed to tax futures trading, the CBoT wrote: "The idea, scheme and theory of contracting for future performance permeates our very lives. It is the blood and bone . . . of our National, personal, commercial and financial existence" (1892, 44). The CBoT went on to argue that the "enormous capital" deployed on the exchanges "is an active, virile, substantial support to the values of agricultural products, and not, as many ignorant or poorly informed persons imagine, a source of depression," thus equating the national prosperity with virility and strength (47). Just as MacKenzie (1896) defined gambling as the resignation of one's manhood, the CBoT argued that futures trading provided virile support for national wealth, while "gambling pure and simple is carried on in bucketshops" and caused the "depression of values" (44–45).

A second, related, argument put forward by the exchanges was that speculating was a natural human enterprise and that futures trading was merely a more sophisticated form of century-old practices. This argument held that speculation had always existed and that futures trading represented the highest possible achievement of civilized man. H. S. Martin, defending the New York Stock Exchange (NYSE), asserted that "speculation was born when men first exchanged one desirable object for another—eatables for wearables, necessities for ornaments" (1919, 1). In 1865, a manual of the NYSE wrote: "The wish of improving his condition, of acquiring wealth, is deeply implanted in man. It is a passion which, duly regulated by sound principles, secures social improvement and national prosperity" (Hamon 1970, 141). Similarly, Chas D. Hamill, president of the CBoT, argued before the U.S. Senate that "the spirit of speculation is inborn in man. The sleepless tendency of all enlightened minds is to speculate upon future conditions and events; and it is to this attribute in man that the highest type of civilization everywhere owes its advancement and stability" (1892, 53). Finally, New York Representative John De Witt Warner argued in an 1894 speech before the House of Representatives that "the business of futures trading is a natural and beneficent one" and an exemplary aspect of the civilized world (Warner 1894). The argument that speculation was the normal and natural result of economic evolution attempted to locate the justification of speculation in (human) nature and tapped into the scientific and biological discourses of the time.

A third argument attempting to legitimate speculation held that gambling and speculation belonged to fundamentally different moral domains. This argument was made, for instance, by New York banker George Rutledge Gibson in a speech to the Association of American Bankers in New Orleans in 1891. While speculation is a business venture, Gibson argued, gambling is mere useless entertainment: "In a moral sense, speculation is not gambling, because, while often resembling it in its uncertainties, the *principle* differs. When one voluntarily gives up his property in a moral way he either exchanges it for another value, which is commercial, or he makes a gift of it, which is benevolent. When he bets on the turn of a card or the result of a race, he relies wholly on chance; he is outside the pale of commerce" (1891, 15, original emphasis). This moral difference, Gibson continued, exists whether delivery of a future contract is intended or not: "The man who buys a hundred shares of stock and sells them the next day may have a gambler's instinct . . . but nevertheless his act is commercial" (16). It is for this reason, Gibson maintained, that bucketshops are immoral and should be outlawed, while trading on the exchanges is moral, albeit sometimes conducted in a "gambling spirit."

The same distinction between "real" business and gambling can be found in the work of the lawyer T. Henry Dewey, who published two manuals documenting legislation concerning futures trading. In the introduction to one of these manuals Dewey wrote: "In speculation and in gambling on prices the result depends upon an uncertain future event. The difference is that, in one the parties are engaged in legitimate business beneficial to both of them, while, in the other, they are engaged in an idle and useless occupation beneficial to only the party winning, and when carried to an excess, injurious to society" (1905, 5). While being important for assigning gambling and speculation to different moral spheres, these arguments remained confused and were unable to effect a clean break between gambling and speculation. As Dewey himself admitted: "As far as the things done in a bucketshop go, it is impossible to distinguish them from the things done in the offices of brokers or commission merchants" (6–7).

A final argument articulating the differences between gambling and speculation was the assertion that speculators proceeded with careful examination and information while gamblers were reckless and ill-informed. In 1903, S. A. Nelson, an associate at the Dow Jones news agency in Wall Street, wrote, "The terms are often used interchangeably, but speculation pre-supposes intellectual effort; gambling blind chance" (1964, 21). A few years later, New York banker John Moody[10] stated the same argument in *The Art of Wall Street Investing*. "The man who speculates in stocks acts on information that he has ascertained and analyzed in one way or another," Moody wrote, "A 'gamble' on the other hand is where a man buys and sells on a blind chance without any particularly sane reason, except that he thinks that a turn in the market up or down is due or that the pools and 'big fellows' mean to give a twist to the stock" (1906, 108). These are the grounds on which bucketshops should be outlawed, Moody argued: "Pure betting is done in bucketshops, is of no use to the community, is destructive to the morals and pockets of young men, and cannot be too severely censured" (146). A final example of the argument that speculative activity required intellectual effort and rational analysis is provided in the work of financial writer Thomas Gibson. Gibson argued that speculators should proceed with "intellectual examination . . . [and] reasoning taking the form of prolonged or systemic analysis" (1923, 6). Gibson's advice to speculators was to "gain immunity from the influence of surface appearances. This can be accomplished only through *knowledge*. The emotions cannot be allowed to play any part in our plans. . . . It is, in short, necessary to realize that the same principles and policies that make for success in any line of business are equally essential in the business of speculation" (1923, 12–13, emphasis in original).

In the various arguments put forward by the exchanges and their supporters, then, we can slowly see emerging a particular representation of the character and identity of financial man. While critics of futures trading had accused speculators of being greedy and reckless gamblers, the defense of speculation cast financial men as coolheaded and rational beings. As early as 1865, the manual of the NYSE argued that speculation, as opposed to gambling, "depend[s] only on political and financial events, which speculators can foresee in proportion to the acuteness of their intelligence. . . . Cool-headed men are the most fortunate speculators, because honest speculation is nothing else than discretion applied to private or public securities" (Hamon 1970, 141–42). This argument was also made by the CBoT, which argued in a 1922 Supreme Court case that federal regulation of financial markets was not necessary, as the board required "character and financial responsibility as qualifications for its membership."[11] Moreover, as Martin argued in a 1919 NYSE pamphlet, speculation should not be condemned because some people were unsuccessful. "The blame," Martin wrote, "should not be placed upon the *kind* of business engaged in, but upon the kind of *man* and the *way* in which he engages in it" (1919, 33, original emphases).

One of the most respected and influential defenders of speculation in the late nineteenth century, who put forward similar arguments concerning the moral character of financial man, was Henry C. Emery. Emery was a former broker who wrote a dissertation on speculation for Columbia University in New York in 1896 (Cowing 1965, 47–49). In his dissertation, Emery argued that the negative effects of speculation were not inherent in financial practices but were caused by amateur participation in the stock markets. "The greatest evil of speculation," wrote Emery, is "the moral evil of a reckless participation in the market by a wide outside public. The possibilities of making quick and large gains from fluctuations in prices lead thousands into the speculative market, who have no knowledge as to its condition, and no real opinion as to the course of prices. Such speculation is the merest gambling in spirit" (1896, 187). In contrast, "real" speculators, Emery argued in an article in the *Political Science Quarterly,* do not enter the market until they have given "full consideration of all knowable circumstances bearing on the future price of their commodities, they enter the market to sell if they expect a fall, and to buy if they expect a rise" (1895, 67). As well as an important defender of speculation, Emery was an influential spokesman for self-regulation of the stock markets and argued that "the highest standard of honor and good faith" should find expression in the rules and regulations of the stock market (1896, 181). Thus, Emery's arguments articulated a powerful distinction between "normal speculation," guaranteed by stock exchange regulations and expressed in the moral virtue of financial professionals, and amateur gambling by the reckless and ill-informed outside public. Emery formulated the moral superiority of financial man as follows:

> The prices determined by speculation are prices for future goods and are made by transactions based on probable future conditions. These conditions are purely matters of estimate, and the farmers as a class are not able to weigh the numberless influences which may affect the future market for their commodities. Only those men who have great experience, wide knowledge and the most improved means of obtaining information, combined with cool judgement, courage and the faculty of quick decision, are competent to forecast the course of future prices and forestall the probable event by their own purchases and sales. And it is the great speculators who combine these qualities in the greatest degree. (1895, 79)

The argument that speculators were rational beings who examined all available evidence before participating in the futures markets provided a powerful and durable defense of stock trading, despite the fact that bucketshop traders, or any other gambler, could equally claim that their trade involved careful study and the collection of information. The exchanges and their supporters were able to make these arguments, because, as Fabian puts it, gambling had become a "negative analogue," or "the one form of gain that made all other efforts to get rich appear normal, natural [and] socially salubrious" (1999, 4–5). In other words, what I have called the moral problematization of gambling, which portrayed gambling in a web of vice that included drunkenness, riots, and prostitution, made it possible for defenders of speculation to posit themselves in opposition to this lawless practice and emphasize the respectableness of the exchanges. Significantly, one way in which this respectableness was asserted was by pointing out that exchanges charged a considerable sum for membership, which in the late-nineteenth-century CBoT, for instance, was around US$25,000. The moral superiority of exchanges was thus assumed guaranteed through financial capacity, a reasoning also detectable in Emery's objections to amateur participation in speculative markets. It is thus no coincidence that the moral problematization of gambling emphasized the evils of "gambling at the margins of society" (Fabian 1999, 2–3). The web of meaning that posited gambling as a problem with particular meaning for the working classes and women contrasted financial irresponsibility, female unruliness, and laziness with financial capability, virile rationalism, and active decision making.

Accordingly, we can recognize Defoe's mastering financial man in Emery's emphasis on courage and quick decision, Hamon's cool-headed speculators, or the CBoT's argument that speculators provide virile support for produce prices. As I argued in the previous chapter, mastering Lady Credit required first and foremost a mastering of the self. This line of reasoning reemerged in the bucketshop debate that cast speculation as a normal and rational business practice, which could however, when carried to excess, have negative effects. For instance, a CBoT pamphlet argued that "the extent to which produce gambling is carried on in the legitimate exchanges of the country is immensely exaggerated. It bears about the same relation to the legitimate commerce and speculation of the country that the froth and foam of the Niagara do to the mighty volume of water underneath. It is the bubble and fuss and fury, the froth and foam upon the surface of trade and commerce that offends—not the trade and commerce itself" (1892, 44). The CBoT's argument that it was the excess of speculation, not speculation itself, which was to be condemned, implied that the moral superiority of financial man should consist of the self-restraint required to refrain from indulging in these excesses. Emphasizing the rational, cool-headed, and studious nature of speculators was one way of communicating that financial professionals possessed such self-restraint, in opposition to reckless and ignorant amateur participants. As Foucault has pointed out, the moral problematization of an issue, and the concomitant construction of "quantitative gradations" of the action, enables the regulation and normalization of the issue (1984b, 45). Articulating a mythical dividing line between normal speculation and excessive gambling (the Niagara and its froth) implies that immorality is not located in the nature of the act (speculation) but is "always connected with exaggeration, surplus and excess" (45). In other words, it is through the emphasis on excess that the *normal* is able to emerge.

Finally, it is interesting to note that even the defenders of speculation in the nineteenth century condemned practices that have become respectable financial instruments in the late twentieth century, including options or "privileges." Options are contracts that give the buyer the option, but not the obligation, to buy a stock or commodity. In contrast to futures, then, options contracts were not always exercised and thus could not claim to always *contemplate* delivery. Congressman Warner in his speech defending speculation, asserts that he expects no one in the United States to defend options and that "the very ones engaged in them would be most prompt to admit that they are gambling, pure and simple" (1894, 5).

PROFESSIONAL RISK BEARERS

Arguably, the most important argument in defense of speculation was the articulation of speculators as professional risk bearers, which accorded them a *productive* role in the economic process. Like the Hammersmith and Fulham ruling concerning *swaps* trading, the bucketshop debate was about the legitimate grounds for making profit. Professional speculators came under attack because they were able to make a profit by buying and selling fictitious commodities without actually being productive in the eyes of their critics. Farmers claimed to toil on the land and feed the nation, while wealthy speculators gambled with their produce. Although proponents of speculation argued that this was no different from buying and selling done by merchants and that speculators' work required knowledge and effort, the defense of speculation remained tenuous because speculators were unable to claim a *productive* part in the economic process.

The articulation of the normal versus the excess, or the regular business practice versus the surplus of gambling, facilitated the articulation of such a productive and economic role for speculators. Beginning in the late nineteenth century, speculators became cast as bearers of *natural business risk,* while gamblers were accused of enjoying the perverted and unnatural creation of chance events. Emery's thesis was one of the first expressions of this argument. "In speculation, as in gambling, the occurrence of a certain event results in gain for one party, while an occurrence of a different kind results in loss. What distinctions can be made between them?" Emery asked (1896, 98), before going on to say: "Both depend on uncertainties, but, whereas gambling consists in placing money on artificially created risks of some fortuitous event, speculation consists in assuming the inevitable economic risks of changes in value" (101).

Although, of course, it is perfectly possible to gamble on natural events, including deaths, births, and catastrophes, as I have discussed, Emery's argument was of particular and durable importance because of the emphasis it placed on *risk*. "It is in the element of risk that we have the key to the function of speculation," Emery wrote:

> It is often said that all business is to a certain extent speculative; in other words, there is an uncertainty as to the ultimate profits. These risks are inherent in all business, and are no more artificial than the whole commercial order in which we live. They are risks which thrust themselves upon business men and which business men must meet. Especially are the risks dependent on changes in value, and it is the assumption of such risks that constitutes speculation. (101)

For Emery, speculators were a professional risk bearing class, "a distinct body of men prepared to relieve [the trader] of the speculative element of his business. . . . Instead of all traders speculating a little, a special class speculates much" (108–9). Emery thus carved off risk from other conceptions of chance and uncertainty by defining it as a natural, inevitable, and essential part of business.

This distinction between gambling and finance was elaborated by Charles O. Hardy, who wrote what is now considered to be one of the first textbooks on the theory of risk. Hardy, a financial economist and vice president of the Federal Reserve Bank of Kansas City, wrote in his *Risk and Risk-Bearing* of 1923 that "gambling is speculating on *artificial* risks" (128, emphasis added). "The only thing which differentiates gambling from 'legitimate' speculation," Hardy argued, "is that in speculation the risks are inherent risks of industry, and must be borne by someone if production is to go on. . . . In gambling, on the other hand, nothing of this sort is true. The risk is an artificial risk, created by the gambling transaction itself. Risk is increased for the sake of risk and for the sake of profiting by one's luck and skill at the expense of another" (128).

The importance of Hardy's argument was not only located in the fact that he cast speculators as professional risk-bearers but also that he emphasized the production of knowledge concerning natural and business risks as the legitimate occupation of that profession. Hardy defined speculators as "responsible men [who] anticipate the wants of the market and take the risks on their own shoulders" (4) and argued that the work of the exchanges consisted in transferring risks to specialists. Thus, even if contracts are being bought and sold purely for speculative purposes, Hardy argued, and delivery of produce is neither intended nor desired, speculators fulfill the economic and moral role of sustaining a market for risks. Holders of speculative contracts, Hardy argued, play "an essential part in the hedging transaction by carrying for a part of the time the risk which ha[s] to be carried by someone all the time" (123). The reason speculators are suited to carry business risks, argued Hardy, is that their specialist function requires them to acquire superior knowledge: "Someone must assume the risks; the fact that the one who assumes them is a specialist may mean that he has superior facilities for judging the situation" (73). Indeed, success in speculation "depends on the ability to forecast price changes, which in turn depends upon the ability to weigh the importance of complicated and conflicting indications of the movement of demand and supply," concluded Hardy (127), thus implying that those not immersing themselves in study would soon be financially ruined.

Hardy thus positioned the concept of risk at the heart of what defines the financial domain and proceeded to offer methods for measurement, classification, and identification of risk. He classified the possible "forms and extent of business risk" according to their origins, discerning, for instance, natural catastrophes, personal injury, and risks inherent in the markets (1–8). Hardy's efforts to arrive at a formal definition and classification of all possible natural risks entailed a normalization and regulation of the financial sphere that was, ultimately, made possible by the moral problematization of gambling. Writing in the 1920s, Hardy was not yet able to express his argument without making explicit the "moral and social evils of gambling." Hardy asserted that "the gambler is in an anti-social position. The whole drift of social evolution throughout the recorded history of the race has been toward the development of moral standards . . . which will promote cooperation. The gambler, however, gains only as others lose" (130). In addition, Hardy argued, gamblers wasted their energy, were irrational, and were engaged in idle and useless pursuits (130–33). However, the main thrust of Hardy's textbook was toward the formalization and objectification of risk management, maneuvering speculation away from its moral problematization and toward what came to be understood as the objective economic sphere.

CONCLUSION

In this chapter I have argued that speculation acquired a moral and economic function by the early twentieth century, thus separating it from gambling. It has not been my purpose to suggest that no distinction *exists* between gambling and speculation but to argue that this distinction is political rather than natural. The possibility of the distinction between gambling and finance hinges on perceptions of morality, character, and excess rather than being inherent in nature or economics. Through the various arguments put forward in the bucketshop debate, speculators became cast as responsible, intelligent, rational, and masculine, in contrast with gamblers, who were portrayed as irresponsible, idle, excitable, irrational, and feminine. Speculating women, by contrast, sat uneasily in this dichotomy: the nickname of the late-nineteenth-century wealthy and successful female speculator Hetty Green, who was known as the "Witch of Wall Street," represents the incredulity of contemporaries who believed that a successful woman on Wall Street had to possess unnatural powers of magic (see Chancellor 1999, 166–67).

By the early twentieth century, risk emerged as a defining feature of financial practices that made possible the articulation of a vital economic role for speculators. Hardy's textbook on risk did not so much provide an objective enumeration of all possible business risks as construct a *legitimate professional domain* for the speculator to occupy himself with, which could thus be closed off from the moral, social, religious, and political ambiguities out of which it had been born. I will further discuss the objectification of the economic domain through professional and numerical practice in the next chapter.

In conclusion, it is important to emphasize that the discursive separation between gambling, speculation, and financial practices remains unstable and continues to haunt modern credit practices. As I mentioned in the introduction, Russian and Japanese legislative bodies have recently struggled to articulate this distinction as the financial exchanges in their countries are being liberalized. At the same time, modern incarnations of bucketshops have caused new worries about popular betting on stock and futures prices. Among recent forms of bucketshops is "spread betting," a form of Internet gambling that allows bets on financial markets without actually purchasing stock or futures. Companies such as the British-based IG Index and USA *Today*'s MoneyExchange in the United States accept bets on the movement of major stock indices, including the Dow Jones, the FTSE and Nasdaq, for amounts lower than the minimum investment levels on exchanges. IG Index does not execute its clients' orders on the financial markets but does buy financial instruments to hedge its client's bets.[12] Companies such as IG Index have caused regulators in the United States and United Kingdom to worry "that private investors will lose their life savings and destabilise the markets" as a result of these gambling practices (Mackintosh and Sanghera 1999).

4

The Dow Jones Average and the Birth of the Financial Market

> *"They came to take the census."*
> *"Yes, and what?"*
> *"And my mother told me to hide."*
> *"What for?"*
> *"What for. That's the point. I didn't know what for. She thought, I don't know what she thought. I went and hid, you know. Two people at the door with clipboards. She said, Get inside, stay down."*
> *"Stay down."*
> *"She said, Stay down. I don't know what I thought and I don't know what she thought."*
> *"It was only the census."*
> *"Don't say only the census."*
>
> DON DELILLO, *UNDERWORLD*

THE POLITICS OF COUNTING

In DeLillo's novel *Underworld,* this dialogue takes place between a white Italian American from the Bronx and a black American from St. Louis, Missouri. Although both men are in their forties and have well-paid corporate jobs, the differences in their backgrounds become forcefully apparent when it seems impossible for the Italian American to understand how the taking of the census can be experienced as a threatening and intruding force by the black family. In fact, the history of census taking in the United States demonstrates the political power of population counting and justifies the black

87

mother's apprehension toward the census takers. In the first U.S. census in 1790, black slaves were recorded as three-fifths of a person for purposes of representation in Congress (Cohen 1982, 159). Furthermore, as Patricia Cline Cohen documents, the 1840 U.S. census found that "the black population of the North appeared to be beset with epidemic rates of insanity, which suggested to some that 'science,' as revealed by tables of figures, had proved freedom to be detrimental to blacks" (1982, 177).

Although the taking of the census is often assumed to consist of objective and unintrusive counting, processes of measuring, counting, and classifying form important operative domains for modern political power. That the politics of census taking are not just a historical aberration is demonstrated by the political controversy surrounding the 2000 U.S. census (Hannah 2001). Because the 1990 census missed an estimated 4 million people, disproportionately from minority groups living in low-income areas, the Clinton administration proposed a new method for census sampling to be used in the 2000 census. This new method was rejected, however, in a January 1999 Supreme Court decision that held that the census should strive for an "actual enumeration," as stipulated in the U.S. Constitution (530). The political stakes of the case were located in the fact that census figures provide the basis on which the seats of the House of Representatives are distributed among the states as well as the basis on which public and private moneys are channeled. While Democrats had hoped to be able to claim more grants for underprivileged and mostly Democratic population groups, Republicans expressed fear that the new counting method would compromise the "integrity of the census" by replacing the actual and individual head count with statistical sampling (Greenhouse 1999; also Holmes 2000).

This chapter discusses the powers of classifying, counting, and calculating that are not only inherent in census taking, but also in statistics in general and financial statistics in particular. While statistics have become accepted as objective and unmediated counting, they are permeated with political origins and consequences. As Hannah puts it, surveys and censuses are "technologies that manipulate or transform what they are supposed to represent" (2001, 516).

Modern credit practices are perhaps understood to be inherently numerical and statistical, more so than the practices of democratic representation. However, as I will argue, the alignment of speculative practices with statistical measurement and management was neither natural nor unambiguous, but provided an important step in the emergence of a professional domain for financial participants. Charts, graphs, and tables of market activity did not so much represent "financial reality" as transform diverse and contingent credit practices into a coherent and measurable financial domain with a life cycle of its own. Furthermore, the virtues associated with statistics provided one way in which the moral superiority of speculators became articulated in the face of political critiques of the exchanges as discussed in the previous chapter.

Of particular importance to the emergence of a coherent and observable professional financial domain was the birth of financial averages in the late nineteenth century in general and the Dow Jones averages in particular. In the 1880s, Charles Dow, founder of the *Wall Street Journal,* was the first to offer price averages of stock groups—initially industrial, utilities, and railway stocks—thus rendering possible a historical charting and studying of prices. Today, the Dow Jones is among the most culturally valued indicators available within the explosion of information at the disposal of financial participants. Dow Jones is not just one of the most important wire companies behind financial news, but its stock market indices are read as authoritative indicators of national economic well-being in general and the financial market in particular. The Dow Jones average is now computed continuously during the U.S. and German stock exchange trading hours (i.e., 13 hours per day), and its movements have become part of standard news broadcasts. Moreover, market indicators have themselves become the bases for new financial instruments, such as index futures and index options (which gain and lose value with the movement of the underlying index), which are widely used for hedging and speculation (see, for instance, Teweles, Bradley and Teweles 1992, 359–79; Mishkin 1992, 298–305). However, today's authoritative and unproblematic existence of the Dow Jones average as public indicator of national well-being obscures its controversial history and contingent compilation.

This chapter begins by discussing the political history of statistics. I will then focus on the nineteenth-century debate concerning the origin of prices and the invention of stock market averages, epitomized by the Dow Jones Industrial Average. As I will argue, these debates rendered possible a professional practice for speculators and investors and the imagination of finance as a coherent domain with a life and history of its own.

STATISTICS AND THE REGULARITIES OF SOCIETY

As I have discussed in the previous chapter, insurance and particularly life insurance were considered illegitimate and immoral until the early nineteenth century. More generally, measuring human life and nature was long considered blasphemous. As Kula documents, Christian European cultures believed that measuring a child would stunt its growth, that medicine which was measured out would not cure the sick, and that calculating harvests was a sin, because "what the lord has provided, even without counting, will find its way into our barns" (1986, 13–14). The Bible teaches that counting God's people was an idea of the devil, and eighteenth-century Christians opposed the taking of the census, both in Europe and the United States. As Zelizer documents in her history of life insurance in the United States, censuses were rejected as "illicit attempts to discover the secrets of God" (1983, 45).

One important reason why insurance was considered blasphemous was that in the religious worldview everything was determined by God. Indeterminacy and chance were not possible: if man did not know what the future held, this was because of men's inadequate knowledge, not because the future was uncertain (Hacking 1990, 1). As long as storms and deaths were seen as acts of God, it was blasphemous to attempt to provide against them. Life insurance in particular was considered blasphemous as it placed a money value on the life of a free man. In the eighteenth-century U.S. South, for instance, it was possible to buy insurance on the lives of slaves, because placing a monetary value on slaves was common practice (Porter 1994, 214). Free men, by contrast, were not allowed to buy policies on their own lives, because, as Zelizer puts it, "this turned man's sacred life into an article of merchandise" (1983, 45).

In order for counting and measuring in general, and practices of insurance and hedging in particular, to become widely accepted and considered morally responsible, a profoundly "altered conception of time and numbers" was needed (Daston 1988, 115). Statistics, or "the science of the state," represents this transformed and typically modern conceptualization of time and numbers, where human agency is seen to be able to have a bearing on a still divinely ordered cosmos.

According to Campbell and Dillon (1993), these conceptual transformations of time, chance, and human responsibility were inextricably connected to colonial conquest. Early modern Atlantic explorations and expansions unsettled the intellectual security of European Christianity, fueling widespread doubt about God's authority. At the same time, however, imperial expansion caused a forceful reassertion of divine will, and "insistence on God's omnipotence left Christian man to confront a universe now dominated not only by a distantiated and inscrutable divine will, but in consequence also by a radical contingency that served to evoke man's awesome powers of self-assertion" (6). The "management of doubt" through the science of statistics was both a rearticulation of divine authority and a powerful new way of ruling and regulating colonial settlements (36).[1]

Although often interpreted as the birth of a modern and secular rationalism, then, statistics nonetheless enabled a powerful reassertion of the ordered cosmos.[2] For example, when the German J. P. Süssmilch published one of the first empirical statistical accounts in 1741, he called it the *Divine Order (Die gottliche Ordnung)* and claimed that it revealed "Providence at work" (Hacking 1990, 20). When bureaucrats started to compile numbers of fires, deaths, and suicides in London and Paris a few decades later and started to make inferences about their occurrence, they substituted the reality and stability of averages for a divinely ordered world. If man did not know *which house* would burn down, or *whose family* would be struck by death, it did become possible to know the regularities of these events over time. In 1795, French mathematician Laplace foreshadowed nineteenth-century belief in societal laws when he wrote: "All events, even those which on account of their insignificance do not seem to follow the great laws of nature, are a result of it just as necessarily as the revolutions of the sun" (11). By comparison, Belgian mathematician and astronomer Adolphe Quetelet, who, according to Hacking was the "greatest regularity salesman of the nineteenth century," wrote in 1829: "We know in advance how many individuals will dirty their hands with the blood of others, how many will be forgers, how many poisoners, nearly as well as one can enumerate in advance the births and deaths that must take place" (105).

This observation of societal regularities entailed the particular technique of power that Foucault calls "governmentality." The compilation of demographics constructs "a population" not just as a representation of inhabitants, but also as a "field of intervention and as an objective of governmental techniques" (Foucault 1991a, 102). The reality accorded to the measured and tabulated phenomena of the population, according to Foucault,

> gradually reveals that population has its own regularities, its own rate of deaths and diseases, its cycles of scarcity etc.; statistics shows also that the domain of population involves a range of intrinsic, aggregate effects, phenomena that are irreducible to those of the family, such as epidemics, endemic levels of mortality, ascending spirals of labour and wealth; lastly it shows that through its shifts, customs, activities etc. population has specific economic effects. (99)

While the science of statistics aims to make regular observations about the population as a whole, including birth and death rates, crime, suicide and poverty, it also claims to speak about each individual member of the population. In Foucault's analysis, then, governing with statistics is both an individualizing and a totalizing power (1982, 213).

It is in this manner that "the economy" emerges as a field of knowledge, as the connection between territory, population, and wealth that can be statistically measured and centrally governed. Toward the mid-nineteenth century, the economy became conceived of as an enormous mechanism, operating with measurable and predictable regularity and expressible in various economic laws. The main instrument through which this shift was brought about was by casting economic phenomena in terms of the natural sciences. In her history of econometrics, Mary Morgan argues that the regularities revealed in statistics were put forward as an appropriate substitute for the experimental method of the physical sciences (1990, 7–8). Indeed, as Philip Mirowski points out, economists began to copy the language of physics term for term in order to guarantee the scientific character of political economy (1991). This allowed economists to reduce the issues of political economy to "mere arithmetical problems" (Poovey 1991, 403).

One important figure in the rearticulation of political economy as economic science was the British economist William Stanley Jevons, whose work, as I will show, influenced Charles Dow. Jevons considered it his explicit goal to make economics scientifically respectable and argued: "I do not hesitate to say, too, that Economics might be gradually erected into an exact science, if only commercial statistics were far more complete and accurate than they are at present, so that the formulae could be endowed with exact meaning by the aid of numerical data" (1911 [1871], 21). Jevons appealed to both the method and subject matter of the physical sciences in order to make economics scientifically respectable. In a paper read before the Statistical Society in 1862, Jevons urged that "all commercial fluctuations should be investigated according to the same scientific methods with which we are familiar in other complicated sciences, such especially as meteorology and terrestrial magnetism. Every kind of periodic fluctuation, whether daily, weekly, monthly, quarterly, or yearly, must be detected and exhibited" (1995, 113). Jevons lamented the fact that economists in general, and financial practitioners in particular, had hitherto shown little interest in collecting and charting commercial and monetary data, and he started to undertake such projects himself.

According to Jevons, graphical representation was the best way to let the economic facts "speak for themselves," and he extensively used tables, charts, and graphs to publicize his collected data. "My purpose," wrote Jevons, is to "ascertain and measure these great changes with some approach to certainty and accuracy, and to establish them as facts of observation. To explain or account for them is a matter which I do not undertake" (1865, 302). The same argument was made by another influential figure in the emergence of economic science, Alfred Marshall. "The graphic method of statistics," Marshall wrote in a paper presented before the International Statistical Congress in 1885, "has the advantage of enabling the eye to take in at once a long series of facts. . . . Ease and rapidity are essential when we want to compare many sets of facts together; because, if the mind is delayed long in taking in the general effect of one set, it meanwhile loses full count of others" (1966, 175).

As Daston and Galison argue, the use of graphs and tables helped guarantee a new brand of scientific objectivity that they call "mechanical objectivity," because numerical and graphical expression were seen as less vulnerable to distortion and bias than language and rhetoric. Increasingly, the scientist was required to display the qualities that were valued in the machine, including, "on the one side, the honesty and self-restraint required to foreswear judgement, interpretation and even testimony of one's senses; on the other, that

taut concentration required for precise observation and measurement, endlessly repeated around the clock" (Daston and Galison
1992, 83). As one French physiologist put it in 1878, "There is no
doubt that graphical expression will soon replace all others when-
ever one has at hand a movement or change of state—in a word, any
phenomenon. Born before science, language is often inappropriate
to express exact measures or definite relations" (81; see also Daston
1994; Poovey 1991, 1998; Porter 1994, 1995b).

Jevons was not alone in his project to make economics scientifically respectable, and Marshall's formulation of the laws of supply
and demand were perhaps even more important in this respect.[3]
Marshall argued that the value of a commodity was not, as earlier
economists had believed, dependent on intrinsic worth or natural
properties, but determined through the laws of the market, which
join supply and demand. The joining point of the supply and demand
curves, argued Marshall, produced the "true equilibrium price."
This is the price that "exactly equate[s] demand and supply (i.e. the
amount which buyers were willing to purchase at that price would be
just equal to that for which sellers were willing to take that price)"
(1961, 333). The equilibrium price was, according to Marshall (332),
the product of an advanced society and integrated markets, and "the
simplest cases of a true equilibrium value are found in the markets
of a more advanced state of civilisation." Marshall compiled and
visualized his economic laws with graphs and statistics and argued
that economics could be made a science through these numerical
methods. Like many scientific economists and statisticians more
generally, Marshall was motivated by social concerns and hoped that
the discovery of the economic mechanisms would enable man to manipulate them to eliminate poverty and scarcity.

The new brand of determinism fostered by the compilation of
numerical regularities created the possibility of individual responsibility that was ultimately to make insurance respectable. The altered
conception of time and numbers associated with statistics and economics is not so much, as Hacking notes, a change from a determined
universe to an indeterminate and malleable one, but a change associated with the "taming of chance." "Where in 1800 chance had
been nothing real," writes Hacking, "at the end of the century it was
something 'real' precisely because one had found the form of laws
that were to govern chance" (1991, 185). If the regularities governing

unfortunate events were still attributable to God, they were now also humanly knowable. By the early nineteenth century, calculation and foresight were articulated as new virtues that underpinned insurance and severed its link with gambling.[4] While gamblers were condemned for desiring short-term gain and forgetting social responsibilities, those purchasing insurance were increasingly praised for taking responsibility for themselves and their family over a long-term future. As François Ewald (1991, 207) has argued, insurance became a moral technology that entailed "no longer resigning oneself to the decrees of providence and the blows of fate but instead transforming one's relationship with nature, the world and God so that even in misfortune, one retains the responsibility for one's affairs by possessing the means to repair its effects."

STOCK PRICES AND THE MEANING OF THE "FREE MARKET"

The question whether trading on the financial exchanges in general and speculation in particular was a distortion or an expression of the newly formulated statistical model of the free market became hotly debated. Currently, the financial market is held out as the perfect model of the free market at work, with a multitude of buyers and sellers interacting directly in order to establish a price under conditions of "pure competition" (Adler and Adler 1984, 2–3; Goux 1997, 162–63). According to Adler and Adler, three conditions are assumed to make stock exchanges the current embodiment of the free market. First, there is a large number of buyers and sellers on the floor of the stock exchange; second, they deal in a homogeneous commodity (i.e., there is no difference between the units of stock of a same company); and third, there is close contact between buyers and sellers, who share knowledge and create prices. Images of stock traders shouting prices and making deals on the floor of an exchange have become powerful representations of the free market. The idea that stock and produce exchanges typify the operation of the free market was first articulated by nineteenth-century economists, and as Stäheli points out, neoclassical, socialist, and Marxist economists were in agreement on this (2002, 118; see also Goux 1997, 163; Langley 2002, 53). Marshall, for instance, named stock exchanges as the ideal example of the operation of the laws of supply and demand and wrote: "Stock exchanges then are the pattern on which markets have been, and are being formed for dealing in many kinds of produce that can be easily and exactly described, and portable and in general demand" (1961, 328).

The casting of the stock exchange as the epitome of the free market, then, has to be seen not as logical corollary to the articulation of laws of supply and demand, but as a political move that served to legitimate exchange transactions. In fact, the nineteenth-century exchanges were under political and moral attack for not representing but *distorting* the free market. It was argued that a small group of "big operators" and monopoly capitalists speculated on the markets and distorted prices to their own advantage. Although the U.S. Supreme Court had ruled in the 1905 Christie case that equalizing produce prices was one of the economic functions of the exchanges, the debate over the origins of stock prices intensified in the early twentieth century and to some extent replaced the contested legitimacy of bucketshops as the core controversy surrounding speculation.

In 1912, a grand-scale investigation was launched by the Committee for Banking and Currency in Washington, with the mandate to establish whether the management of U.S. corporations and financial institutions was "rapidly concentrating in the hands of a few groups of financiers" (Pujo Committee 1912, 6). It was feared that these financiers, particularly J. P. Morgan, were so powerful in the financial markets that they were able to determine prices as well as "to control the security and commodity markets; to regulate the interest rates for money; to create, avert and compose panics" (6). Samuel Untermyer, chairman of the investigative committee that become known as the Pujo Committee, made it clear that in his view, there was little difference between speculation and price manipulation. In a paper presented before the Annual Meeting of the American Economic Association in 1915, Untermyer argued that since the disappearance of "pure" bucketshops, which did not execute their transactions on the exchanges, price manipulation of stocks had become the main problem of speculation. The multitude of small brokers that replaced the bucketshops *did* execute their speculative orders on the exchanges and thus influenced price movements. As a result, argued Untermyer, "the dealings on the Exchange have become mainly speculative and . . . prices are regulated, not by intrinsic values, but by the technical phase of the market created by the manipulation of the particular security by the big interests" (1915, 46). Untermyer pleaded passionately for federal regulation of the stock markets and proposed to curtail the rights of brokers to advertise their services. Regulation, according to Untermyer, would enable rather than hamper the natural functions of speculation. Only when price manipulation has ceased "can we have open, honest speculation based upon conceptions of value," concluded Untermyer, "then and only then will speculative transactions furnish a guide to values" (52).

In response to Untermyer and others before him who had made similar arguments, defenders of speculation argued that the exchanges were nothing but neutral marketplaces, enabling a multitude of buyers and sellers to meet and determine the right price for securities. For instance, Horace White, chairman of the Hughes Commission, an earlier investigative committee into stock market practices that, contrary to the Pujo Committee, had found no need for federal legislation, argued in 1909 that "an exchange is a common meeting-place of buyers and sellers. Such meeting-places have existed from earliest times. The Agora in ancient Greece was an open-air market before it acquired any political or juridical character" (1909, 529). The economic function of these markets, which are natural products of economic evolution, White went on to argue, "is the ascertaining and publishing of prices, so that producers may know what they can obtain for their products, and purchasers what they must pay for them" (530). Indeed, White echoed the reasoning of Marshall when he argued that "prices are made by the competition of buyers and sellers in open market under the spur of self-interest, and there is no other way they can be legitimately made" (530). Still, when it came to the definition of manipulation and the influence of speculation on prices, White's argument remained confused. "The physical, or external causes are the controlling ones in the long run," White asserted, "but the governing force at any particular time is the state of opinion prevailing on the exchange. This may be in part artificial or 'manipulated,' but it represents the law of supply and demand at the moment" (530).

It is important to understand that the resolution of this debate did not depend on the *discovery* of the true and natural origins of stock prices, but on the construction of a discourse of "true prices" as being independent of human influence and control. Such true and natural prices were assumed determined by the movements of the economic mechanism that resembled the movements of the sun and stars. Increasingly, the existence of true and natural prices was simply asserted. The following exchange between Untermyer and Frank Sturgis, a governor of the New York Stock Exchange (NYSE), during the Pujo hearings, illustrates how exchange transactions were rearticulated as being expressions of economic truth:

Q. [UNTERMYER] What is the purpose of short selling?

A. [STURGIS] Generally speaking, to make a profit.

Q. To make a profit by what process?

A. By repurchasing the short sale at a declining price.

Q. That is, by selling a security that you have not got and gambling on the proposition that you can get it cheaper and deliver the thing that is sold. Is that not it?

A. That is the usual process—selling *when you think the price is too high and repurchasing when you think it has reached the proper level.* (53, emphasis added)

Sturgis's answer does not so much disagree with Untermyer as reformulate the question by asserting the existence of natural and transcendental prices. An 1892 pamphlet of the New York Cotton Exchange similarly argued that speculators had no influence on price levels, but merely acted in accordance with economic laws. "The great law of supply and demand," the Cotton Exchange Committee wrote, "regulates values of everything and is no more to be resisted than the tides of the ocean. A short seller in making his engagements will either derive profit or suffer loss as the ultimate facts prove him to be right or wrong" (New York Cotton Exchange 1892, 6–7). In another pamphlet, James Bloss, president of the Cotton Exchange, argued that if speculators had any influence on price movements, it was a negligible one. Speculation, Bloss argued, "is really no more than a fly upon the wheel that rides along with the vehicle that is moving" (1892, 14).

Interestingly, the discourse of the "right" and "proper" price, which was assumed to exist above and beyond human action, was used by both defenders and opponents of speculation. For example, after sharp fluctuations in the sugar price in 1923, a case was brought before the Supreme Court by the U.S. government, which argued that the New York Coffee and Sugar Exchange conspired to manipulate prices for sugar and consequently was in breach of the Sherman Anti-Trust Act of 1890. The petition against the New York Coffee and Sugar Exchange argued that futures sales made on the exchange did not intend delivery and that "the Exchange thus put in the hands of gamblers the means of influencing directly the prices of sugar to be delivered, and thereby of obstructing and restraining its free flow in trade between Cuba and the United States." Like Untermyer, the petition equated speculation with manipulation and asserted that the exchange dealings did not represent the true and natural prices for sugar. The governors and members of the sugar exchange, the petition argued, "have established artificial and unwarranted prices, not governed by the law of supply and demand, but based wholly on speculative dealings not involving the delivery of the quantities of sugar represented thereby, but altogether carried on for the purpose and with the effect of unduly enhancing the price of sugar to the enrichment of said defendants and their principals and to the detriment of the public." With the suit, the government sought to dissolve the sugar exchange and restrict dealings in sugar to those persons who actually possessed sugar and those who "in good faith" intended to buy and pay for that sugar.[5]

In response to the petition, the Coffee and Sugar Exchange argued that in spite of the fact that it was occasionally vulnerable to gamblers who attempted to manipulate its prices, futures trades generally stabilized and equalized prices. The 1923 fluctuations in the sugar price, argued the exchange, were due to "a probable shortage in the supply of sugar" as well as to the fact that "the previous estimate of the amount of the next Cuban crop was too high by several hundred thousand tons." The Supreme Court found in favor of the New York Coffee and Sugar Exchange and pointed out that the legality of futures trading had been affirmed in the 1905 Christie case.

Another court case that debated the origins of stock prices was the 1923 case over the constitutionality of the Grain Futures Act, which was passed in 1922 with the purpose of regulating and recording the trade in grain futures (Hieronymus 1971, 313–14). The act stipulated that futures trading was invested with a "national public interest" and that transactions on the CBoT were "susceptible to speculation, manipulation and control." Less than a year after the passing of the act, however, the CBoT legally contested it, arguing that the government had no constitutional right to interfere with the private business of the board and that transactions on the board did not distort the natural prices of grain. The CBoT argued before the Supreme Court that a large part of future trading was "done by speculators . . . who make a study of the market conditions affecting prices, and try to profit by their judgement as to future prices; [and] that few of such speculators have capital enough to make large single purchases in any way affecting the market; . . . [and] that the law of supply and demand regulates prices and prevents violent fluctuations."[6]

Clearly, then, the very concept of what constitutes the "free market" was under discussion in this court case. One of the witnesses cited by the defense was Herbert Hoover, who spoke in his capacity as Food Administrator when he asserted that speculation did have an effect on price fluctuations and that he regarded a proportion of exchange transactions "as an attempt to dislocate the normal flow of the law of supply and demand and any attempt to *dislocate a free market* must be against public interest" (emphasis added). The Supreme Court found in favor of the government and upheld the constitutionality of the Grain Futures Act. The court affirmed the beneficial functions of futures trading as formulated in the 1905 Christie case, but agreed with the U.S. attorney that manipulation posed a real danger to the operation of the markets, with the power to "exert a vicious influence and produce abnormal and disturbing temporary fluctuations of prices that are not responsive to actual supply and demand." Moreover, the Supreme Court affirmed that futures sales did in fact have a bearing on produce prices and that the argument of the CBoT in this matter was contradictory. "It is said there is no relation between prices on the futures market and in the cash sales," Justice Taft said in the decision of the court. However, Taft objected: "This is hardly consistent with the affidavits the plaintiffs present from the leading economists . . . who say that dealing in futures stabilizes cash prices. . . . [I]t is very reasonable to suppose that the one influences the other as the time of actual delivery of the futures approaches, when the prospect of heavy actual transactions at a certain fixed price must have a direct effect upon the cash prices in unfettered sales."

The tension in the CBoT's argument noted by Taft resulted from the fact that in order to fight accusations of price manipulation, financial practitioners increasingly asserted the objective existence of "true" and "right" stock prices, independent from the actions of any specific agents. However, this line of reasoning contradicted earlier claims that held that financial practitioners *produced* stock prices. The productive function of financial practitioners was most notably articulated in the 1905 Christie case, which ruled that the exchanges were the legitimate owners of the price quotations, which were to be regarded as a trade secret. This contradiction is also apparent in the work of Emery, who, as I argued in the previous chapter, argued in the late nineteenth century that the greatest evil of speculation was the reckless participation of amateurs in the markets and that speculation was best left to experts. However, in a 1915 article written in response to Untermyer, Emery argued that expert speculators did not at all occupy privileged positions in the markets and that brokers merely fulfilled the neutral function of executing orders on the exchanges. "Is it not obvious that these brokers are, after all, merely our agents; that their powers are very much limited?," asked Emery, before going on to answer: "Say what one may about 'insiders' and 'manipulation,' it is the public which makes prices. It is you and I who determine in the end what we think the value of any security to be; and who by our purchases and sales establish the price for that security which is registered on the Stock Exchange" (1915, 78).[7]

THE DOW JONES INDUSTRIAL AVERAGE

Perhaps the most important step in the imagination of the financial market as an independent mechanism with its own laws and regularities was the development of stock price averages in the late nineteenth century. The construction of the Dow Jones took place within the context of the invention of statistical averages and normalities during the nineteenth century, and it has to be understood as a technology that did not simply represent financial reality but fundamentally transformed the operation of modern credit practices, making it possible to image the financial market as a coherent entity. Charles Dow aspired to the standardization, quantification, and objectivity of financial news. Although commercial journalism was not new in the late nineteenth century, it had hitherto been a paper extension of small social circles and personal contacts. Financial newsletters often consisted of little more than lists of rates and prices, initially for private use, such as the letters of the Fugger family (McCusker and Gravesteijn 1991, 21–41). In England, one of the earliest financial publications in London, John Castaign's *Course of the Exchange &c.*, founded in the 1690s, relied on the "good credit and esteem" of its publisher within the small circle of stockbrokers who met in London coffee houses (McCusker and Gravesteijn 1991, 312–14). Impersonal news was not just hard to come by, it was also not valued as such during most of the seventeenth and eighteenth centuries. "What reason was there," Porter points out, "to put faith in an anonymous document?" (1995b: 46).

What was new about late-nineteenth-century financial publications, most importantly the *Wall Street Journal* in New York and the *Financial Times* in London, was that they emphasized personal detachment and numerical representation of financial news. The first edition of the *Financial Times* in 1888 declared itself "the friend of the honest financier, the bona fide investor [and] . . . the legitimate speculator" and the enemy of "the gambling operator," and it adopted as its banner: "Without Fear and Without Favour" (quoted in Kynaston 1988, 17). Similarly, according to Dow, personal contact and involvement on Wall Street were the origin of fraud and stock manipulation (Rosenberg 1982, 5–6). In the first edition of the *Wall Street Journal* in 1889, Dow stated its purpose and principles to be:

> To give fully and fairly the daily news attending the fluctuations in prices of stocks, bonds and some classes of commodities. It will aim steadily at being a paper of news and not a paper of opinions. It will give a good deal of news not found in other publications, and will present in its market article, its tables, and its advertisements a faithful picture of the rapidly shifting panorama of the Street. (quoted in Stillman 1986, 14–15)

The first edition of the *Journal* in 1889 printed a list of the "average movement of prices," which traced the prices of twelve stocks on the NYSE over the past year. Dow attempted to read a pattern in the price movements, and in the accompanying comment he wrote: "The bull market of 1885 began July 2, with the average price of 12 active stocks 61.49. The rise culminated May 18, 1887, with the same 12 stocks selling at 93.27. Prices gradually declined for about a year, reaching the next extreme low point April 2, 1888, the 12 stocks selling at 75.28" (16–17). The fact that Dow did not mention which stocks were included in his average or mention the unit of account of the prices contributed to the reification of the average. This table of 12 stocks was the predecessor of the Dow Jones Industrial Average (DJIA), which was first published in the *Journal* in October 1896 and consisted of a list of twelve industrial stocks that were named by Dow.[8] At the same time that the DJIA emerged, Dow compiled a railway average, consisting of the average price of twenty railroad stocks.[9] Dow's emphasis on numerical representation and tabular arrangement was in line with the emerging scientific consensus that numerical representation and statistics were better able to guarantee scientific objectivity than language and rhetoric, as had been argued by Jevons and Marshall.

In fact, Dow's attempts to discover regular price movements represented by the averages were directly inspired by the work of Jevons, who in the late nineteenth century claimed to have discovered cyclical economic movements called "sun-spots." In a series of papers published in the journal *Nature* between 1878 and his death in 1882, Jevons articulated his sun-spot theory and proposed that commercial fluctuations were directly related to "the varying power and character of the sun's rays" (1878, 36). He analyzed two centuries of data concerning the prices of corn, wheat, and other agricultural products, and announced that he had found a "true but mysterious periodicity" (34). Jevons determined the interval of the periodic commercial crises to be, on average, 10.466 years, and stated: "I am perfectly convinced that these decennial crises do depend upon meteorological variations of like period, which again depend, in all probability, upon cosmological variations of which we have evidence in the frequency of sun-spots, auroras, and magnetic perturbations" (1879, 588).

Dow was familiar with Jevons's work on sun-spot cycles and agreed that commercial and stock exchange panics showed periodic movements. In an editorial written shortly before his death in 1902, Dow argued that stock exchange panics were periodic because "the business community has a tendency to go from one extreme to another" (1920, 97). According to Dow, such commercial cycles consisted of five or six years of confidence, followed by five or six years of hopelessness. "This ten year movement," Dow continued, "is given in detail by Professor Jevons in his attempt to show that sun-spots have some bearing upon commercial affairs. Without going into the matter of sun-spots and their bearing upon crops, commerce, or states of minds, it may be assumed that Professor Jevons has stated correctly the periods of depression as they have occurred in England during the last two centuries" (97–98). Dow went on to argue that the United States had in fact seen commercial fluctuations identical to those Jevons found for England since the early eighteenth century. "Judging by the past and by the developments of the last six years," Dow concluded, "it is not unreasonable to suppose that we may get at least a stock exchange flurry in the next few years" (101). Dow's conclusion has been interpreted as correctly predicting the 1907 financial crisis in the United States (Hamilton 1922, 27).

Dow's construction of market swings and regularities were premised on the imagination of the financial sphere as a coherent and natural system with its own internal dynamic. In 1899, Dow began a series of editorials in the *Wall Street Journal* that discussed market developments to expose this internal dynamic. Downward swings in the market, Dow argued in the first of these commentaries, generally last at least four years. "The time involved in these turns," Dow wrote, "is determined by natural causes. The cause is that the stock market reflects general conditions and it takes several years for such a change for the better or for the worse to work its way through the community" (1899, 1). In another of these editorials in 1901, Dow argued that the movements of the stock market were comparable to the natural fluctuations of the sea and that his price averages offered a method of comprehending and predicting such fluctuations:

> A person watching the tide coming in and who wishes to know the exact spot which marks the high tide, sets a stick in the sand at the points reached by the incoming waves until the stick reaches a position where the waves do not come up to it, and finally recede enough to show that the tide has turned.
>
> This method holds good in watching and determining the flood tide of the stock market. The average of twenty stocks is the peg which marks the height of the waves. The price-waves, like those of the sea, do not recede at once from the top. The force which moves them checks the inflow gradually and time elapses before it can be told with certainty whether the tide has been seen or not. (quoted in Wendt 1982, 67–68)

The image of the stock market as a natural system and the price averages as the barometer of this system became increasingly important. In 1903, Samuel Nelson, an associate at Dow Jones news agency, argued that the function of the stock exchange was its role in the measurement of commodity and produce values. "Stock Exchange prices register values and the state of trade," wrote Nelson, "precisely as a thermometer registers heat or cold" (1964, 24). When *Wall Street Journal* editor Peter Hamilton wrote a book on Dow's work and theories in 1922, he called it *The Stock Market Barometer*. Hamilton wrote that financial crises and panics were caused by "too much imagination" and that what the financial world needed were "soulless barometers, price indexes and averages to tell us where we are going and what we may expect. The best, because the most impartial, the most remorseless of these barometers, is the recorded average of prices in the stock exchange. . . . Continuously these have been kept by the Dow-Jones news service for thirty years or more" (1922, 4). Reading the price movements was an entirely objective and detached exercise, Hamilton went on to say, just as "a barometer predicts bad weather, without a present cloud in the sky. It is useless to take an axe to it merely because a flood of rain will destroy the crop of cabbages in poor Mrs. Brown's backyard" (4). This argument was also used by Henry Crosby Emery, who argued that price movements are like a weather vane: "The vane may change at any time. But the vane does show how the wind is blowing at a specific instant. It seems to me that the fallacy of many people who wish to change methods that provide for the smooth working of a free and open market for securities is the fallacy of one who thinks that he can change the wind by interfering with the weather vane" (1915, 78).

Still, Dow's averages were not immediately regarded as unproblematic representations of the financial market. After the 1929 crash, total losses were measured in absolute terms and not in index point losses. In a 1930 speech concerning the crash, the president of the NYSE, E. H. H. Simmons expressed skepticism with regard to averages and indictors: "Almost everyone interested in [price levels of the share market] is bound to use stock indexes or stock averages, and to depend upon them. Yet a close examination of such price averages shows how unrepresentative they often are, and in what an offhand manner they are frequently composed" (1930, 5). At the same time, however, the controversies following the crash gave a boost to the political importance of perceived objectivity in finance.

Because of the great political interest in the movements of the New York stock market, the NYSE economist J. Edward Meeker argued:

> There is today a particular need of statistical yard sticks with which to measure its activities. For only by recourse to definite figures can a basis be provided for a serious and unprejudiced study of the activities and functions of the Stock Exchange. The need of adequate statistics is all the more important because mass psychology is regularly so considerable a cause of most stock market phenomena. (1930, 3)

Meeker announced the monthly compilation of statistics concerning the trading activity on the NYSE, including the publication of aggregates and indices. These new statistical records would be made "as promptly and as generally available to the public as possible" and would be published "entirely without comment, for while the Stock Exchange wishes to make every effort to discover and make public factual evidence concerning stock market conditions, it leaves it to others to interpret and comment upon this material" (18). Compilation and publication of statistics, Meeker argued, is the way in which investing and speculating can be made into a science. "It is the beginning of wisdom," Meeker concluded, "to recognize quite clearly and frankly the defects of the statistical record we already have, and to purify these necessary economic agents of ours as far as possible by painstaking care in collection and compilation, patient experimentation and critical impersonal analysis. These, after all, are the methods of true science" (19–20).

It was the political controversy over stock market practices in general, and the critique of speculation after the 1929 crash in particular, then, that created the need for statistics in finance, as they made possible claims to scientific detachment and professional study. According to Porter, standard index numbers represent "the public aspect of statistics. . . . They epitomize the social role of objectivity" (1995b, 81). The publication of financial statistics "without comment" by the NYSE illustrates how indices became regarded as embodiments of truth concerning the financial markets, which speak for themselves. Despite their public role however, the compilation of index numbers can be obscure and arbitrary. "Index numbers could never simply be observed," Porter writes, "they normally involved intensive data collection and often difficult or at least tedious calculation. Their credibility required that they be calculated, even from bad data and it has never been acceptable to adjust a number on the basis of one judgement alone, however expert" (81). Meeker's 1930 speech offers a glimpse of the difficulty and arbitrariness of the compilation of numbers. Problems have arisen, Meeker said, concerning the determination of the correct prices of infrequently traded issues and concerning the historical variation of issues traded on the exchange. Similarly, Preda notes the problems with the standardization of financial price publications during the nineteenth century. "The problem was not so much the gathering of data on stock prices," Preda writes, "the problem was the accuracy of this data: which prices should be listed? Opening prices, or midday ones, or the prices at 2pm?" (2000, 219). Still, Meeker was keen to ensure his audience that as a result of the meticulous work of his statistical department "the amounts of listed issues that enter into the monthly compilation are not guesses or estimates, but accurate figures" (1930, 5).

TIME AND PREDICTABILITY

Dow's compilation of price averages and charting of financial cycles offered a professional practice to speculators, who were to engage in careful study and prediction of stock prices. While financial price charts had been in use since the 1830s, what was new about Dow's charts and compilations was that they made it possible to visualize price changes over time and thus encouraged constant vigilance of one's portfolio of stock. This was partly made possible through the 1867 invention of the ticker tape on the NYSE, which recorded and communicated stock prices instantly and continuously (Preda forthcoming). The professional practice of investors and speculators came to include, according to Preda, "permanent attention to market events [and] . . . permanent attention to one's own doings" (30). For example, Dow instructed the financial trader to

> keep a chart of the price movements of these stocks so as to know their swings for months or years, and thus be able to tell readily where in the general swing his particular stocks appear to be. He should keep with his price movement a record of the volume of transactions and notes of any special facts bearing on that property. . . . He should observe the movement of the general market as indicated by the averages given daily in the *Journal* as this shows the market more clearly than is shown by any one stock. (quoted in Stillman 1986, 104)

Such study and administration, Dow believed, did not just inform speculators of past price movements but enabled him to some extent to foresee the future. "Within limitations, the future can be foreseen," Dow wrote in an essay entitled *Scientific Stock Speculation,* "the present is always tending toward the future and there are always in existing conditions signals of danger or encouragement for those who read with care" (1920, 15). Similarly, an 1892 article in the *Political Science Quarterly* asserted that with the right knowledge and information, speculators were able to accurately predict future price movements. "The successful speculator must have accurate knowledge from every available source," Albert Clark Stevens wrote, "being successful, he has merely foreseen causes which made prices go up or down" (1892, 429).

Dow's emphasis on foresight and predictability demonstrate the radically altered conception of time and numbers that underpinned the new professional practices of stock analysts and investors. Modern credit practices in general, and the commercialization of futures in particular, have a special relationship with cultural understandings of time, which are at the heart of the controversies over the morality of exchange trading. For example, the charge against medieval merchants, observes Le Goff, "was that their profit implied a mortgage on time, which was supposed to belong to God alone" (1980, 29). Indeed, medieval prohibitions on usury turned on arguments against "selling time" (29; also Maurer 2001a, 9). In contrast, Le Goff argues, the time of the merchant became an "object of measurement" and, slowly, the merchant "superimposed . . . an oriented and predictable time on that of the natural environment, which was a time both eternally renewable and perpetually unpredictable" (1980, 35). These controversies over the proper understanding of time played out, as I have argued above, particularly in relation to the legitimacy of insurance: where it once was considered blasphemous to provide against the future, it slowly became considered irresponsible *not* to insure oneself against Fortune's blows.

The possibility and legitimacy of exchange trading in general and the trading of futures in particular also hinged on particular notions of time. The construction of "scientific public time" in the late nineteenth century was an important transformation in cultural understandings of time that facilitated the commercialization of the future (O'Malley 1996, 60). Until the late nineteenth century, there was no public standard time in the United States, and great varieties in local timekeeping existed, which proved increasingly problematic to the railroads in particular. Despite the publication of voluminous travel schedules, O'Malley (1996, 63) argues, confusion over proper timekeeping increased: "What time prevailed when two or more standards conflicted? Did the railroad and steamship set the time, or did the local sun?" Rail travelers frequently had to adhere to a railroad time that was different from local times, and one railroad official went as far as to suggest that two sets of hands should be put on watches for this purpose.

The debate on the reform of timekeeping lasted decades, and advocates of standardized time feared upsetting century-old local traditions. In 1882, a U.S. Senate Report on the matter concluded that "it would appear to be as difficult to alter by edict the ideas and habits of the people in regard to local time as it would be to introduce among them novel systems of weights, measures, volumes and money" (quoted in O'Malley 1996, 104). However, in 1883, the U.S. railroads adopted a system of standard time zones, similar to the one still in use today. The time zones of the railroads were backed by scientific authority and were expected to have a disciplining effect on travelers. As William Allen, who played an important role in the adoption of a central railroad time, wrote: "Railroad trains are the great educators and monitors of the people in teaching and maintaining exact time" (quoted in O'Malley 1996, 115). Standardized and commodified time, according to one proponent, promised to replace "human frailty and propensity for error with automatic, consistent, mechanical observation" in timekeeping (85). One year later, an international time standard was set at the Prime Meridian Conference in Washington, which "determined the exact length of a day, divided the earth into twenty-four time zones one hour apart and fixed a precise beginning of the universal day" (Kern 1983, 12).

Some cities, including Pittsburgh, Louisville, and Detroit, however, refused the adoption of railroad time in the 1880s, and a number of court cases were fought disputing the authority of railroad time, particularly in relation to the expiry of contracts. The opposition to standard time was greatest, according to Bartky (1989) in places where the clock adjustments were biggest. What opponents of standard time objected to was, first, the assumption that time was arbitrary and subject to business interests. For instance, the Iowa Supreme Court decided in 1899 that local timekeeping was still valid and declared: "We are not quite ready to concede that, for the mere convenience of these companies, nature's timepiece may be arbitrarily superseded" (quoted in O'Malley 1996, 139). The cities resisting standardized time disputed the authority of the railroads to set local times and argued that time should be set by the movement of the sun and stars instead. Some clergy argued that "the local time of their region was God's time and that the new time was a falsehood" (Bartky 1989, 51–52). One newspaper opposing standard time joked in 1883, "We presume the sun, moon and stars will make an attempt to ignore the orders of the railway convention, but they will have to give in at last" (quoted in O'Malley 1996, 136).

Second, opponents of standardized time objected to the regulatory and disciplinary effects the new techniques of timekeeping had on industrial workers. As Foucault documents, the use of timetables in education, factories, and other disciplinary institutions is an important instrument of modern power (1979, 149–56). Although timetables were developed to regulate ascetic life in medieval monasteries, their role in the organization and disciplining of modern life was increased and refined during the eighteenth and nineteenth centuries (Adam 1995). A more detailed division and allocation of time emerged; timetables began to count in "quarter hours, in minutes, in seconds" and stipulated tasks for each recorded time unit. The "three great methods" of timetables, according to Foucault, were to "establish rhythms, impose particular occupations, regulate the cycles of repetition," and these were an important part of the power exercised in schools, poorhouses, and workshops (1979, 149).

The adoption of standard time was not simply the result of economic logic, driven by local time's impediments to interstate and international businesses and railroads, but bound up with a cultural change that no longer saw time as a divine loan but as a commodity that could be bought, sold, and made profitable. Like no other previous development, standardized futures contracts divided and commercialized time and banked on the future. Just as futures trading was facilitated by the standardization of quantities and qualities of grain, it was facilitated by the standardization and increasingly precise measurement of time. Although transformations in (work) time were "evolutionary, not revolutionary" (Stein 2001, 119), some

U.S. populists objected to the disciplinary power associated with regulated timekeeping and the introduction of standard time and instead "insisted on nature as the source of time and natural imperatives as guides to using it" (O'Malley 1996, 141).

These conflicting cultural understandings of time are at the heart of a 1909 short silent movie by U.S. filmmaker D. W. Griffith, called *Corner in Wheat* (Figure 5). This film was based on the work of American novelist Frank Norris, in particular on Norris's short story "A Deal in Wheat," published in *Everybody's Magazine* in 1902 (Gunning 1999, 133–35). Norris tells the story of a Kansas wheat farmer who is forced to sell his farm and move to the city when the price of wheat is below its production costs. Once in the city, the price of wheat has risen dramatically due to speculation on the Chicago Board of Trade, and the farmer finds he cannot afford to buy bread and is forced to join a nightly breadline. Norris's story contrasts the "roar of a hundred voices . . . the rush of a hundred men . . . [and] a hundred hands in eager, strenuous gestures tossed upward from out the brown of the crowd" in the wheat pit on the exchange, with a sad and solemn image of the breadline, "this interminable line of dark figures, close-pressed, soundless; a crowd, yet absolutely still; a close-packed silent file, waiting, waiting in the vast deserted night-ridden street" (1936, 574, 578). Norris's critique of the "operators" who traded on the exchange concluded: "The farmer—he who raised the wheat—was ruined upon one hand; the working man—he who consumed it—was ruined upon the other. But between the two, the great operators, who never saw the wheat they traded in, bought and sold the world's food, gambled in the nourishment of entire nations . . . went on through their appointed way, jovial, contented, enthroned and unassailable" (579).

Griffith's film is regarded as embodying new artistic representations of time and sequencing—it develops a reordering of the "linear narrative" and shows "events occurring in different places simultaneously." (May and Thrift 2001, 11; also Kern 1983, 30). In the film, the parallel lives of the farmer, the worker, and the speculator are presented as three narrative strands that never meet—and may even be ignorant of each other's existence—but that are connected through their relationships to wheat. According to Erik Ulman's (2001) analysis, this technique "represents the new topography of modern capitalist economics, and its lack of face-to-face

Owing to the
advance in the
price of flour
the usual 5￠ loaf
will be 10 ct's.

Corner
in Wheat

& Selected
Biograph
Shorts
1909-
1913

ALL WITH
DIGITAL
STEREO SCORES

The New York Hat

The Mothering Heart

Figure 5. D. W. Griffith, Corner in Wheat, *1909.*

encounters with the forces which determine our lives" (cf. Gunning 1999, 136). Different perceptions of time are at the heart of the film: at the beginning of the film, the world of the farmer is portrayed in a shot of farmers and horses in the field, sowing, and plowing. This shot lasts over a minute, symbolizing the amount of work and time involved in growing the wheat and "confronting the viewer with the real time of the action" (Ulman 2001). The world of the speculator, in contrast, is shown as a hectic place where fortunes are quickly made and lost. As in Norris's story, the image of the wheat pit on the exchange is a manic one, with men frantically shouting, waving their arms, pushing and shoving, men looking euphoric and desperate, one man fainting from shock and another tossing a coin to determine his bid. The second contrast offered in Griffith's film is that of the wheat king's lavish banquet intercut with scenes of a bakery where a sign announces: "Owing to the advance in the price of flour the usual 5^{ct} loaf will be 10$^{ct's}$" (see Figure 5). The wheat king is a celebrated man; his dealings on the exchange are not seen as fraudulent or morally ambiguous by his contemporaries, who gather to celebrate his success. As the bulletin accompanying the release of the film put it, the Wheat King "is lauded for his acumen, wined and dined, and regarded as a man among men, little thinking of the misery and suffering his so called genius has induced" (quoted in Gunning 1999, 130–31). The scene of the Wheat King's party, however, is intercut, first, with a scene of a poor woman and her daughter who can no longer afford the bread; and second, with a famous frozen shot of the poor waiting in the breadline.

In contrast to Norris's story, the film ends with the speculator's death by being buried under his own grain in the grain elevator, while simultaneously a riot breaks out at the breadline. Griffith saw in the Wheat King's death vengeance through the hand of God, because "one of the sins that cries to heaven for revenge is denying food to the hungry" (*Corner in Wheat* bulletin, quoted in Gunning 1999, 131). But the scene of the dying Wheat King is intercut with images of the riot of the hungry being violently suppressed by a policeman, and as Ulman (2001) concludes: "The death of the Wheat King may be deserved, but is not sufficient to right the wrongs that he and the system he represents have caused." The final shot returns to the land and shows a lone farmer sowing—the film thus concludes with the natural cycle of the wheat. Griffith's contrasting images of the slow, cyclical, and monotonous time of the land with the short time horizons of the exchange, and the "constant movement and liveliness" of the Wheat King's party with the somber frozen shot of the breadline reflect the controversies over "natural" time versus "commercial" time in the railroad debate (Gunning 1999, 139).

Despite these controversies, however, by the late nineteenth century prediction of stock prices and the commercialization of the future it implied had become not just possible but respectable. The professional practice of the stock analyst and investor consisted of prediction and constant scrutiny of both the movement of stock prices and his own actions, which discursively protected him from accusations of gambling and idleness. Especially after the 1929 crisis, the publication of manuals advising how to invest in the stock market proliferated. The popular fallacy concerning stock trading, one such manual pointed out in 1934, is that in the stock market it is possible to "get something for nothing" (Schabacker 1967, 3). Those who believe the stock market to offer opportunities for easy profit, Schabacker argues, fail to "estimate the long study, careful analysis, the systemic planning that account for Mr. So-and-So's success" (1967, 3). Instead, Schabacker goes on to say, stock trading is a business that requires "time, study, thought and planning . . . just as one would expect to do in any other type of business, and thus to make eventual and consistent profit a logical reward rather than an unmoral gift of luck" (6). Schabacker's manual consists of advice on technical study, including charting price movements, analyzing financial data, and calculating risk. This practice of study and prediction was in part made possible through the Dow Jones averages, which visualized the history of price movements and invited speculation concerning their future. Instead of being an objective representation, however, I will argue in conclusion to this chapter, these averages performatively constituted the financial market and transformed modern credit practices.

THE DOW JONES AS PERFORMATIVE

Like statistics, modern (financial) rationality is not wholly secular and disinterested, but is premised upon faith in a divine or cosmological order. For example, by locating the origins of prices among the movements of the sun and stars, Jevons displayed faith in a cosmological order while making these economic factors scientifically knowable. Indeed, in modern economics the laws of the market appear to possess a transcendental authority comparable to that of a provident divinity. As Hilton points out, during the nineteenth century commercial cycles were frequently interpreted as the work of God, providing "timely reminders of the existence of providential government," and reminding businessmen of their "ambivalent moral status" (1988, 125). Moreover, the new orientation toward the future embodied in standardized and commodified time, is not, according to Loy, an expression of secular timekeeping. Instead, "the future-directness of linear time" expresses modern spiritual need by promising—as Christian theology does—"fulfilment in the future" (Loy 2001, 264). In his *Genealogy of Morals* of 1887, Nietzsche objected to Victorian science precisely on the grounds of its apparent rejection of spiritualism. According to Nietzsche, scientific asceticism did not constitute the renunciation of ideals, beliefs, and hopes but was on the contrary the expression of a very specific kind of faith and morality:

> Science today . . . constitutes not the opposite of the ascetic ideal but rather *its most recent and most refined form*. . . . What *compels* these men to this absolute will to truth, albeit as its unconscious imperative, is the *belief in the ascetic ideal itself*—make no mistake on this point—it is the belief in a metaphysical value, the value of *truth in itself*. . . . Strictly speaking, there is absolutely no science "without presuppositions," the very idea is inconceivable, paralogical: a philosophy, a "belief," must always exist first in order for science to derive from it a direction, a meaning, a limit, a method, a *right* to existence. (1996, 125–27)

Indeed, it must be emphasized that the new scientific asceticism was both gendered and particular to the upper classes. Paradoxically, the self-discipline or willful self-elimination required of the scientist, while claiming to tame subjectivity, exemplified the highest form of autonomy and personal strength. Only the fully independent, well-educated, and self-conscious agent was regarded to have the strength to consciously take distance from himself and to renounce his desires and hopes. Keller (1985, 1994) has pointed out that there is a pervasive historical association between articulations of masculinity and objectivity. It is precisely the subjection of sexual desires to reason that is seen to make man fully autonomous and in control of his person. The similarities with seventeenth-century gentlemanly science and Defoe's mastering financial man are obvious here and demonstrate the historical continuity between literary representations and scientific discourses. During the nineteenth century, Keller concludes, the discourse of self-mastering rendered possible "the progressive disembodiment and dislocation of the scientific observer," constructing "the illusion that [scientific] knowledge is not man-made—not crafted, articulated or constructed, but *discovered*" (1994, 316, 321, emphasis added).

With regard to exchange trading, faith in a divine or natural order is expressed, for instance, in the work of Dow's successor Hamilton, who argued that although Dow was the first to make an attempt to "elicit and set forth the truth contained in the fact of the stock market" (1922, 16), the law that governs the stock market is ahistorical, unchangeable, and not dependent on political organization or geographical location. "The laws we are studying," concluded Hamilton, "are fundamental, axiomatic, self-evident. And in this higher truth surely there is something permanent that would remain if the letter of the Constitution of the United States had become an interesting study for the archaeologist, and the surviving writings of our day were classical in a sense their authors never dreamed. Such a foundation is permanent because truth has in it the element of the divine" (20).

The search for a true and accurate statistical representation of the financial market intensified during the twentieth century. The DJIA was increased to twenty stocks in 1916 and to thirty stocks in 1928 (where it remains today). These thirty stocks are carefully selected to constitute a representation of the U.S. stock market—the selected stocks are considered leaders in their industries and are selected on the basis of their long-term performance. The lack of transparency in the selection process—the index composition is seldom changed and only at the discretion of the *Wall Street Journal* editors—contributes to the authority of the Dow and its public role of objectivity. "We change the Dow as seldom as we possibly can," says John Prestbo, who currently administers the Dow Jones Averages, "it helps with the trust factor" (quoted in Moreau 1999). In addition, many more stock market indices have been designed since the first publication of the Dow Jones averages, each one more complexly compiled and calculated in the hope of giving a more accurate representation of the market. Today, almost all countries have their own national share index, which are all differently calculated. The British equivalent of the DJIA, the Financial Times 30 Index, consists of thirty leading industrial companies and dates back to 1935. In the United States, Standard and Poor's 500 Index consists of 500 stocks listed on the NYSE, the American Stock Exchange (AMEX), and the Over the Counter (OTC) market, and originated in the 1940s. Since 1970, there are world stock market indices, such as the MSCI World Index, which is based on the share prices of 1477 companies listed on 19 of the world's stock exchanges (Ross 1992, 583–586).

The explosion of indices during the twentieth century is a logical result of the market philosophies of people like Dow and Meeker, who believed that technological progress and calculative sophistication were all that were needed to arrive at a true and undistorted representation of market value. Indeed, the current trend toward using broader market indices, such as the Wiltshire 5000 index watched by Alan Greenspan, implies that objectivity in indexing can progressively be attained. "The more inclusive is the index," the *New Palgrave Dictionary of Finance* writes, "the closer it is to the ideal of an index that includes all wealth" (Ross 1992, 587). The ideal of an "index that includes all wealth" expresses a desire to arrive at a true, undistorted, and nonarbitrary representation of the financial market. However, this ideal is as attainable as the map that represents phenomena on their true scale and negates the political processes of selection, computation, and representation at the heart of statistics in general and the stock market indices in particular.

Indeed, although the calculation of indices becomes increasingly complex and computerized, the problems of representation have not been remedied. On the contrary; the construction of ever more complex financial indices has created its own problems. For instance, in December 2000, the financial indexing company MSCI, which computes various stock market indices worldwide, announced a change in the calculation of its indices. In the future, MSCI will only include shares available through the market in its valuation of companies. The recalculation was seen by the *Financial Times* to provide a "more realistic picture of tradeable assets, by reflecting the proportion of a company accessible to investors" (John 2000). However, the recalculation will have a negative effect on companies partly owned by national states, for instance, Deutsche Telekom of Germany, where the state owns 40 percent of shares. Thus, the change is expected to devalue former public companies in European welfare states and Japan, while it benefits companies in more liberalized economies such as the United States and United Kingdom.

Thus, while these techniques profess to give unproblematic representations of financial reality, they offer particular and political representations of the financial domain. Measurement tools, argues Callon, "do not merely record a reality independent of themselves; they contribute powerfully to shaping . . . the reality that they measure" (1998, 23). Financial statistics and averages, like population statistics before them, exert power because they "[render] aspects of existence thinkable . . . calculable and amenable to deliberated and planful initiatives" (Miller and Rose 1990, 3). Thus, avenues for action in the financial domain are rendered possible, logical, and rational through particular representations of financial truth, just as other avenues are foreclosed through such representations. In particular, the Dow Jones embodies a concept of the financial market as a closed system with its own laws and regularities, which can be studied and observed. While no prepolitical or self-evident definition of "the financial market" exists, financial indicators have assumed the role of defining the markets and embodying their objective movements.

It is in this sense that the Dow Jones can be considered to be a *performative*. Rather than a more or less accurate representation of the market, financial indices in general and the Dow Jones in particular *create* the financial market as a unified, observable, and measurable phenomenon (cf. Preda 2001, 223–27). The market acquires a life and a history through stock market indices, and the particular strength of the DJIA is that its records go back to the late nineteenth century (see Figures 6 and 7). In spite of the problematic nature of its composition and historical comparability, then, the Dow Jones *performs* the history of the financial market. Repetition of indices in news bulletins is not just incidental to their performativity, but at the heart of it. As Butler explains: "Performativity must be understood not as a singular or deliberate 'act,' but, rather, as the reiterative and citational practice by which discourse produces the effects that it names" (1993, 2). This citational practice that creates the financial market, in turn, makes (policy) action by financial participants possible and thus affects the material reality it purports to objectively measure and observe.

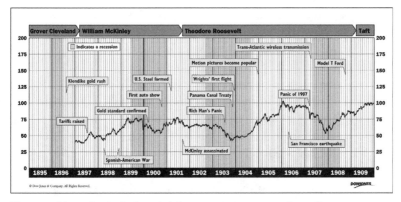

Figure 6. Dow Jones Industrial Average, 1895–1909. http://
www.djindexes.com/downloads/1895–1909.pdf.

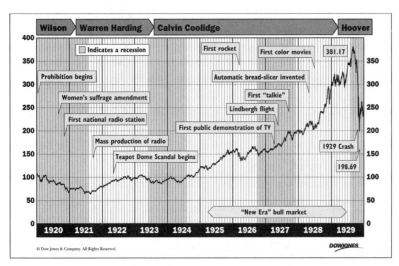

Figure 7. Dow Jones Industrial Average, 1920–1929. http://
www.djindexes.com/downloads/1920–1929.pdf.

CONCLUSION

The statistical compilation of stock price data and the development
of financial charts offered a professional practice to the investor and
speculator. This practice of speculators and analysts came to include
statistical tabulation and calculated foresight, which underpinned
the new respectability of speculation. However, financial charts in

general and the Dow Jones in particular did not so much represent financial reality as transform diverse and contingent credit practices into a coherent and measurable financial domain with a life cycle of its own.

Present reification of financial statistics has almost silenced critical questioning of their origins, compilation, and cultural significance, even by those critical of financial capitalism. For instance, Doug Henwood's (1997) recent work on Wall Street, while highly critical of and very knowledgeable about financial practices and instruments, does not question the categories of knowing and defining the financial domain offered by the financial industry. To a large extent, Henwood's book accepts and reproduces the rules of the legitimate production of financial knowledge. For instance, Henwood accepts that financial statistics, including price levels, interest rates, and stock returns, compiled over certain historical periods, are unproblematic representations of financial reality (even if he does not like that reality). About the Dow Jones, Henwood notes that it is the most famous average, but "far from representative of the whole market. A broader index . . . is the Standard and Poor's 500, an index of industrial, service and financial stocks" (21). By abstracting the Dow Jones from its political history while implicitly accepting that a representative average of the entire stock market is possible, Henwood undermines his own scope for criticism. Although he is critical of the increasing mathematization of finance and economics, Henwood does not include statistics among the techniques of financial governance he discusses, nor does he advocate questioning and rethinking financial standards and measures among the possible strategies of resistance to the power of finance. In contrast, it is my contention that questioning finance and financial practices must involve a critical attitude toward the unwavering scientific authority of financial statistics as well as toward the ways in which financial knowledge is produced more generally.

5

Regulation and Risk
in Contemporary Markets

Normalization becomes one of the great instruments of power at the end of the classical age.

MICHEL FOUCAULT, *DISCIPLINE AND PUNISH*

STOCK MARKET REGULATION

As I have argued, the political contestations surrounding the boundary between finance and gambling, the morality of speculation, and the meaning of the free market lasted well into the twentieth century. Although the argument that speculation was an intelligent, responsible, and professional practice was established by the turn of the century, the 1929 stock market crash caused a resurgence of critique of the financial sphere. For example, the U.S. political magazine *Atlantic Monthly* regularly published critiques of speculation and the stock market in 1930 and 1931 and called for reform of the financial system. In a 1931 issue, Samuel Spring argued that financial practices such as speculation were the enemy of modern scientific achievements and incompatible with "foresight and cautious calculation," the very virtues that defenders of speculation sought to be associated with (1931, 477). "The demon of speculation," Spring wrote, "scattering wild booms and still wilder panics, hovers over us as the abiding affliction of our machine age. . . . Seemingly a savage jest is being played upon our self-sure, scientific generation" (477). Spring accused investment bankers of having sinned against business morality and prudence. "If there be an inherent weakness in the human mind or in the human heart involved in speculation," he wrote, "this weakness primarily is not mob greed and mob stupidity, but rather it is the failure of our business leaders—primarily our investment bankers—to refrain from making dazzling, though largely fugitive, paper profits by exploiting unto the edge of disaster the possibilities of a mad market" (482–83). Spring thus refuted Emery's thesis that amateur participation in the markets was cause of the evil of speculation, while using a discourse of temptation and greed to explain the 1929 crash.[1]

As a result of critiques in the wake of the 1929 stock market crash, the U.S. Senate authorized hearings on the financial system in March 1932 to be carried out by the Committee on Banking and Currency of the Senate. The report delivered by the committee, which came to fifteen volumes and was not completed and published until 1934, provides a thorough examination of U.S. stock market practices. The "Stock Exchange Practices Report" led to the adoption of two regulatory acts bearing on stock trading. In 1933, U.S. Congress adopted the Securities Act, which requires public disclosure of information pertaining to securities that are publicly offered and which seeks to prohibit fraud. Second, in 1934 the Securities Exchange Act (SEA) was adopted, which created the Securities Exchange Commission (SEC) as the federal regulator of the stock exchanges.[2] These regulatory acts responded to the moral and economic critiques of speculation voiced in *The Atlantic Monthly,* among other places. President Roosevelt declared that the acts were designed to implement a "national policy to restrict, as far as possible, the use of . . . exchanges for purely speculative purposes" (quoted in Werner 1975, 1244–45). Similarly, a senator who supported the laws stated their purpose to be "to make the stock market places for investors and not places of resort for those who would speculate or gamble" (1245).

In the United Kingdom an investigative committee that was appointed in 1929 to examine the monetary dealings of the 1920s also found itself, as documented by Gordon (1972), investigating the Great Depression and the surging unemployment after the 1929 stock market crash. The Committee on Finance and Industry, known as the Macmillan Committee, was established by the British Chancellor of the Exchequer, Philip Snowden, who denounced the U.S. stock market crash before a Labour Party Conference by asserting that "there has been a perfect orgy of speculation in New York during the last twelve months" (quoted in *Banker's Magazine* 1929, 907). The Macmillan Committee became preoccupied with distinguishing the working of the "real" economy from the "veil of money," and it asked its witnesses to state "their opinions as to whether and to what extent Britain's difficulties were due to monetary factors" (Gordon 1972, 965). After hearing statements from the leading economists of the time, including Keynes, the Macmillan Committee concluded that the main monetary evil was the instability of the general price level, and its report advised active government intervention in financial matters. The Macmillan report, which was delivered in 1931, concluded: "We may well have reached the stage when an era of conscious and deliberate management must succeed the era of undirected natural evolution" (970).

It is generally argued, then, that the 1930s saw a profound change in international financial practices entailing, as Helleiner puts it, "an important . . . break with [the] liberal tradition in finance" (1994, 28). "The 1931 international financial crisis," writes Helleiner,

> marked the beginning of a kind of socio-ideological "structural break" in financial affairs. As one German financier noted at the height of the crisis: "What I have just experienced means the end of a way of life, certainly for Germany and perhaps other countries as well. . . . The common vision of the future has been destroyed." Largely discredited by the crises, the private and central bankers who had dominated financial politics before the 1930s were increasingly replaced at the levers of financial power. (22)

In short, the financial changes of the 1930s are often interpreted as entailing a submission, prohibition and regulation of financial practices. It is assumed to be a period of political defeat of financial interests, signifying an end to the freedom of financial capitalism.

However, in contrast to this interpretation of qualitative change, the regulatory efforts of the 1930s, the creation of financial supervisory agencies, and the adoption of broad-based financial laws can also be seen as the normalization and legitimization of financial practices (see MacKenzie 2002, 29–33). While financial practices had been profoundly and openly contested in previous decades, the regulatory efforts of the 1930s made possible a depoliticization of these practices. As lawyer Walter Werner has argued with respect to the 1933 and 1934 U.S. acts that established the SEC, for example, these did as much to create the moral and legal space for financial markets to operate as they did to curb speculation. The Exchange Act, Werner points out, "confirmed the validity of existing exchange commission rate and membership practices" (1975, 1251). In consequence, it became possible to abstract stock trading from the field of political contestation, which in turn consolidated and legalized a professional domain for financial speculators.

Foucault argues that normalization is one of the most important forms of modern power, with the examination and the audit among its most significant operative techniques. "The examination," writes Foucault, "is a normalizing gaze, a surveillance that makes it possible to qualify, to classify and to punish" (1979, 184). This interpretation is made possible through comprehending power as a producing and enabling force, instead of a purely negative and prohibiting force. "We must cease once and for all to describe the effects of power in negative terms," Foucault writes, "it 'excludes,' it 'represses,' it 'censors,' it 'abstracts,' it 'masks,' it 'conceals.' In fact, power produces; it produces reality; it produces domains of objects and rituals of truth" (194). It is in this sense that we can understand the power entailed in the adoption of federal stock market regulation as a *producing* and *enabling* power. The regulatory efforts of the 1930s produced a legitimate professional domain for speculators; they produced regimes of financial truth embodied by rules for disclosure and registration, and they enabled the silencing of the political contestation over speculation that had predominated in previous decades. It is interesting, in this respect, that the SEC's Web site notes that the 1933 Securities Act is "often referred to as the 'truth in securities' law."[3] Financial truth, in this sense, does not exist uncontested and before interpretation but, paradoxically, emerges through legal and regulative requirements that designate the domain of finance. More precisely, it was not until the formulation and consolidation of the limits of the financial sphere in law following the 1929 crash that it became possible to reify financial practices by erasing traces of their controversial, religious, cultural, moral, gendered, and political origins.

However, despite their normalization, traces of the contingent discursive moves that legitimized speculation continue to haunt financial discourse today, especially in times of perceived crisis. In this chapter, I discuss how the near bankruptcy of the U.S. hedge fund Long-Term Capital Management (LTCM) demonstrates the continuing tensions in and controversies over modern credit practices and illustrates the politics of regulation and risk in contemporary finance. LTCM had been regarded as a bastion of financial credibility and included some of the most respected and prominent members of the modern financial world, but it was forced to seek assistance from the New York Federal Reserve in September 1998 to avoid bankruptcy.[4] I am less interested in finding explanations for why the fund failed than in discussing the rationale behind the fund's operations and trades that preceded and outlived it. In particular, I will argue that the mathematical models and market philosophies associated with the fund's founders are at the heart of contemporary financial practices. Rather than being a reassertion of a homogenous or unitary force, the "reemergence of global finance" since the collapse of Bretton Woods has taken specific institutional forms through political debates on risk, mathematical modeling, and the legitimacy of derivatives trading, which in part built on debates discussed in my earlier chapters (Helleiner 1994).

SCIENTIFIC FINANCE

In chapters 3 and 4 I argued that the scientific study of stock prices emerged as a moral imperative during nineteenth-century political controversies over financial practices in the United States and United Kingdom. Financial study and scientific endeavor became a way for speculators to assert their productiveness and intelligence in the face of growing opposition to their trades as fraudulent and gambling. Jevons's and Dow's metaphors cast the workings of financial markets in terms of natural universal laws, making possible the scientific study of finance. Another contemporary of Dow and Jevons who proposed to understand financial practices in terms of physics was French physicist Louis Bachelier. Bachelier wrote in his doctoral thesis of 1900 that "it is possible to study mathematically the static state of the market at a given instant, i.e., to establish the law of probability of price changes consistent with the market at that instant" (1964, 17). Given the nature of economic markets, Bachelier argued, it is possible to compare the movement of stock prices to the movement of dust particles under influence of millions of tiny pushes given to them by molecules. In Bachelier's analogy, the aggregate behavior of millions of speculators influences the movement of prices at any given moment. This comparison teaches that the movement of stock prices can be predicted as the diffusion of smoke in a room that proceeds mathematically along the normal distribution (or bell curve) (Dunbar 2000, 9–12).

Although Bachelier's "Theory of Speculation" had little impact at the time of writing, it has more recently been heralded as one of the most influential treatises in financial science. Most notably, LTCM founder Professor Robert Merton credits "Bachelier's magnificent dissertation on the theory of speculation" as being very influential on his own work (1994, 451–52). A direct lineage runs from Bachelier's studies of the movement of share prices to the mathematical trading techniques employed by LTCM. Paradoxically, the fundamental randomness of stock price movements as argued by Bachelier made the market inherently calculable. Simply put, Bachelier's suggestion that stock price changes are entirely random means that the expected range of movements of stock prices over a given time can be calculated. If the starting point of a stock price movement is given (for instance, the current stock price), it is possible calculate the propensity that stock prices will move by a stated amount in any given period of time (Bernstein 1996, 144–50).

At the heart of this reasoning is the conviction that markets are efficient, that is, that they reflect all available information at any one time, producing an equilibrium price for securities. This equilibrium will be readjusted when stock prices move, for instance, in response to new information that is introduced randomly into the stock markets (Bernstein 1992, 126–45). This model of the market has been called the "efficient market hypothesis," developed, among others, by University of Chicago professor Eugene Fama. Fama defined an efficient market as a place "where there are large numbers of rational, profit-maximizers actively competing, with each trying to predict future market values of individual securities" (1965, 56). Competition between investors will cause, according to Fama "the full effects of new information on intrinsic [stock] values to be reflected 'instantaneously' in actual prices" (56). Simply put, Fama argued that because of the combined intelligence of stock market analysts and investors, market prices "will reflect predictions based on all relevant and available information," thus making it impossible for any individual investor to spot opportunities where stock prices diverge from their "intrinsic" values and thus make profits

(Bernstein 1992, 134–35). This image of rational, efficient, and equili-
brating markets was the ideological addition that Bachelier's dry
mathematical thesis needed before it could gain popularity in the
1960s and 1970s.

Despite Fama's arguments that it is the combined intelligence of
investors that makes markets efficient, arguments on the statistical calculability of future stock prices, made possible by the work
of Dow and Bachelier, forcefully demonstrate the tension between
two possible formulations of financial rationality. On one hand,
financial rationality is cast as the impartial reading of financial
information, making scientific and computerized calculation in
finance possible. On the other hand, financial professionals assert
their legitimacy in terms of professionalism, experience, and unique
insight, which suggests that financial decision making cannot be
delegated to a formula or machine. This tension in financial discourse has become increasingly important during the twentieth century. For example, Bernstein (1992, 28–38) documents how in the
1930s Dow's successor Peter Hamilton and the speculator Alfred
Cowles expanded Dow's assertions that the market was inherently
measurable and predictable by analyzing data from the 1920s and
1930s stock market with the help of one of the first IBM calculating machines. Cowles himself had suffered substantial losses in the
1929 stock market crash and joined the legion of researchers, both
public and private, who tried to unearth how this crash could have
happened and how similar events could be avoided in the future.
From his analyses, Cowles concluded that stock prediction by financial analysts was nearly worthless, and he found that "the best of a
series of random forecasts made by drawing cards from an appropriate deck was just as good as the best series of actual forecasts"
(Bernstein 1992, 35).

In the 1960s and 1970s financial mathematicians continued to
voice their beliefs that "a blindfolded monkey throwing darts at a
newspaper's financial pages could select a portfolio that would do
just as well as one carefully selected by the experts" (Malkiel 1990,
24; see Fama 1965). In 1971, one of the most influential figures
in the postwar development of financial science, Fischer Black,
suggested that "it . . . appears that most investment management
organizations would improve their performance if they fired all
but one of their security analysts and then provided the remaining

analyst with the Value Line Service [a statistical investment model]" (quoted in Bernstein 1992, 136). Merton himself dismisses pre-1960s security analysis as profoundly unscientific: "During most of this period, finance was almost entirely a descriptive discipline with a focus on institutional and legal matters. Finance theory was a collection of anecdotes, rules of thumb and shufflings of accounting data" (1994, 452). Naturally these conclusions angered finance professionals; it implied that well-paid investment advisors delivered inherently useless advice. During most of the Bretton Woods years financial professionals were able to dismiss mathematical finance by arguing that academics were bad investors and had no real market experience. Financial mathematicians were confined to academic institutions such as the Cowles Commission for Research in Economics at the University of Chicago.[5]

In the 1973 articulation of an option pricing formula by Black and LTCM co-founder Professor Myron Scholes, however, academic finance theory and finance practice would find a very profitable meeting ground. With the help of Bachelier's teachings on stock price movements, Black and Scholes reasoned that option prices could be calculated if one knew the current stock price and the average volatility of a particular stock. Black and Scholes expressed dissatisfaction with existing option pricing theories, as these all included unknown or unmeasurable components such as "the expected value of the stock price" at the time of expiry of the option, or the utility preferences of investors (1973, 639–40). As finance professor Zvi Bodie later said in a BBC documentary about LTCM: "The mathematical models that were being developed during the fifties and sixties depended on inputs that were completely unobservable in the real world like expectations of investors which might differ very much from one investor to another" (Horizon 1999). Black and Scholes eliminated all such unmeasurable factors from their equation and articulated a way in which to reduce the importance of the one remaining unknown component, the level of risk, through the continuous hedging of their positions. Although Merton did not co-author the original 1973 piece, he did cooperate closely with Black and Scholes and provided an alternative justification for the Black-Scholes equation in the same year (Bernstein 1992, 203–30).

At the time that Black, Scholes, and Merton worked on their equations, derivatives were still not regarded as a legitimate part of finance practice. I have already discussed how options were considered to be gambling instruments, as they are not binding contracts and thus could not be said to "contemplate" delivery.[6] Options on commodities had been banned in 1934 as a result of federal investigations into the 1929 stock market crash, but stock options were traded in small volumes from restaurants near Wall Street (Dunbar 2000, 33). Suspicion of derivatives trading lasted until well into the 1970s, and the practice, as before, was associated with gambling and female promiscuity. For example, when in 1976 a futures market in U.S. Treasury bills opened at the Chicago Mercantile Exchange (CME), *The Economist* wrote:

> Like Linda Lovelace, the girl with the deep throat [and character in the 1971 pornographic film *Deep Throat*], the International Money Market (IMM) of the Chicago Mercantile Exchange tries to make money by being more outrageous than its rivals. Now that its currencies futures market is well established—it was opened in 1972 by women in fancy dress—the IMM has this month opened a trading pit in United States treasury bill futures. Bidding for the government paper takes place on the same floor as for pork bellies, live cattle and three-month eggs. (1976, 106)

One participant in the debates over the legitimacy of derivatives was Leo Melamed, president of the CME, who campaigned vigorously for the creation of financial futures markets. "Why is there a need for a futures markets in currencies?" Melamed (1972) asked in a speech to securities analysts, "might this not merely be the invention of a legalized form of gambling?" On the contrary, Melamed (1974b) argued, the existence of fixed exchange rates is incompatible with a globalizing world and "with the demise of Bretton Woods . . . a new era was dawning, not only with respect to flexible exchange rates, but in the very essence of American psychology." With the help of a 1971 paper written by Milton Friedman, Melamed argued that a futures market in currencies where businesses could hedge their currency risk was urgently needed. Melamed justified derivatives markets with all the arguments developed at the beginning of the twentieth century. The existence of professional speculators was indispensable to derivatives markets, he argued, because "it is the speculator who is willing to accept and offset the risk of the commercial user" (Melamed 1972). Indeed, "to us, speculators are as welcome as hedgers" Melamed (1974b) said in another speech, "our philosophy is never to differentiate between a commercial or private motivation for making a trade. . . . In a free society, everyone ought to have this right." Moreover, "a futures exchange will act as a public weather vane and instant barometer of the market," according to Melamed (1972), and its development would be in the national economic interest (see Melamed 1974a, 1974b). But Melamed's motivation also included institutional expansion, and he rightly anticipated the profit opportunities of the commercialization of risk. In a recent interview Melamed explains: "I was on a holy mission to diversify the [CME's] product line. . . . We tried everything. We tried shrimp. We tried scrap steel. We tried turkeys. We tried apples. We tried potatoes. None of those turned out to be very good" (Wasendorf 2003). The new big idea was the creation of futures markets in financial products, of which the market in currencies (the IMM) that opened in May 1972 was just the first step.

The Black-Scholes option pricing formula was not incidental to the growth in derivatives markets, but at the heart of it. According to the Chicago's exchange council, the model helped legitimize options trading and spurred the growth of the Chicago Board Options Exchange (CBOE), which was founded in 1973:

> Black-Scholes was really what enabled the [CBOE] to thrive. . . . It gave a lot of legitimacy to the whole notion of hedging and efficient pricing, whereas we were faced, in the late 60s–early 70s with the issue of gambling. That issue fell away, and I think Black-Scholes made it fall away. It wasn't speculation or gambling, it was efficient pricing. . . . [Soon] I never heard the word "gambling" again in relation to options. (quoted in MacKenzie and Millo 2003, 121)

MacKenzie and Millo (2003, 124) document how traders on the CBOE trading floor started using printed sheets with prices as calculated by the Black-Scholes formula, and Bernstein (1992, 227) notes that Texas Instruments soon developed a calculator programmed with the formula. The option price as given by the formula, then, became the industry standard and was used by traders and speculators who did not understand its underlying mathematics or assumptions. Indeed, Black himself was critical of this development and wrote in a 1989 article: "Traders now use the formula and its variants extensively. They use it so much that market prices are usually close to formula values even in situations where there should be a large difference" (8).

Moreover, at the heart of the Black-Scholes model was the assumption that with the help of options a portfolio that was not correlated to the fluctuations of the overall market could be created; in other words, a *riskless* portfolio, in which each position was hedged by an option in the opposite direction. Merton's innovation was called dynamic hedging and entailed a continuous computerized adaptation of one's portfolio in order to hedge out the risks (MacKenzie 2003a, 844–51). "I looked at this thing," said Merton in an interview with MacKenzie in 1999, "and I realised that if you did . . . dynamic hedging . . . if you actually [traded] literally continuously, then in fact . . . you could get rid of the risk" (850). This argument legitimized and fueled the international expansion of options markets in the 1980s and 1990s. One broker interviewed for the BBC Horizon (1999) documentary explained it as follows:

> The basic dynamic of the Black-Scholes model is the idea that through dynamic hedging we can eliminate risks, so we have a mathematical argument for trading a lot. What a wonderful thing for exchanges to hear. *The more we trade, the better off the society is because the less risk there is.* So we have to have more contracts, more futures exchanges, we have to be able to trade Nikkei futures in Japan, we have to be able to trade options in Germany. Basically in order to reduce risk we have to trade everywhere and all the time. (emphasis added)

The Black-Scholes formula, in short, directly legitimated the growth of post-Bretton Woods financial markets by arguing that derivatives could reduce societal risk. The formula's influence on the financial markets has been widely acknowledged, and by 2002 the aggregate notional amount of derivatives trades was more than US$160 trillion, or around US$27,000 for every human being on earth (MacKenzie 2003a, 832). As Goldman Sachs trader Emanuel Derman put it: "The Black-Scholes equation was to finance what Newtonian mechanics was to physics. Black-Scholes is sort of the foundation on which the field rests" (quoted in Stix 1998).

Rather than as a contestable construction of the fair price of financial instruments, then, the Black-Scholes formula was heralded as the scientific discovery of financial truth. Such interpretation of their work was consolidated by the 1997 decision of the Nobel

Academy to award Scholes and Merton the Bank of Sweden Prize in Economic Sciences (Black died in 1995). In the press release accompanying this decision, the Royal Swedish Academy of Sciences wrote:

> Effective risk management requires that [financial] instruments be correctly priced. Fischer Black, Robert Merton and Myron Scholes made a pioneering contribution to economic sciences by developing a new method of determining the value of derivatives. Their innovative work in the early 1970s, which solved a longstanding problem in financial economics, has provided us with completely new ways of dealing with financial risk, both in theory and in practice. Their method has contributed substantially to the rapid growth of markets for derivatives in the last two decades. (Royal Swedish Academy 1997, 1)

Around the same time, *The Economist* (1997) lauded Scholes and Merton with the accomplishment of having "turned risk management from a guessing game into a science" that could be considered "among the most useful work that economics has produced."

LTCM AS A SITE OF CRITIQUE

Perhaps challenged by the oft-posed question to academics, "If you're so smart, why aren't you rich?" (Malkiel 1990, 131), Scholes and Merton entered investment practice in 1994 in cooperation with former Salomon Brothers bond trader John Meriwether[7] to set up the hedge fund LTCM.[8] Predicated on the philosophies of scientific finance in general and dynamic hedging in particular, the hedge fund started trading in 1994 with US$3 billion in capital. Armed with new and sophisticated versions of their financial formulas and US$20 million worth of computer equipment, LTCM traders scanned the global markets for profit opportunities. As the LTCM prospectus stated: "We want to be global, and we want to have an ability to employ this technology in any country around the world" (quoted in Dunbar 2000, 126). LTCM's preferred financial strategy was called arbitrage, which assumes that in integrated financial markets the same or similar financial contracts have to be priced equally. Should discrepancies in these prices exist, for instance, between different countries, an arbitrage dealer can make enormous profits when buying the underpriced and selling the overpriced contract, providing he or she has enough money at his or her disposal because profit margins are very small. Arbitrage reasoning underpins the model of financial markets as integrated, efficient, and rational: price differences can never exist long in this model because these profit opportunities would be exploited. It is in this sense that arbitrageurs can be considered to be the "border guards . . . between economics and sociology. . . . The . . . plausible assumption that pricing discrepancies will be eliminated by arbitrage allows the development of elegant and influential economic models of markets," according to MacKenzie (2003b, 350). In 1995 and 1996, LTCM returned over 40 percent net profits to its investors, and "the list of firms investing or trading with Long-Term ultimately became a who's who of international finance" (O'Brien and Holson 1998, C22).

However, LTCM started incurring losses in early 1998, which accelerated as a result of Russia's default in August and culminated in single-day trading losses exceeding US$500 million in August and September 1998 (GAO 1999, 39). The Federal Reserve, led by Alan Greenspan and New York Federal Reserve President William McDonough, subsequently organized a recapitalization for the hedge fund by bringing together its creditors and pressuring them into keeping the fund afloat for the general benefit of the international capital markets. LTCM's managers were dismissed, the fund's positions were slowly wound down, and it eventually stopped trading in 2000. At the time of its bankruptcy, *The Economist* compared LTCM's demise to the sinking of the Titanic and wrote: "Like the Titanic, Long-Term Capital Management was supposed to be unsinkable" (1998, 127). *The Economist* continued: "The hedge fund's dramatic downturn and bail-out last week was the stuff of Hollywood disaster movies: fortunes laid waste, proud men (Nobel laureates no less) cut down to size, giant tidal waves threatening to drown some of Wall Street's snootiest institutions" (127).

In October 1998, as a direct result of LTCM's failure, a hearing on hedge fund operations took place before the U.S. House of Representatives. This hearing was used as a platform by a few members of Congress to voice critiques of the legitimate bases of profit making in modern finance, which can be considered a reopening of the older, similar debates examined in previous chapters. Most notably, Independent Congressman Bernard Sanders from Vermont, who can be counted among Greenspan's most outspoken critics, said in his opening speech during the first hearing, held in October 1998:

What we have here are banks that are willing to lend billions of dollars to one man so that he could gamble on whether interest rates go up by a half a percent or whether they go down by a half percent. But meanwhile these are the very same banks that refuse to loan money for economic development and job creation in communities all over America. Evidently there is not enough money in these banks to invest in job-creating small business, in job-creating family farming, in job-creating manufacturing, but there are unlimited amounts of money to be lent to gamblers in their nonproductive efforts to guess if interest rates will rise or fall. (HBC 1998, 24)

Sanders went on to express his concern over the "extraordinarily unfair distribution of wealth that exists not only in our country, but throughout the world. . . . According to the United Nations . . . the world's 225 richest individuals have a combined wealth of over a trillion dollars, equal to the bottom 47 percent of the world's population. Two hundred twenty-five people have as much wealth as almost half of the world's population" (HBC 1998, 101). Similarly, Congressman Maurice Hinchey linked the unequal distribution of wealth in the United States to the possibility of such an event as the LTCM failure. "The fact that you have an extraordinary amount of money in the hands of a very few people," Hinchey argued, "[means] that they are inclined to take risks with that money which they would not ordinarily do if the amounts available to them were appreciably less; and in that exercise they perhaps are endangering the rest of us more than they are themselves" (HBC 1998, 126).

Former SEC President David Ruder also spoke out in favor of hedge fund regulation on the grounds that "our capital markets should not be held hostage to the activities of a group of risk-takers who can operate in secrecy without regard to possible systemic effects" (HBC 1998, 188). Finally, labor union leader Lawrence Parks questioned the productive bases of financial institutions such as LTCM when a second hearing on hedge funds was organized in March 1999. "What benefit to society," Parks asked, "could possibly justify Long-Term Capital's, other hedge funds', and particularly banks' and brokerage firms', ability to reap so much money from this activity [speculation]? Does this 'trading' result in any good or service that improves anyone's life?" (1999, 2).

On the other hand, Greenspan and McDonough, who were asked to justify the Federal Reserve's role in LTCM's recapitalization before the Banking Committee, argued that the situation the fund found itself in was extraordinary and an aberration in the markets. McDonough argued that "while hubris may have set LTCM up for a fall, it was the extraordinary events of August in global markets that appear to have tripped them" (HBC 1998, 31). The Federal Reserve's involvement, as McDonough repeatedly pointed out, "has to be understood in the background of the extremely dangerously disturbed financial markets" (HBC 1999, 31).[9] Objecting to those who wished to make the LTCM failure a rallying point for critique of speculative capitalism, Greenspan justified LTCM's trading strategies with the argument that they support efficient and rational markets, and he dismissed the market turmoil associated with the LTCM disaster as irrational and rare. Greenspan's justification built on the arguments concerning price production developed over a century ago:

> Many of the things which [hedge funds] do in order to obtain profit are largely arbitrage type of activities which tend to refine the pricing system in the United States and elsewhere, and it is that really exceptionally and increasingly sophisticated pricing system which is one of the reasons why the use of capital in this country is so efficient. It is why productivity is the highest in the world, why our standards of living, without question, are the highest in the world. (HBC 1998, 93)

So what if hedge funds earn "an extra bit of return on capital" for providing this social service, Greenspan asked (1998, 2). Such was also the reasoning of hedge fund president Leon Metzger, who offered the following rationale for hedge fund activity in his plea to avoid regulation: "Hedge funds play a positive role in maintaining the smooth operation of the financial markets. . . . Hedge funds search out assets whose prices are temporarily out of line with fundamental values, helping to reestablish the true market value of securities by selling short an overpriced instrument and buying an underpriced one" (HBC 1999, 61).

As a result of the hearings, Congress adopted the Hedge Fund Disclosure Act, which stipulates quarterly reporting requirements for hedge funds concerning their assets, positions, leverage, and risks. However, like the 1930s regulatory efforts, this act must been seen as a depoliticization and normalization of hedge fund activity, rather than as a fundamental restraint of it. Indeed, the act was designed specifically for this purpose, and in an accompanying press release Representative Richard H. Baker, chairman of the House Capital Markets Subcommittee, stated: "After considering the report and testimony at several hearings held by the House Committee on Banking and Financial Services . . . I have concluded that the most appropriate response to the treatment of hedge funds is a measured, market-oriented approach of enhanced disclosure."[10] In short, the Hedge Fund Disclosure Act created a legitimate domain for hedge funds to operate, stabilized the controversy surrounding hedge funds, and, most importantly, silenced the critical questioning concerning discourses of entitlement and wealth distribution that took place during the hearings.

RISK AND MARKET PHILOSOPHY

Central to the House hearings was the question whether LTCM's rationale and activities were exceptional or typical of contemporary financial practices. Although many have denounced LTCM as "an anomaly within the industry" (HBC 1998, 209), I argue that the market philosophy and risk models employed by LTCM and designed by its associates are exemplary of modern financial risk management. First, it is important to note that LTCM's trades and techniques were widely copied in the financial industry, despite the fund's claims to secrecy. In the 1990s, hedge funds specializing in arbitrage proliferated, and one fund called Convergence Asset Management raised US$700 million from investors who had been denied a chance to participate in LTCM (Dunbar 2000, 197). In addition, LTCM's trades were being imitated by the large investment banks, such as Merrill Lynch, to such an extent that LTCM's managers worried that their profit opportunities would vanish. Indeed, one of the events that triggered LTCM's losses was Salomon Brothers' unwinding of similar arbitrage positions (Dunbar 2000, 190–97; Lewis 1999). To MacKenzie, this explanation of the fund's collapse is the more convincing one and illustrates a wider point about the social nature of arbitrage and financial trading in general: instead of a purely rational or mathematical logic, arbitrage opportunities are identified and exploited through a social "arbitrage community": "Arbitrageurs often know each other and are affected by each other" (2003b, 371). In fact, Meriwether has retrospectively argued that "his mistake was that he failed to see so many other investors were mimicking his trades . . . [and] he was trampled by the herd" (Silverman and Chaffin 2000, 9). As early as 1999 Meriwether started to raise money in order to set up a new hedge fund called JWM, which, he claimed, "can withstand extreme events of the type experienced in 1998" (quoted in Lowenstein 2001, 236).

At the same time however, Meriwether's indignation at the financial industry's imitation of LTCM's positions may also be seen as indicative of the fund's commitment to a particular and unreflexive model of economic science. LTCM had become a very significant part of the markets it traded in—by the time of its collapse in 1998, the fund was committed to more than 20,000 transactions and conducted business with over 75 counterparties (GAO 1999, 7). But the thought that its trades and reputation may have a bearing on the markets it exploited was inconceivable to LTCM's participants. This attitude was not just an aberration in comparison to the fund's size, but the logical conclusion of its faith in modern risk management. As I argued in chapter 4, the nineteenth-century metaphor that cast stock price movements in terms of natural laws paved the way for the moral application of scientific methodology to financial markets and underpins the discursive move that abstracts the observer from the financial system he or she studies. LTCM's computerized trading in the international derivatives markets was predicated on the assumption that it could objectively measure and manage its risks, and it had no space for the social dimension of markets (see Lewis 1999). That Meriwether views the social dimension of markets as something rare and irrational is illustrated by his following remark: "There are times when markets can be much more chaotic than one would ever predict, driven in a sense by human behaviour" (quoted in Silverman and Chaffin 2000, 8). Human behavior, for Meriwether, is something illogical that has no proper place in the financial markets.

But more important than Meriwether's new hedge fund or the fact that LTCM's specific trades were copied by other market participants are the ways in which LTCM's models and market philosophies were representative for contemporary finance. This is illustrated in three specific ways. First, the Black-Scholes model remains unquestioned and is used in the markets on a daily basis. Second,

the risk models used by LTCM were typical for the financial industry as a whole. Third, the market philosophy articulated by Scholes
and Merton underpins the unprecedented commercialization of
risks in contemporary markets.

First, the financial theory of those associated with LTCM, and
especially the Black-Scholes model itself, has not come under scrutiny and remains used in the markets on a daily basis. I have already
discussed how the price given by the Black-Scholes formula has
become the industry standard. The "right" price for options for
which Black and his colleagues had been searching—and which
the Royal Swedish Academy (1997) confirmed as their "scientific
achievement"—instead became reflexively constructed in their own
formulas. As long as everyone trading in options-markets is using
the same formula, this reflexivity poses no practical problems. However, it should be understood that the Black-Scholes model delivers
a normative prescription in the name of scientific objectivity: the
philosophy of continuous finance and dynamic hedging entails, as
the broker quoted above succinctly points out, an authoritative and
mathematical argument for "trading a lot." As MacKenzie (2003a,
854) argues, the model has contributed to its assumptions becoming
more realistic: its assumed "ideal conditions" of zero transaction
cost, the possibility of purchasing stock on credit, and the absence
of penalties for short-selling now approximate actual market practices more closely than they did in the 1970s, partly because of the
legitimation the model provided. Second, to estimate its overall risk-
position in the markets, LTCM used a technique called value-at-risk
(VaR), which was not specific to the fund itself but has become an
industry standard (Izquierdo 2001; Tickell 2000). VaR was developed by J. P. Morgan in reaction to the 1987 stock market crash to
offer the daily calculation of a broad, aggregate figure of potential
losses. Calculating VaR involves assigning probabilities to future
events, such as price changes and market movements, as well as
forecasting the volatility of markets and correlations between various financial instruments held by a firm. According to this model,
the losses LTCM incurred were calculated to occur once every 800
trillion years or 40,000 times the age of the universe (Jorion 1999,
13). In particular, Russia's default on its ruble-denominated debts
in August 1998 was regarded as "shocking" and unpredictable
(MacKenzie 2003b, 362). But what seems to have eluded commenta-

REGULATION AND RISK IN CONTEMPORARY MARKETS · 139

tors who dismiss the events of the fall of 1998—Russia's debt mora- torium and LTCM's default—as abnormal and aberrant, is that *normality is constructed in the very mathematical models that are supposed to measure it.* In other words, when the LTCM collapse is assumed triggered by "non-normal behaviour" of capital markets (Young 1999, 70), the fact that VaR constructs a contingent image of normality according to specific historical data is disregarded (see Maurer 2002).

Historian of science Ian Hacking notes this profound tension in the "scientific" conception of the normal. Although it is articulated as a mean or average in mathematical measurements, the normal reflexively denotes not how things *are* but how things *ought to be:* "The normal stands indifferently for what is typical, the unenthu- siastic objective average, but it also stands for what has been, good health, and for what shall be, our chosen destiny. That is why the benign and sterile-sounding word 'normal' has become one of the most powerful ideological tools of the twentieth century" (Hacking 1990, 169). Their objective ambitions notwithstanding, articula- tions of normality in financial practices offer normative claims con- cerning financial stability, efficiency, and rationality. Such a norma- tive concept of normality allows the retrospective denouncing of the events of autumn 1998 as irrational and abnormal. However, the elusiveness of financial normality in practice is nicely illustrated in the words of Scholes, who argued after LTCM's collapse that there is now a greater need for consideration of extreme events in finan- cial modeling. Scholes's summing up of "periods of extreme mar- ket stress, such as 1987 around the world, 1990 in Japan, 1991 in Europe, 1992 in Sweden, 1994 in the United States, 1995 in Mexico, and 1997–1999 in Asia, and the Americas, Europe, and the United States," leaves one to wonder when, if ever, financial normality can be assumed to exist (2000, 19).

In fact, VaR and the associated technique of stress-testing, can be seen as exemplary of what Niklas Luhmann calls the construction of a "secondary normality," or the desire to show that the unexpected and unanticipated have "an order of [their] own" (1993, i). By trying to calculate and tabulate the unexpected, these techniques demon- strate reluctance to accept domains of unpredictability in financial practices. Instead, they desire to reduce the unexpected, the irratio- nal, and the rare to calculable probabilities. LTCM, for instance, stress-tested its portfolio by calculating the consequences of "extreme" hypothetical events "such as a huge stock market crash, bond default by the Italian government, devaluation by China, or . . . failure of EMU" (MacKenzie 2003b, 359). However, would it have been possible for LTCM to test for *all* possible unexpected events— including Russia's default on ruble-denominated debt? Or is the definition of events to be included in stress-testing exemplary of what Stephen Green calls "the epistemological confidence of the modern risk order," namely "the assumption that risk can be calculated. It is just a question of the right mathematics and enough information" (2000, 86). Instead, should the definition of the unexpected not be precisely that it is *unexpected*?

Third, and directly related, is the importance of the philosophy behind options pricing to the growth of commercial risk markets. What Merton, in particular, argued was not only that a formula for pricing complex options could be scientifically calculated, but also that "the underlying conceptual framework . . . can be used to price and evaluate the risk in a wide array of applications, both financial and non-financial" (1998, 324). For example, a share can be interpreted as an option on the firm, which means the share price can be calculated with the option pricing formula (when shares are infrequently traded). But also uncertainties related to product development, almost any type of insurance, uncertain future income streams, and even dilemmas of movie production can be understood and priced through options theory, according to this reasoning. As Merton put it: "'Option-like' structures were soon seen to be lurking everywhere. . . . The future is uncertain . . . and in an uncertain environment, having the flexibility to decide what to do after some of that uncertainty is resolved definitely has value. Option-pricing theory provides the means for assessing that value" (1998, 336, 339). Merton's ideal was a world of continuous and complete markets in which every thinkable uncertainty can be bought and sold at an intrinsic fair price. Such complete market utopia had been earlier proposed by Stanford economist and Nobel laureate Kenneth Arrow who, as one journalist put it, "had a vision of a world in which everything was assigned a value on a market. In this utopia, every possible state of the world, past, present and future, from a stormy July evening in Patagonia to England winning the World Cup had a financial payoff associated with it" (Dunbar 2000, 42).

Merton called his market vision the "financial-innovation spiral" in which limitless amounts of custom-designed financial contracts spiraled toward the utopia of "complete markets and zero marginal transactions costs" (1994, 456).

It is important to understand the commercial consequences of finance's desire to tabulate the unexpected and to quantify every imaginable uncertainty. Only quantifiable risks can be hedged, and thus, bought and sold on the financial markets. "Risk management as a system of interlocking technological, institutional and social forms of action," Green writes, "has become entrenched in global markets because of its basic ability to combine the modern ambition for certainty about the future and capitalism's willingness to bring imagined futures into the realm of the market" (2000, 81–82). In other words, risk management combines the political legitimacy of speculation (providing security) with opportunities for unprecedented profit. Thus, contestable mathematical models rapidly become the basis for real financial practices and markets. As Porter puts it: "[New] instruments move from a mathematical model in a financial analyst's computer to being the basis of vast markets in the space of a few years. Once the instruments are accepted as routine, these markets come to be taken for granted as the baseline reality around which other practices are oriented" (1999, 142). To Merton, this is a positive effect of his equations: "Options-pricing technology has played a fundamental role in supporting the creation of new financial products and markets around the globe" (1998, 324). After the fall of LTCM, Scholes defended the use of complex risk modeling in similar terms: "Better risk management models reduce costs, and as a result, financial firms develop new products and activities that make their constituents better off" (2000, 21).

Who, indeed, is better off with the philosophy of complete markets? According to Ulrich Beck, "Risks are a 'bottomless barrel of demands,' unsatisfiable, infinite. . . . Demands, and thus markets, of a completely new type can be *created* by varying the definition of risk, especially demand for the avoidance of risk" (1992, 56). While financial speculation is justified as providing security in the face of an uncertain future, new risk products and markets provide security only to those who can afford to purchase them, and mostly to those who design and sell them. Large companies increasingly seek to hedge themselves against not just traditional insurable uncertainties such as fires, accidents, or exchange rate fluctuations, but also against newly identified risks such as fluctuations in the company's stock prices and assets or fluctuations in the weather. French food group Danone is one example of a company that seeks such continuous insurance and is in the process of developing a financial risk strategy that seeks to "protect the group's bottom line from any type of risk" (Booth 1999). But there is a circular argument propping up the financial sphere: while professing to provide security for an uncertain future, the financial industry invents more and more uncertainties to be hedged.

The LTCM case demonstrates that the combined effects of the complex technologies of financial risk management do not guarantee the security and risk reduction they purport to provide. Enron, for example, was one firm that profited from the logic of complete markets and was involved in buying and selling all kinds of uncertainties, including weather derivatives (allowing companies to hedge against or simply speculate on changes in the weather), credit default swaps (allowing financial institutions to resell the risk of a borrower default), and advertising risk management (allowing companies to hedge against fluctuating prices of advertising space).[11] The goal of Enron, as one manager put it to *The Economist* only months before the firm collapsed, was "the commoditisation of everything" (2001, 90). There is some evidence, then, that complex risk modeling increases overall risk in international financial practices, as it allows, in the words of one critic, "relying on something with false confidence and *running larger positions* than you would have otherwise" (Nassim Taleb, quoted in Kolman 1997, emphasis added; see also de Goede 2004; Izquierdo 2001, 82).

CONCLUSION

The possibilities for increasing commercialization of risk in contemporary financial practices—and the massive growth of international derivatives markets since the end of Bretton Woods—have not emerged naturally, "like a Phoenix from the ashes," but have been made possible and have been given specific institutional and legal structures through political debates and financial modeling techniques (Cohen 1996). The objectified and authoritative discourses of scientific finance, which rest on historical formulations examined in previous chapters, underpin the distribution of legal and economic entitlements in contemporary markets. Specifically, the discursively constructed legitimacy of risk management as a masculine and scientific practice that provides security in the face of the uncertain future renders possible the massive monetary entitlements of those engaged in large-scale speculation. Not only has arbitrage slowly been legitimized as a market perfecting enterprise, but the discourses of science and objectivity to which LTCM's Nobel laureates appealed reign as the epitome of modern authority and respectability.

These discourses, however, are subject to moments of destabilization and reaffirmation. The debates—congressional and otherwise—in the wake of the LTCM failure provide such a site of potential destabilization. Instead, then, of accepting the discourse that casts the LTCM default as an aberration of financial logic and a tragic but isolated event, a profound questioning of the discourses of entitlement that allow LTCM to exist in the first place must be thought possible. Such possibilities are opened by examining the cultural and political roots of scientific finance that show that present financial structures are not immutable facts of (human) nature. The next and final chapter will go on to think through ways in which financial discourses of entitlement can be repoliticized.

6

Repoliticizing Financial Practices

There is no single locus of great Refusal, no soul of revolt, source of all rebellions, or pure law of the revolutionary. Instead there is a plurality of resistances, each of them a special case: resistances that are possible, necessary, improbable; others that are spontaneous, savage, solitary, concerted, rampant or violent; still others that are quick to compromise, interested, or sacrificial; by definition, they can only exist in the strategic field of power relations.

MICHEL FOUCAULT, *THE WILL TO KNOWLEDGE*

A PLURALITY OF RESISTANCES

The purpose of this final chapter is to discuss how resisting a linear and frictionless history of finance opens up possibilities for political dissent and alternatively imagined financial futures. I have argued that financial practices exist as exclusionary discourses—which, historically and continually, exclude that which is deemed external to the financial domain. Thus it has become possible, as discussed in chapter 1, to formulate authoritative measures of economic well-being that praise Britain for its economic efficiency while one in five British children live in poverty. William Connolly points to the wider implications of such exclusionary practices for the conditions of democracy. "Equality must be viewed not simply as an end in itself," writes Connolly, "but also as a condition of democratic pluralization . . . economic equalization is a pre-requisite to effective

145

democracy, but effective democracy is also a pre-requisite to equali-
sation. Each must be fostered for the other to occur" (1995, 80–82).
Connolly points not just to the barriers of democratic participation
experienced by those without entitlements, but also to the deliberate
withdrawal of the wealthy from participation in social life through
commissioning private facilities, including health and education,
and private security in the form of, for instance, gated communities
(80–85; see also Davis 1990). The connections between contemporary economic rationality and the proliferation of private security
are not incidental, according to Connolly, but indispensable: "New
forms of discipline, regulation, and surveillance are introduced to
promote economic growth under difficult conditions of realization
and to control or neutralize those populations excluded from its
benefits" (84). Hence, argues Connolly, the attachment of "the legitimations of disciplinary society" to "the hegemony of the growth
imperative" (25) that defines contemporary economic discourse.[1]

Addressing the economic inequality fostered by contemporary
financial practices coincides with the preoccupations of many authors in the field of political economy. However, in contrast to some
of the literature in political economy, this chapter will argue that
"global finance" as a sphere of thought and action is never secure
and stable, but is subject to continuous articulation, affirmation,
and rearticulation by financial practitioners. It is precisely in these
spaces of (re)articulation that financial practices are vulnerable to
criticism and change.

This chapter commences by discussing the differences in modes
of resistance identified within some political economy literature and
those identifiable through a Foucauldian framework. It then goes on
to observe and encourage a plurality of resistances that are taking
shape in the era of liberalized finance: from the challenge to the logic of
modern debt and credit posed by Jubilee, to the existence of multiple
measures and multiple moneys in daily life and in art that invite reflection on the meaning and morality of money, to an alternative imagination of the secure financial future through the values of Fortuna.

THE CONSTRUCTION OF "GLOBAL FINANCE"
AND THE POLITICS OF RESISTANCE

Recent approaches in political economy have understood finance as a
uniquely mastering force, or "a Phoenix risen from the ashes" (Cohen

1996, 2000). Global finance is thus constructed as a powerful monolith, directing and constraining the policy choices of national governments. In response to the risen Phoenix of global finance, many authors have proposed the reregulation of the financial sphere and have emphasized (concerted) state action as the way to submit and control the activity of financial institutions. Cohen articulates a core question: "If states were so pivotal in the globalization process, could they also turn back the clock if they wish?" (1996, 276). By comparison, Cerny argues in favor of "new, authoritative market-constraining measures to prevent both old and new kinds of market failure, i.e. to control and counteract perverse, unintended conse-quences that may have been caused by the original deregulation" (1995, 241). The platform on which reregulation of financial mar-kets should take place, Cerny goes on to say, "must become more internationalized and/or transnationalized" (242–43).

There is a profound nostalgia for the Bretton Woods era in many critical assessments of the newly liberalized financial sphere. In the words of Helleiner, quoting Richard Gardner, the purpose of the Bretton Woods agreement was to "make finance the servant, not the master, of human desires—in the international no less than in the domestic sphere" (1993, 20). Since the 1970s and 1980s, how-ever, Helleiner concludes, "Bankers . . . have become 'masters of the universe' rather than the 'servants' of Keynes and White's early plans" (40). Hence, as Cohen's question above expresses, a pre-occupation with "turning back the clock." Martin, for example, exemplifies Bretton Woods nostalgia when he writes: "Whatever the form, the case for re-regulation is strong: the power of global money over national economic space has already been allowed to extend too far" (1994, 275; see also the essays in Bello, Bullard, and Malhotra 2000). Thus, Bretton Woods becomes constructed as a kind of "golden age," and its specific (international) power structures, such as the gender inequality promoted by Fordism's concept of the family wage, are obscured.

The assumption that reregulation of financial markets on a global scale and through state cooperation is the *only* viable re-sponse to liberalized finance is flawed, for three reasons. First, as I have argued with regard to the regulatory efforts that took place in the United States and United Kingdom during the 1930s, regula-tion entails a depoliticization of financial practices. Regulation and reporting requirements determine the domain of financial truth and normality, which is thus placed beyond political debate. "Too often," Thomas Keenan (1997, 172) writes, "a demand for politics takes the form of an evasion of the political." Keenan's statement seems particularly relevant in relation to the demand for regulation within the literature of political economy. Cerny, for example, holds out depoliticization as the way in which reregulation of global finance *should* be brought about. "The substance of any agreement" concerning international financial regulation, Cerny writes, "must be limited enough in scope that it can be treated as a *technical issue* and dealt with by experts away from the political limelight. Politicization, whether at an intranational or an international level, might well prove to be an insuperable barrier, if not always to the conclusion of any specific agreement, then to its effective implementation" (1995, 243, emphasis in original).

In fact, Cerny's scope for politicization of financial practices is profoundly limited by the concept of financial markets his work implies. As quoted above, the reason Cerny (1995, 241) advocates financial regulation is, in the first instance, to prevent "market failure" and to prohibit market distortion. Thus, Cerny offers an understanding of "markets" as pregiven, clearly bounded, and autonomous entities. However, there is nothing natural or self-evident about understandings of the (free) market. On the contrary, the meanings and measures of what constitutes the free market have been subject of political debate and contestation and have been stabilized only through those regulatory structures that render legitimate financial transactions possible and create the space for the free market to operate. What eludes Cerny, therefore, is the point that the market and regulation are not forces pulling in opposite directions but are mutually constitutive and do not exist independently of each other. My argument that regulation entails a depoliticization must not be seen as a principled rejection of *all* regulatory efforts, but instead it seeks to emphasize this mutually constitutive role of law and market and advocates an increased openness to wide-ranging practices of financial politicization within the study of political economy.

The second reason why holding out reregulation as the only viable alternative to liberalized finance is flawed is that the objectives of regulation share their epistemological assumptions with financial rationalism itself. The objectives of reregulation are cast most commonly in terms of preventing financial crises and providing financial stability. "My particular question . . . is," Strange writes, "where are the truly serious flaws in the system that threaten its stability and even survival?" (1998, 18). Strange (1986, 1998) takes the 1929 stock market crisis and the depression of the 1930s as benchmarks of disaster and is preoccupied with identifying strategies and policy choices that can prevent such events in the future. Underpinning Strange's call for financial stability is a concept of security that connects certainty to autonomous state action. Although there is a marked difference between Strange's work, which repeatedly insists that "we do not—cannot—know the future," and the degree of faith in predictability displayed by the financial industry, preoccupations with future stability and certainty within the literature of political economy fail to pose a profound challenge to the notions of security and predictability that underpin financial practices (1998, 179).

A third reason why Bretton Woods nostalgia and calls for reregulation are inadequate is because they can sometimes entail a degree of defeatism that in its own way has a depoliticizing effect. In 1997, Pauly thought "a revival of the more flexible exchange rate mechanism of the Bretton Woods system" to lack the "slightest political momentum" (141–42). Strange also expressed doubts about whether it is "practicable" to "[turn] the clock back to a time of strict exchange controls, state intervention in investment and production, and the closing—in effect—of international financial markets and the channels that link them together" (1998, 187).[2] Since the Asian financial crisis, however, demands for global financial regulation are seen as more viable and have taken the form of a call for a new international financial architecture (e.g., Bello, Bullard, and Malhotra 2000; Noble and Ravenhill 2000).

More generally, however, the representation of finance as a homogenous and clearly bounded system attributes to the power of financial institutions a degree of effectiveness and autonomy that seems impossible to refuse. Gill and Law (1988, 78), for example, conceptualize the power of capital as structural power in which the material and normative aspects of authority converge to form a consistent "framework of thought," which conditions "the way individuals and groups are able to understand their social situation, and the possibilities of social change" (74; also Gill and Law 1993).

Structural power is defined through its consensual rather than coercive nature, and comprises the powerful processes by which certain interests are articulated as universal interests. Gill quotes Gramsci's definition of the hegemonic "moment" as "bringing about not only a unison of economic and political aims, but also intellectual and moral unity . . . thus creating the hegemony of a fundamental social group over a series of subordinate groups" (1990, 45). Thus, the identification of a financial hegemony implies a consistent, unitary and coherent regime of government, firmly directed by financial institutions and a financial ruling class. Microtechnologies of disciplinary power and "the intensification of surveillance in the workplace and in the streets" are interpreted by Gill (1995, 40; 2000) as the progressive extension of the power of capital into daily life. Gill's argument here bears important similarities to Connolly's assertion that economic inequality and the privatization of security are linked. However, Gill's identification of the progression of disciplinary neoliberalism into all domains of life awards the power of capital a degree of homogeneity and structural coherence that is problematic.

Indeed, it can be argued with the words of Gibson-Graham, that "the project of understanding the beast has itself produced a beast" (1996, 1). Gibson-Graham argues that discourses of Marxism and critical political economy have themselves constructed capitalism as a unified, singular, and totalizing system that permeates all aspects of daily life. For example, through the use of architectural metaphors, "Capitalism becomes not an uncentered aggregate of practices but a structural and systemic unity" (255). This representation, in turn, makes imagining resistance daunting and difficult. "If the unity of Capitalism confronts us with the mammoth task of systemic transformation," Gibson-Graham writes, "it is the singularity and totality of Capitalism that make the task so hopeless" (256). Perhaps the starting point for resistance is to disaggregate the capitalist discourse and encourage a plurality of possible resistances. "If there is no singular figure," Gibson-Graham concludes, "there can be no singular other" (14; cf. Langley and Mellor 2002; Thrift 2001b).

A genealogy is motivated precisely by finding insecurities and uncertainties in that which is represented as stable, coherent, and self-perpetuating. Politicizing "global finance" requires a historicity that "disturbs what was previously considered immobile; . . . fragments what was thought unified; . . . shows the heterogeneity of what was imagined consistent with itself" (Foucault 1984a, 82). Rather than being completely oppressive, one-directional, and all-encompassing, orders of reason always entail, according to Foucault, the possibility of freedom or revolt. Put simply, if financial practices prescribe "normal" and "rational" choices and behavior, this still implies a field of choice or possibility, even if some choices may lead to financial exclusion or predicates of madness. "When one defines the exercise of power as a mode of action upon the actions of others," Foucault wrote,

> one includes an important element: freedom. Power is exercised only over free subjects, and only insofar as they are free. By this we mean individual or collective subjects who are faced with a field of possibilities in which several ways of behaving, several reactions and diverse comportments may be realised. . . . Consequently there is no face to face confrontation of power and freedom which is mutually exclusive (freedom disappears everywhere power is exercised), but a much more complicated interplay. (1982, 221)

It is important to understand the differences between Foucault's understanding of the complex interplay between freedom and power and the representation of financial power as hegemonic or universal. For instance, concepts of hegemony as articulated within political economy frequently presume a one-directional power relationship between the ruler and the ruled. In a Gramscian hegemony, individuals either have power *or* are subjected to it, largely by virtue of their class position. Keenan summarizes this view in which power and freedom are mutually exclusive: "Power, understood as domination or the imposition of constraint, works by 'fraud, illusion, false pretences,' by preventing our purposes and desires from reaching fulfilment (or perhaps even formulation) and then masking that fact" (1997, 139–40).[3] Similarly, formulations in Gramscian political economy emphasize the misleading cunning of power and imply a notion of "false consciousness" by which the subordinated come to believe in normative propositions that are antithetical to their genuine (class) interests (see Germain and Kenny 1998; Jessop and Sum 2001, 93–95).

In contrast, in Foucault's understanding individuals both exert and undergo power. "There is no binary and all-encompassing opposition between rulers and ruled at the root of power relations,"

Foucault argues, "One must suppose rather that the manifold relationships of force that take shape and come into play in the ma-
chinery of production, in families, limited groups, and institutions,
are the basis for wide-ranging effects of cleavage that run through
the social body as a whole" (1998, 94). Indeed, subjects are constituted in and through relations of power, as Campbell explains:
"Foucault's being human is necessarily implicated in and produced
by those relationships of power. . . . [This] means that relations of
power in and of themselves can neither be avoided nor considered
'bad,' for without them . . . society could not exist" (1998b, 511–12).
In Foucault's formulation, power is no longer understood as forbid-
ding and misleading, purposely wielded by one group over others,
but as producing and regulating the network of social relations.

The indispensability of power relations for society does not mean
that it has become futile and irrelevant to study power relationships.
On the contrary, Foucault points out, this new point of departure
"makes all the more politically necessary the analysis of power relations in a given society, their historical formation, the source of their
strength or fragility, the conditions that are necessary to transform
some or to abolish others. For to say that there cannot be a society
without power relations is not to say either that those that are established are necessary, or, in any case, that power constitutes a fatality
at the heart of societies, such that it cannot be undermined" (1982,
223). While there is no power without the possibility of resistance—
"violent resistance, flight, deception, strategies capable of reversing
the situation"—Foucault points out elsewhere, "states of domination do indeed exist. In a great many cases power relations are fixed
in such a way that they are perpetually asymmetrical and allow an
extremely limited amount of freedom" (1989b, 441).

While power relations made possible through financial discourses
are undeniably asymmetrical, strategies of resistance and repoliticization must not just be thought possible in a distant future but must
be identified and encouraged in the present. Just as power does not
emanate from one clearly defined source, resistance may emerge
from multiple sources and in many possible ways. Instead of "a
single locus of great Refusal," says Foucault, "there is a plurality
of resistances, each of them a special case: resistances that are possible, necessary, improbable; others that are spontaneous, savage,

solitary, concerted, rampant or violent; still others that are quick to compromise, interested, or sacrificial; by definition, they can only exist in the strategic field of power relations" (1998, 95–96). In contrast, Robert Cox, for example, holds out a broad-based counter-hegemonic challenge as the desired form of resistance against the financial establishment. "The practical problem," Cox writes, "remains of forging links among divergent disadvantaged groups that would bind them together in a counter-hegemonic formation" (1999, 15). However, reducing the multiplicity of possible refusals and resistances to a single force or movement can be seen as an exclusionary political project in itself.[4] Instead, political economy might open itself to theoretically supporting a plurality of resistances. Accordingly, the following sections will discuss a few of the many possible sites of rearticulation and repoliticization that demonstrate the emergence of new responsibilities in the era of liberalized finance. Starting with a discussion of the Jubilee campaign and the logic of debt, the chapter will go on to think about alternative logics of numbers and money, the politics of disturbance through art and money, and finally, alternative conceptions of security.

JUBILEE AND THE LOGIC OF DEBT

The Jubilee 2000 initiative, a global campaign that was founded in 1996 to demand the cancellation of all international debt owed by poor countries in the millennium year, can be seen to repoliticize the relations between creditor and debtor. Spaces of freedom have always existed in relations of financial power, and in contrast to modern credit-rating practices and tightly regulated repayment schemes, historical evidence suggests that debt enforcement has often been erratic and irregular. In chapter 3, I showed that nineteenth-century U.S. courts were not afraid to side with ruined traders and annul futures contracts. By comparison, in his satirical dialogues describing the seventeenth-century Amsterdam money markets, Joseph de la Vega mentions the possibility of an "appeal to Frederick," which effectively allowed the annulment of contracts for short sales if buyers were about to lose from them. According to de la Vega, most people would appeal to Frederick "only when compelled to do so, I mean only if unforeseen losses occur to them in their operations" (1996 [1688], 153). But some, de la Vega complains, abuse the possibility of this appeal, and consider their personal advantage more valuable than their credit and their honor. De la Vega concludes: "The fact is . . . that, while Adam was ashamed of his nakedness, there are men at the exchange who are not ashamed that (to the disadvantage of their creditors) they have kept hold of their money" (154). De la Vega, in other words, constructs a moral discourse around the practice of appealing to Frederick, and asserts that those making use of it were frequently "gullible" and "gamblers" (153).

By comparison, in seventeenth- and eighteenth-century Britain, debt sanctuaries existed, to which debtors could escape when they were unable to repay their debts (Barty-King 1991, 5–8, 73–84). At this time debtors were jailed and were frequently worse off than their fellow inmates because prisoners had to pay for food and lodging to the prison warden. Debt sanctuaries were legal enclaves where debtors could not be arrested and taken to prison. These sanctuaries had ecclesiastical origins and were directly linked to Christian prohibitions on usury. One sanctuary, for instance, was located in Edinburgh's Holyrood Park, which provided refuge for all sorts of criminals, but from 1560 onward for debtors only. Some debtors lived in the refuge temporarily, some permanently, as is mentioned in Charles Mackie's description of Holyrood palace and grounds: "The whole of this Park still affords an Asylum to insolvent Debtors, whose persons dare not be seized at the instance of their creditors so long as they reside within its precincts" (1819, 105). According to Mackie, "The privilege of this sanctuary is strictly limited to civil debts. No protection is afforded for breaches of the peace, or crimes of any description. There are accordingly a number of persons either insolvent, or who have experienced sudden reverses of fortune, which they hope to retrieve, constantly resident in the houses within the boundary" (1819, 109).

De la Vega's moral sense that it is not precisely the *money* that was at stake in the negation of financial contracts but the honor and credit of the debtor can also be found in descriptions of the eighteenth-century debt sanctuaries. For example, the Whitefriars sanctuary in London features in Sir Walter Scott's novel *The Fortunes of Nigel,* when in the second volume Scott's hero suffers a blow to his fortune. The moral fiber of Whitefriars' inmates was questionable, according to Scott, who composed the following initiation song for its entrants:

From the blight of the warrant . . .
From the Bailiff's cramp speech,
That makes a man thrall,
I charm thee from each,
And I charm thee from all.
Thy freedom's complete . . .
To be cheated and cheat,
To be cuff'd and to cuff;
To stride, swear and swagger,
To stare and to stab,
And to brandish your dagger.
(1822, 146)

Indeed, Scott's description of Whitefriars firmly establishes the lost honor of debtors who decided to seek refuge and failed to confront their creditors. The inhabitants of Whitefriars are portrayed as drunken, loud, and lawless gamblers—and once again, financial irresponsibility is associated with female unruliness and prostitution. In "the ancient Sanctuary at Whitefriars," according to Scott,

> the wailing of children, the scolding of their mothers, the miserable exhibition of ragged linens hung from the windows to dry, spoke the wants and distress of the wretched inhabitants; while the sounds of complaint were mocked and overwhelmed in the riotous shouts, oaths, profane songs, and boisterous laughter, that issued from the ale-houses and taverns, which, as the signs indicated, were equal in number to all the other houses. And, that the full character of the place might be evident, several faded, tinselled, and painted females looked boldly at the strangers from their open lattices. (1822, 128–29)

Thus, while the possibility existed for debtors to abscond their legal financial obligations, they were still regarded as moral outlaws of society.

In 1869 the new Debtors Act prohibited imprisonment for debt except in cases of fraud, and most imprisoned debtors were released. The act was a product of decades of political struggle and debate, during which the responsibilities of the debtor and the moral relations between debtor and creditor were at stake (Barty-King 1991, 119–49). While some participants in these debates claimed that "credit is . . . imprudently given, to the real injury of the customer who is induced to buy what he cannot pay for" (127), the responsibility for the relationship between debt and credit was overwhelmingly assigned to the debtor. "These thriftless persons," wrote one journalist in 1859, "are often driven in the end to do very shabby things. They waste their money as they do their time; draw bills upon the future; anticipate their earnings; and are thus under the necessity of dragging after them a load of debts and obligations which seriously affect their action as free and independent men" (142).

Still, it is precisely with the ending of debt imprisonment, and the emptying of the debt sanctuaries that the (moral) relation between debtor and creditor became entrenched as a technology of power in the Foucauldian sense. This is foreshadowed, for instance, in the writings of James Neild, treasurer of the "Society of for the Discharge and Relief of Persons Imprisoned for Small Debts Throughout England and Wales," a charitable institution that collected funds to have debtors released and that supported reform of insolvency laws. In 1802, Neild wrote that imprisoning debtors seldom led to the repayment of the debts and that it was in the best interests of creditor and debtor alike to abolish such laws. "If therefore imprisonment could be avoided," Neild continues, "a man in distressful and precarious circumstances, convinced that the greatest evil which could befall him under a reverse of fortune would be to give up all his property for the payment of his debts, would then, with a calm and honest firmness, submit to his creditors [and] make a true disclosure of his circumstances" (1802, 23–24). Neild thus advanced his case for debt forgiveness by emphasizing the moral obligation and responsibility of the debtor to honor his financial contracts and further pointed out that the Society for Relief of Imprisoned Debtors maintained a moral distinction between deserving and undeserving debtors, "preferring to relieve those whose characters best warrant attention," and using a debt classification system as "the means of checking the career of the thoughtless and extravagant" (26–27).

According to Nietzsche (1996, 44), there is a connection between the concept of "guilt" as sin or bad conscience and "the very material concept of debt," which are both denoted by the German word *Schuld*. The pleasure of corporeal punishment, Nietzsche argues, frequently took the place of material repayment in European history. "In order to instil trust for his promise of repayment," Nietzsche writes, in order to impress repayment as a duty and obligation sharply upon his own conscience, the debtor contractually pledges to the creditor in the event of non-payment something which he otherwise still "possesses," something over which he still has power—for example, his body or his wife or his freedom or even his life. . . . In particular, however, the creditor could subject the body of the debtor to all sorts of humiliation and torture—he could, for example, excise as much flesh as seemed commensurate with the size of the debt. For this purpose, there have existed from the earliest times precise and in part horrifically detailed measurements, *legal* measurements, of the individual limbs and parts of the body. (1996, 45–46, emphasis in original)

After the abolishment of slavery and imprisonment of nonpaying debtors, the debtor's obligations, previously regulated by punishment, came to be regulated through the guilty conscience and the "powers of freedom" (Rose 1999). The moral duty to observe financial obligations can be considered among the "values and presuppositions given in the name of freedom and liberty" that act upon and regulate free subjects in modern society (Rose 1999, 11). The corporeal freedom for debtors, then, was made possible through technologies of debt management and credit rating. We have seen that in the eighteenth century Defoe was one of the first to articulate financial rationality in this way by making a connection between good bookkeeping and a clear conscience. As Barty-King recounts in his history of debt and debtors, credit management became institutionalized not long after imprisonment for debt was abolished, and the accountancy profession became preoccupied with "organising respectable credit for respectable people" (1991, 166). The new technologies of credit rating and debt honoring, however, operate with unprecedented force and consistency and have made the occurrence of debt forgiveness and jubilees (almost) unthinkable.

Despite the abolition of slavery, torture, and imprisonment for nonpaying debtors, a strict regime of guilt and punishment still underlies modern debtor-creditor power relations. Indeed, according to Nietzsche, the modern regulation of debt/guilt *(Schuld)* is dependent upon "the spiritualisation and intensification of *cruelty*" (1990 [1886], 159, emphasis in original). Nietzsche's argument that modern debtor/creditor relations depend not upon a relaxation of punitive measures but on an internalization and intensification of cruelty seems nowhere more appropriate than in regard to the current international debt problematic. Loans made to "developing" countries in the 1970s by Western banks and governments continue to paralyze the poorest countries in the world, with some countries owing more than twice their gross domestic product (GDP) in debt (Dent and Peters 1999, 10–11). Most loans were made with flexible interest rates, and when in the early 1980s international interest rates soared, many countries found themselves unable to keep up payments. Despite a number of rescheduling efforts, many sub-Sahara African and Latin American countries still struggle to keep up interest payments and can no longer hope to be able to service the debt principals themselves. In fact, many debtor countries have by now paid a manifold of the principal amount of their debts in interest. At the same time, through the accruement of interest and the devaluation of debtor currencies, international debt obligations are greater than ever (Kamp 2000, 40). This has led to a situation in which there is a net flow of payments from African countries to the International Monetary Fund (IMF), which has gained effective governance over many indebted countries (Pettifor 1998, 120). Many indebted countries, Oxfam has documented, spend more on interest rate payments than on "health, education and basic nutrition" (Strange 1998, 113).

In 1996, James Wolfensohn, president of the World Bank, launched a debt relief initiative aimed at large-scale reduction of the levels of international debt of highly indebted poor countries (HIPC). The initiative, Wolfensohn noted in an accompanying statement, "deals with debt in a comprehensive way to give countries the possibility of exiting from unsustainable debt. It is very good news for the poor of the world."[5] Despite the fact that the HIPC initiative in scope and aims does go beyond earlier debt relief initiatives, such as the Brady Plan of 1989 (Felix 1994, 368), a logic of guilt and calculated punishment can still be demonstrated to underlie the new initiative. Under the initiative, countries have to qualify for debt relief after a "Debt Sustainability Analysis," prepared by staff of the World Bank and the IMF, which measures debt-to-export levels and determines "whether a country is facing an unsustainable debt situation after the full application of the traditional debt relief mechanisms." This new framework, the World Bank goes on to say, "not only adds greater certainty to the calculations, but will *in most cases* increase the amount of relief actually provided."[6] The complex calculations of debt sustainability analyses aim to determine the *minimum* amount of debt reduction that would provide "a solid basis for HIPCs to . . . strengthen their development efforts, particularly in the area of poverty alleviation" (World Bank 2001, 3). In one instance, Dent and Peters (1999, 55) note, this careful calculation and changing of balance sheets led to a reduction of Mozambique's yearly debt service burden from US$104 million to US$100 million. In contrast, Daly argues that debt quantification "appears increasingly absurd and arbitrary. . . . The foreign debt . . . is beyond calculation and is exorbitant in relation to any possibility of actually being met" (2002, 127).

Instead, fears of debtor irresponsibility can be perceived at the heart of Western opposition to debt cancellation. It is feared that developing countries that have incurred debts in the 1970s but "squandered" the money on luxuries and corruption are not properly punished for their sins and may even be encouraged to continue such irresponsibilities after the debt relief. The calculated punishment of the HIPC initiative and the fears of leniency expressed by Western governments and creditors illustrate Connolly's arguments concerning "a call for revenge" underlying modern discourses of justice and responsibility. According to Connolly "a call to revenge forms the least discussed and most pervasive force in the desire to punish" (1995, 42). This call to revenge, Connolly goes on to show, is regulated through the forgetting of all ambiguity and porosity of "responsible agency" as a category: "The porous category of responsible agency provides perhaps the largest container into which the spirit of revenge is poured in contemporary moral and legal practices" (46). While authors such as Foucault and Butler have demonstrated the problems of the category of sovereign agency, "The most compelling practices of merit, desert and respect within Western cultures require attributions of responsibility to maintain themselves," writes Connolly (46). "There are powerful cultural pressures then," Connolly concludes, "to obscure this tension between the social indispensability of responsibility and the problematical desert or merit of those to whom it is applied" (46).

Thinking through the problem of international debt with the help of Connolly's arguments, it becomes clear that "a call for revenge" underlies the constitution of debtor states as responsible agents who must be punished for their sins of corruption and financial irresponsibility. As Popke puts it, the actions of the IMF and the World Bank in relation to debtor countries are "scripted as the fault of individual countries. Like the unruly child or the credit card junkie, the problems of these countries are the result of certain avoidable actions against which they have been cautioned. By emphasizing individual responsibility, the IMF deflects attention away from the harmful policies of the industrialised nations" (1994, 265–66). Casting debtor states as individual responsible agents allows the calculated punishment measured out by the World Bank, which remind of the precise measurements of flesh excised from the bodies of premodern debtors. Future lending by the IMF is made conditional upon the debtor countries' demonstration of responsibility through pursuing austerity programs. Meanwhile, the discourse of individual responsibility allows the forgetting of the shared responsibility underlying the debt crisis.

The objectives of the Jubilee 2000 coalition stand in sharp contrast to the allocation of individual responsibility, calculated punishment, and the desire for revenge underlying creditor actions. Jubilee campaigns for the uncalculated cancellation of all unpayable HIPC debts. According to Jubilee, international debt relations are a new form of slavery, and its campaign emphasizes the comparable brutality of the debt crisis and the Atlantic slave trade.[7] By emphasizing this historicity, Jubilee disturbs the normalized performance of financial practices. According to campaign president Ann Pettifor, the Jubilee initiative is explicitly intended to question the right of international creditors to uphold their standards of financial rationality above all other concerns. "International financial relations are dominated at all stages by creditors who decide on the conditions for repayment, closely monitor the implementation of conditions, and determine whether to offer rescheduling," Pettifor argues. "Creditors act as plaintiff, judge and jury in their relations with debtors" (1998, 119–20). The asymmetrical power relations based on the moral superiority of creditors have been institutionalized in international financial relations and, according to Pettifor, debt servicing by poor countries has become "accepted by public opinion as an unpleasant but necessary by-product" of economic rationality (121).

The Jubilee 2000 campaign challenges existing articulations of the relation between creditor and debtor. As two of the founders of the Jubilee campaign explain, the Jubilee in the Old Testament teaches that the creditor has a moral duty to forgive the debt when the debtor cannot pay. In biblical teachings, say Dent and Peters, this is related as the "natural and proper thing to do with unpayable debts" (1999, 23). Similarly, Dent and Peters urge financial institutions to refrain from collecting debt if it is "only repayable at a social cost which no honourable banking institution would seek to impose" (30). Thus, Western creditors have to take responsibility for promoting the loans and imposing excessive interest rates on them, according to the Jubilee coalition. As Pettifor puts it, "The Coalition does not use the phrase 'debt forgiveness' in its campaigning. This would imply that the 'sin' of falling into debt was committed solely by elites in debtor countries. Rather, the elites of the more powerful nations are considered co-responsible. . . . Most credits are aggressively promoted to encourage poor countries to buy British goods—particularly arms" (119). Jubilee opposes the calculative and punitive regime that underlies the World Bank initiatives and emphasizes the lack of historical continuity between the borrowing governmental elites of the 1970s and 1980s and those servicing interest payments now. Jubilee's rearticulation implies that debtor counties cannot be treated as responsible sovereign agents (Pettifor 2001).

Through its broad-based campaigning, Jubilee has effectively repoliticized a number of issues conventionally beyond public and political debate. The relations between debtor and creditor, the priority of financial rationality, the calculations of the World Bank, and the accountancy principles underpinning international debt flows have become questioned and scrutinized in Jubilee's publications. In contrast to many authors in the discipline of political economy, who take the containers and calculations of financial rationality as "material" starting points to their inquiries, and who, as I have demonstrated, sometimes even advise depoliticization as effective strategy, Jubilee has called for broad-based public knowledge and debate on the principles of financial rationality. Jubilee believes that everyone "can understand and grapple with supposedly complex financial matters," as Pettifor writes in Jubilee's December 2000 report (Barrett 2000). Challenging complex and mathematical financial knowledge, then, becomes one of the most important sites of politicization in contemporary finance, as in the following examples of multiple measures and multiple moneys.

MULTIPLE MEASURES

As Keenan explains, Foucault's work demonstrates that there is no uncontaminated or innocent space in which "pure" or scientific (and financial) knowledge can develop, away from power structures. "Where knowledge is concerned, power relations do not simply say 'no,'" writes Keenan, "on the contrary, according to Foucault's hypothesis, they stimulate, excite, incite knowledge" (1997, 149). This argument makes it possible to think of critique not as the progressive liberation from false knowledge but as the simultaneous production of *different knowledges*. Here, I will consider how multiple measures have the ability to challenge the authority of dominant stock market indicators such as the Dow Jones. Stock market indices are important, I argued in chapter 4, not only because they are read as reflections of national economic well-being but also because they have become definitions of *the market*. In other words, while no prepolitical or self-evident definition of "the financial market" exists, financial indicators have assumed the role of defining the markets and embodying their objective movements. In addition, financial indices have become the basis of a number of new financial instruments and investment opportunities. Since the 1970s, it has become possible to invest in "index funds," which technically replicate the market's composition and are assumed to provide safer investment strategies than the purchase of a carefully selected basket of stocks. These investment strategies are based on assumptions of continually rising market indices, and, as Bernstein explains, "to perform as well as the index [is] to perform well above average, and at lower levels of risk" (1992, 248–49). The emergence of index funds has given rise to a number of index-based speculative instruments, such as index futures.

Financial Times journalist Philip Coggan demonstrates that ambiguity continues to exist around the construction of indices within the financial industry, despite their scientific and authoritative image. The indices are increasingly important, Coggan (2000a, 2000b) writes, because they are used as benchmarks for investment performance. In other words, if index funds have made it possible to buy a portfolio consisting of the entire market, funds that invest differently are obliged to show better performance. However, Coggan (2000a) points out, "some people argue that the leading indices not only fail to reflect the true performance of the market but have led to dangerous distortions, particularly in the form of the dominance of the technology and telecommunications stocks." Coggan's (2000a) preoccupation with guaranteeing that the index is a "true measure of market performance," however, demonstrates his belief that technological progress and calculative sophistication are ultimately able to deliver an undistorted representation of market value.

However, Coggan's acknowledgment of the problematic nature of many current indices unwittingly offers a site in which financial measurements can be politicized and questioned. What, indeed, is represented by current authoritative indices and economic measurements? What are the normative judgments obscured in their scientific image? Such questions have been poignantly raised concerning the validity of the GDP as a measurement of national economic wealth and well-being by *Washington Monthly* editor Jonathan Rowe, among others.[8] Pointing out that traffic jams, pollution, litigation services, and hospitals all contribute to growing GDP and that the "fastest growing occupations in [the United States] include debts collectors and prison guards," Rowe (1999) politicizes established economic knowledge and statistical measurement. Rowe seizes on historically disqualified knowledges to support his political argument by reminding that the Nobel Prize winning economist Simon Kuznets, who designed and compiled the national accounts on which the GDP are based, had deep reservations about this indicator. As early as 1934, Kuznets argued before the U.S. Congress that "the welfare of a nation . . . can scarcely be inferred from a measurement of national income" (quoted in Cobb, Halstead, and Rowe 1995). Kuznets's reservations were dismissed by economists looking for "concepts that can actually be measured," and the GDP has acquired the "appearance of empirical certitude and expert authority" (Cobb, Halstead, and Rowe 1995). In contrast, Rowe and his colleagues have designed proposals for a different measurement of national wealth, which includes household and volunteer work but discounts for the depletion of natural resources, security expenditures, and increases in the inequality of income distribution.

Current economic and political obsession with continually rising stock market indicators similarly obscures the fact that environmental degradation, increased economic inequality, and the spread of disease and disaster may all contribute to a rising stock market. In chapter 4 I discussed how Dow's initiatives in compiling stock market indicators were specifically designed to abstract financial practices from such political and social critiques and move them into a domain of scientific and disinterested study. While Dow emphasized in his writings that his average would go up as well as down, current continuous calculation of the Dow Jones average and newer, more complex indices have intensified pressures for listed companies to deliver continually rising stock market value.

At the same time, however, different knowledges *are* being produced by those who criticize the short-term growth imperative of modern financial practices. While alternative measures in their own way affirm faith in the objective representation of economic activity and are easily allied with social conservatism, it is important to observe and encourage such challenges to technical financial authority. Indeed, the existence of a plurality of possible indicators undermines the supposed objectivity of the ones that dominate the news, thus prying open space for doubt, choice, and democratic discussion of financial issues.

First, the Dow Jones company itself, which owns and produces leading stock market indices, has developed a "sustainability index" in response to growing consumer demand for investment opportunities into companies with good social and environmental performance (Cowe 2000, 22). In contrast to the continually calculated Dow Jones Industrial Average, The Dow Jones Sustainability Group Index (DJSGI) in the United States—and the comparable FTSE4Good Index in the United Kingdom—emphasize long-term growth and transparency of its calculation. The DJSGI includes companies that have integrated "long-term economic, environmental and social aspects in their business strategies" and are evaluated for performance on environmental and human capital issues.[9] There are specially tailored indices that exclude alcohol, tobacco, and arms companies, and there is also a Dow Jones Islamic Index, which excludes businesses that violate Islamic law, including those dealing with alcohol, pork, and financial products (Maurer 2003). While both the sustainability index and the Islamic index are problematic because through them financial institutions "come to occupy a pivotal position in determining the criteria that define what practices are regarded as 'ethical,'" (Langley 2002, 160), the existence of these multiple measures implicitly raises questions about the politically problematic nature of other leading indices.

A second example of multiple measures that offers a more profound questioning of financial practices and the economic growth imperative is the work of the economic think tank the New Economics Foundation (NEF), based in London. Starting from the premise that "what gets counted, counts," the NEF has developed a number of alternative measures and indicators that redefine understandings of well-being and progress and that attempt to find "ways to make the invisible value of things which are essential to quality of life visible and measurable."[10] The NEF's measures include, for example, the Index of Sustainable Economic Welfare (ISEW), which forms an alternative to GDP, and the *Prove It!* tool, which measures the welfare of (inner city) communities and gives residents an opportunity to select their own index components, thus opening up economic indicators to democratic participation. The NEF has further developed the "Inner City 100" index, which lists and awards enterprises supporting inner city investment and renewal. At the same time, the NEF seeks to question current accountancy practices and valuation models, striving for more socially and environmentally aware accountancy.[11] While not strictly breaking with the logic of statistical measurement and objective representation, then, the NEF's alternative indicators challenge the priorities of modern financial practices and exemplify the possibility of numerical dissent, often absent in political economy literature.

MULTIPLE MONEYS

In addition to multiple measures that question the logic of dominant indicators, it is possible to identify multiple moneys, that have the potential to question the dominant logic of credit and debt. Local exchange trading schemes (LETS), are most commonly held up as examples of alternative monetary practices that challenge not just the way in which money is used and valued but that have the potential to recast "people's worth" through a "communitarian morality" (Langley 2002, 161; see also, for example, Boyle 1999; Douthwaite 1996; Hutchinson, Mellor, and Olsen 2002, 184–92; Leyshon and Thrift 1999b; Maurer 2003; North 1999; Seyfang 2000). LETS are local currencies that enable the exchange of services and products within a community of members without the intervention of "real money," and they are often based on a standard of value in terms of labor time, such as the successful Ithaca Hours scheme in upstate

New York. Rather than as a potential means to overthrow the monetary order, LETS and other alternative moneys are interesting from the perspective of this chapter for the way in which they challenge naturalized credit structures and make their participants reflect on the faith and value of money (Maurer 2003, 335; Tickell 2003, 119). The problem of money for local and inner city communities, one participant in the Manchester "Bobbin" project argued, is that "it moves mostly away from us, away from our communities, and it's always produced by somebody else" (quoted in North 1999, 76). This remark reminds of Congressman Sanders's critique of banking practices, when he observed that those banks willing to grant LTCM enormous loans were the same as those unwilling to make available cheap credit for job creation in local communities. The way that credit is created and channeled comes under scrutiny through LETS, and it can provide a means of credit for those unable to obtain it through formal channels. The solution to the scarcity of credit, according to the Manchester participant, is to "create your own money" (North 1999, 76).

Indeed, the creation of alternative currencies has a long history and was used during the Great Depression to overcome shortages of money in local communities in Austria and the United States. So-called scrip money, first designed by Austrian Silvio Gesell, discouraged hoarding by charging interest for *holding* the money: after a certain amount of time, a 2 or 3 cent stamp had to be affixed to the paper money in order to revalidate it. According to Douthwaite, in the United States by 1933 "more than three hundred communities had introduced some form of barter system, scrip or local currency to try to overcome the nationwide currency shortage" (1996, 99). While the Roosevelt administration was initially sympathetic, it forbade further issuance of scrip money in 1933 because Harvard Professor Russell Sprague advised the government that scrip money represented not just a means to job creation but an attempt to restructure and democratize the American monetary system (Kennedy 1995, 38–43; Douthwaite 1996, 99).

However, the development of alternative currencies and barter networks in the wake of financial crisis persists. For example, the current financial crisis in Argentina that has caused the freeze and devaluation of the savings of significant sections of the population has encouraged the growth of sophisticated barter clubs as "survival strategy" (Pearson 2003, 214). By mid-2002 it was estimated that 20 percent of the Argentinean population was involved in barter trading, and the success of the *Clubes de Trueque* is partly dependent on the involvement of such a large section of the population, offering not just home-baked bread or home-grown produce, but professional services including public relations, health care, and educational services (Pearson 2003, 218). "Argentina has a large class of professional people who are in financial difficulties," a professor at the University of Buenos Aires explained, "in other countries with a large middle class there is not the same necessity" (quoted in Bellos 2001). Although it is possible to interpret the barter clubs as temporary and trivial coping mechanisms—and indeed, according to Pearson (2003) most participants come to the *Clubes* out of economic necessity rather than ideological commitment to the network's values—their significance lies in their ability to generate discussion on the morality and meaning of money and to confront consumers, or *prosumers* as they are called in Argentina's barter network, with the possibility of multiple moneys in their everyday lives.

It is not just the consciously political creation of alternative moneys, then, that can be seen as a practice of dissent in the era of liberalized finance: survival and coping strategies, bartering, and the earmarking of money in everyday life can all be understood as spaces of resistance involving "cultural (not just economic) strategies and the development of new identities" (Marchand and Runyan 2000, 19; see also Amoore 2002, 137–57). For example, Zelizer (1994) shows how the social differentiation of money, in terms of welfare, loans, gifts, tips, donations, alimony, bonuses, etc., stands in sharp contrast with the concept of money as neutral and fungible within economic and financial theory. Wrapping up money in special paper or pouches, "love tokens," greeting cards, and little poems called "dollar ode[s]" are all ways in which gift money is personalized and distinguished from everyday rent and food payments (Zelizer 1994, 72). Gift money also involves the invention of new currencies, such as vouchers, certificates, and special Christmas money orders and is, moreover, often differentiated at the receiving end, being kept in special boxes or savings accounts for special purchases (105–11). People surviving on small budgets historically often earmark moneys by separating amounts for rent, food, clothes, insurance, and church money, according to Zelizer (1994, 171–72), and this was both a coping strategy and a way of personalizing charity or welfare money that often came with "strings attached." Finally, Zelizer discusses how women's earnings were historically both lower and "treated as more frivolous, less serious" (62) than men's money and may be earmarked for separate expenditures, for instance, on items for children or luxuries.

Earmarking money, then, exemplifies the profound importance of social and cultural practices for the definition and use of money and can be regarded as a way in which the assumed neutrality of standardized currencies is being challenged within "the domain of dailiness" (Bleiker 2000, 187). While alternative currencies and earmarking may have many meanings and motivations, what they have in common as practices of dissent is that they involve a reflection on the meaning and morality of money that contrasts with the calculative logic and assumed rationality of modern financial practices. They are, in Roland Bleiker's (2000, 201) words, "practices by which people can re-appropriate the space controlled through the existing discursive order."

MONEY ART AND THE POLITICS OF DISTURBANCE

Multiple measures and multiple moneys are also created, often playfully, in increasing numbers of art projects relating to money and the stock exchanges. I have already discussed how Boggs's money performance art raises questions concerning what money is and how it acquires value. Here, I offer a discussion of a number of artists and artworks to explore how art can politicize financial practices. Art as a site of dissent stands in opposition to the historical figure of the mass uprising or the heroic act, according to Bleiker, because it can challenge and undermine, slowly and without urgency, normalized practices on an everyday level. "There are no quick and miraculous forms of resistance to discursive domination," Bleiker writes, "dissent works by digging, slowly, underneath the foundations of authority" (2000, 270–71). Or, in Connolly's words, the *politics of disturbance* can question normalities and expose "the deleterious effects of their naturalizations upon difference" (1995, xxi). The many examples of money and stock market art, some of which will be discussed here, have the ability to do just that.

Boggs's performances stand in a long tradition of art and literature that questions the value of money—including, as discussed previously, films, poems, stories, and cartoons critical of financial practices. Artists before Boggs have used signatures or scribbles to pay for items, and in 1919 Marcel Duchamp famously paid his dentist with a drawing of a check drawn on the mythical "Teeth's Trust Company" (Wenschler 1999, 40–41; Velthuis 2002). Artists have long experimented with the fictionality of (paper) money—for example, the work of Thomas Nast discussed in the introduction or Paul Cotton's "joke note drawn on 'the Bank of the Imagi-Nation'" from 1970 (Shell 1995, 84). Indeed, as Shell observes in his *Art and Money*: "Both artist and politician seem to be able to take an apparently valueless piece of paper and, by virtue of words and drawings, make it as valuable as exchange note or the valuable 'original' for which the note is purportedly exchangeable" (1995, 84). This was unfortunately not the case for art student Bada Song, whose story poignantly brings together money art and financial need. In 2001, after two years of struggling to pay, Song drew her own currency to cover the £6,950 for her tuition fees at the Camberwell College of Art in London. Each banknote, in denominations from £5 upward, showed her portrait and detailed her life story "written out in miniature" (Crace 2001, 11). The college refused to accept Song's currency, but proposed a deal in which the student would be allowed to "meet the real invoice with 'art money,' so long as she meets an 'art invoice' with real money" (11).

Giving and the gift are often considered to form the antithesis of the calculative logic of modern financial practices and form a recurrent theme in money art. In his autobiographical account *Hand to Mouth*, American novelist Paul Auster (1997) tells the story of a certain "Doc" who seeks to bring down the U.S. financial system by giving away cash to passersby on the streets of Manhattan. "Money is a fiction, after all, worthless paper that acquires value only because large numbers of people choose to give it value," Doc explains in Auster's novel. "And what would happen if that faith were undermined? . . . The fifty-dollar bills he handed out to strangers weren't just gifts; they were weapons in the fight to make a better world. He wanted to set an example with his profligacy, to prove that one could disenchant oneself and break the spell that money held over our minds" (41). Compare the work of French artist Jonier Marin, whose "Money Art Service" in the early 1970s "[aimed] to both sell money at half price and throw it into the streets." "To distribute money," says Jonier, "is for me a form of art" (quoted in Shell 1995, 115).

The gift was also at the heart of a 2001 show called *Capital* in the Tate Gallery in London by artists Neil Cummings and Marysia Lewandowska. The exhibition explored the institutional histories and spaces of the Bank of England and the Tate, both of which regulate local, national, and international economies of value—they help determine what value is, how it is produced, and distributed. For the duration of the show randomly selected visitors of the Tate and the Bank of England Museum were given a special gift of a limited edition print by the artists. "Indirectly," Cummings and Lewandowska write, "we hope to open up questions surrounding perception of value, its coagulations (as capital), its releases and consequences; to connect with the myriad pressures that move values through the otherwise distinct economies of the Bank and Tate" (2001, 31). The gift, Jeremy Valentine points out in the accompanying essay, is not without obligation: "Giving is indistinguishable from the obligation to return and thus debt" (2001, 44). However, the gift creates complex social relationships that form "the basis of community" and can underpin a logic of generosity rather than calculated repayment (Valentine 2001, 49; also Osteen and Woodmansee 1999, 28–32).

A final work of art that forms an interesting example here, also at the Tate in 2001, is Lise Autogena and Joshua Portway's ironically named *Black Shoals Stock Market Planetarium*. The Black Shoals Planetarium projected onto a domed ceiling the movements of stock prices as the movements of stars in a planetarium, thus playing with the scientific and naturalistic assumptions of contemporary stock market practices and forecasting technologies. The project links early modern theories of astrology with the latest financial technology and seeks to examine "the urge to understand our environment, the desire to predict, recognise patterns and impose structure and the limits of this ambition."[12] "In Black Shoals," Julian Stallabrass (2001) wrote in the essay accompanying the exhibition, "viewers look upon the sublime spectacle of the markets in action as the ancients glazed at the night sky, immersed in data and searching for patterns that might disclose the future." The project thus comments on the everyday understanding of the stock market as an opaque mechanism that has unprecedented but mysterious influence on our lives as well as providing a "tart comment on the aspiration to grasp and reduce all data to a single frame" (Stallabrass 2001).

The link between art and money is a complex, and of course not always politicizing, one. Instead of providing a critique of money, art can be and has been, as Shell points out, "comfortably traded or treated as money" (1995, 116). In the 1980s, for example, there was a "frenzy of buying" that reduced the work of critical painters interested in everyday life and cooperative artists' communities, such as van Gogh, to investment tools for large companies (116). Still, (performance) art commenting on money and stock exchanges has the ability to question, disturb, and help undermine naturalized financial practices by raising the questions that need to be silenced in order for money and financial practices to operate on a daily basis.

RETHINKING FINANCIAL SECURITY: REVALUING FORTUNA

If the modern faith and social relationships invisibly underpinning monetary instruments need to be subject to moments of disturbance, so too does the logic of security underpinning the spiraling risk commercialization in contemporary markets. I concluded chapter 5 by observing that there is a circular argument propping up the financial sphere: while pretending to eradicate uncertainty from business ventures, finance identifies and invents more and more possible uncertainties to be hedged. In the name of security, an infinite number of risks are identified and translated into commercial contracts with the help of the Black-Scholes option pricing formula. Here, I will discuss how questioning the logic of financial security has the potential to delegitimize this spiraling risk commercialization.

As well as a military and strategic term, security is properly understood to be a financial term.[13] The financial meaning of security originates from the pledge, promise, or caution given in relation to an obligation or debt that reminds of Nietzsche's remarks on the pledging of life and wife to the creditor in case of nonpayment. The *Oxford English Dictionary* records the following entry as far back as 1592, "Without good securitie they will lend Nobody mony." This sense of security as a loan collateral is also related to the meaning of the term "bond" as promise or pledge in financial dealings. The meaning of security evolved to mean a creditor's document, held as a guarantee for repayment, and subsequently became a noun, a general term for stocks and share certificates. Financial practitioners came to be called "security analysts," and when in 1934 U.S. Congress established a federal regulator for financial markets as a result of investigations into the 1929 stock market crash, it was called the Securities Exchange Commission (SEC). More recently, securitization is the name given to the process by which financial assets such as loans are transformed into marketable instruments. In this process, a large number of small loans (for instance, mortgages) are bundled and sold to a financial investor (for instance, a pension fund) (Mishkin 1992, 305–7). Securitization has increasingly come to mean the constructing, assembling, and selling of tailor-made financial instruments for large investors and speculators, and it has in recent decades encouraged an increase in speculation (Sassen 1991, 70–78).

According to Michael Dillon, "We stand too uncritically under the prejudice of the opposition between security and insecurity" (1996, 120). The political significance of a search for security, argues Dillon, is that it seeks to expel and exclude that which is defined as causing insecurity. "It is evident," writes Dillon,

> that any discourse of security must always already, simultaneously and in a plurality of ways, be a discourse of danger too. For example, because security is engendered by fear (fundamentally aroused by the uncanny, uncertain, different, awesome, and uncalculable), it must also teach us what to fear when the secure is being pursued. . . . Because security is engendered by fear it also calls for countermeasures to deal with the danger which engenders fear. Hence, while it teaches us what we are threatened by, it also seeks in its turn to proscribe, sanction, punish, overcome—that is to say, in its turn endanger—that which it says threatens us. (120–21)

Throughout this book, I have argued that the security provided through financial practices seeks to expel and punish that which is associated with Fortuna, who has been the personification of disorder, chance, and chaos since the Middle Ages. She is traditionally associated with time and is sometimes seen to do the work of time, such as controlling the seasons, causing ruin, and presenting opportune moments (Patch 1967, 115–17). In financial debates in the eighteenth and nineteenth centuries, the dangers represented by Fortuna also became embodied by the gambler. In the words of one author, the affinities between gambling and Fortuna's cult are clearly detectable. "Gambling is wholly based on superstition," wrote MacDougall in his *Speculation and Gambling,* "[it] is a practice ill adapted to an age of science. It has its early origin in the practice of divination and sorcery. . . . It is the dark jungle-land from whence there still issue untamed beasts of prey to make havoc among citizens" (1936, i). As I have argued, female unruliness, deviance, and prostitution are recurrent themes in the construction of discourses of danger and gambling that underpin the articulation of financial rationality.

In conjunction with these particular and gendered notions of danger, then, a particular notion of security was constructed to carve off a legitimate realm of finance. A specifically masculine and supposedly scientific notion of certainty and foresight became articulated in opposition to Fortuna's dangers. This notion of security operates by "synchronising security, safety and certitude" (Constantinou 2000, 288). In other words, financial security is predicated on the presumption that "to be secure is to be safe is to be sure. To secure is to protect from danger is to *know* the danger and how to go about doing the protection. This constitutes the security problematic as automatically and exclusively a question of providing safety and producing knowledge" (288, emphasis added). Thus, financial man is cast as the confident dispeller of doubt. Such was, for instance, the argument of banker George Rutledge Gibson when addressing a Bankers' Convention in 1891:

> The stock broker, if at all fitted for his vocation, takes a wide interest in affairs, nothing escapes his observation, and he is constantly on the watch for news and opinions that may have any bearing upon any of the securities dealt in on the exchanges. . . . He reflects upon the past and peers into the future to discover all the springs which move the money market, public sentiment and national prosperity or adversity. As a rule, he is genial in manner, liberal in his views, generous in his nature, a warm friend, a good liver and a keen observer. (1891, 30–31)

Increasingly, the knowledge assumed to enable financial security depends on mathematical and scientific study of stock prices, which has a depoliticizing effect.

However, the concept of security that connects safety and certitude is only one of multiple possible meanings that can be given to

174 · REPOLITICIZING FINANCIAL PRACTICES

security. Current notions of security have prevailed over other possible definitions, such as the one noted by Der Derian (1992, 75) of
security as "a careless, hubristic, even damnable overconfidence,"
as in the following Oxford English Dictionary reference from 1575,
"They . . . were drowned in sinnefull securitie." We have seen that
it is precisely such overconfident security that was punished by
Fortuna, who reputedly lashes out to those believing themselves
happy, rich, and secure. The moral condemnation of those who attempt too rigidly to control, hedge, and predict the future has been
written out of contemporary financial discourses. Reopening this
historical meaning of security, which suggests that it is not always
desirable to actively control and submit the future in order to attain
a (false) sense of security, chips away at the legitimacy of modern
financial risk managers and their desires to mathematically predict
and commercialize the future.

An alternative concept of security that does not legitimize spiraling risk commercialization could be what Constantinou (2000,
290) calls the condition of being "secure-in-danger": "where one
can dwell . . . next to one's enemy in security, without surrender-
ing, or dominating, or making friend of the foe." The state of being
"secure in danger" can be interpreted as a different way of dealing
with Fortuna; pertaining not to the desire to dominate and master
her, but to a desire to learn to live with instability and to respect
the indeterminacy of life as a locus of democratic openness. In this
alternative sense, "Security is . . . not a given or permanent condition but continuous, spiritual, seafaring agon. To emerge secure,
one must free oneself and withdraw from the obsessive mental cares
one is commonly submerged to. To remain afloat one must . . . learn
to live with fluctuidity and instability" (292). Not surprisingly, this
alternative notion of security echoes representations of Fortuna,
whose vicissitudes were often associated with the sea (McWilliam
1995, cxxxvi).

One outspoken critic of the claims to certainty and security made
by the financial industry is hedge fund manager and philanthropist
George Soros. Soros has repeatedly argued that "economic theory
set itself an impossible task when it tried to imitate physics" because
financial actors play an active role in shaping the future that they
are supposed to reflect (1999, 24). The notion of market equilibrium
that underpins the analogy between physics and economics, Soros

argues, is a theoretical construct "rarely observed in real life" and entirely inappropriate for understanding financial markets (36). Instead, Soros argues that financial practices are reflexive because "prices are not merely the passive reflection of independently given demand and supply: they also play an active role in shaping those preferences and opportunities" (1997, 50). In contrast to prevailing notions of security and knowledge, Soros has argued that "we must lower our expectations about our ability to explain and predict social and historical events" before a real change in financial practices becomes possible (1998, 39). Soros's critique echoes subjugated notions of security as "damnable overconfidence" that question the rights of those who confidently predict and commercialize the future. Instead of a new model or a new universally valid law, Soros's argument introduces an element of "indeterminacy into social events. . . . It interprets social events as a never-ending historical process and not as an equilibrium situation" (1994, 2). Soros's conclusions point to the necessity for greater political skepticism toward calculative and expert financial practices. While Soros's arguments have been dismissed by established economists as unscientific, ill-informed, and unacceptable,[14] they provide an important provocation for those working in the field of political economy.

Respect for the indeterminacy of life and criticism of expert financial knowledge must not been seen as a rejection of care for the future or a passive resignation to Fortuna's blows. On the contrary, while defining security in terms of certainty and knowledge underpins a legitimacy deficit in financial practices and (financially) rewards those able to make claims to accurate prediction, different orientations to danger and security promise to reopen these practices to political discussion. Recognition of the limits of human capacity to predict and control the future enables, in Sanjay Reddy's words "enlarged room for social and political contestation [of] . . . the indeterminate future. It enables the indeterminate future to be transformed into an open political domain, rather than existing as an undemocratically and scientistically defined and mapped out horizon of alternatives" (1996, 228). By comparison, to Edkins, "perhaps the key to retaining the political is living with insecurity" (2002, 80). For Edkins, critical political practice needs to disturb the depoliticizing effects of "securitisation" that is a "disciplining . . . process that legitimates what we call political control" (79). In finance, moving away from a profound belief that mathematical predictability is able to deliver (financial) security would allow more room for democratic debate and would question the need for modern risk commercialization.

CONCLUSION

In this chapter, I emphasized a multiplicity of ways and a multiplicity of sources from which the seemingly secure knowledge of financial practices is being questioned and disturbed. Instead of looking for a single locus of "great Refusal" or the emergence of a "collective will" that opposes the power of capital (Gill 2000, 138), this chapter has identified ways in which "new conceptual horizons are opened" by an ensemble of practices that subvert, rearticulate, and challenge financial rationality (Butler 2000, 14). Dissent and resistances to financial practices should not be understood as a subversive collective, working in unison toward the eventual overthrow of financial orthodoxies. Resistances themselves work in different, contradictory, and insecure ways: as I have argued, Jubilee questions the contemporary logic of credit and debt; alternative measures reveal the contingent construction of value and offer numerical dissent; multiple moneys can represent a conscious rejection of contemporary finance, but can also be complementary currencies, coping strategies, or inadvertent appropriations of supposedly neutral money; money art disturbs the image of finance as dwelling in the sphere of science and rationality; revaluing Fortuna undermines the logic of risk commercialization. There is thus no clear confrontation between domination and resistance but multiple resistances. However, all practices of dissent discussed here invite reflection on the meaning and morality of money and thus promise an increased democratic openness in relation to modern credit practices.

Conclusion
Objectivity and Irony
in the Dot-Com Bubble

The for-profit nation-state, with a globally dispersed citizenry of share-holders, is the next stage in the evolution of political economy.
JONATHAN FRANZEN, *THE CORRECTIONS*

In the midst of current controversies, triggered by the end of the so-called dot-com boom, the collapse of Enron, and the U.S. analysts scandal, the legitimacy of financial practices is to be rescued again with appeals to objectivity and disinterestedness. At first glance, Eliot Spitzer, the New York Attorney General who has cast himself as the champion of the rights of small investors and who has conducted high-profile investigations into the work of the stock analysts of large investment banks, seems like an unlikely ally for Wall Street. For example, Spitzer's investigation into Merrill Lynch found that the firm's "supposedly independent and objective investment advice was tainted and biased by the desire to aid Merrill Lynch's investment banking business" (Spitzer 2002a). Spitzer found that during the dot-com boom, Merrill Lynch's research division not once issued a "sell" recommendation for the securities it analyzed and that analysts' public recommendations of stocks contradicted their private opinions. Famously, one investment analyst is said to have privately called the stock of a particular internet company a "piece of junk," while publicly recommending the stock as a good investment opportunity. As *The Economist* (2002a) wrote about the scandal: "Investment banks . . . are in disgrace . . . for the way in which [they] shamefully abused privileged information and misled clients . . . during the stockmarket bubble." Analysts such as Jack Grubman and Henry Blodget have been dismissed in the wake of Spitzer's investigations and have come to embody the excesses of the dot-com boom. Investment banks as well as individual analysts were forced to accept responsibility and blame for the millions of dollars lost by individual investors.

At the same time however, Spitzer's investigations seek to reaffirm the dominant discourse of financial knowing that casts investment analysis as an objective, disinterested exercise. In fact, both sides to the analyst debate assume that financial researchers observe an external financial reality, examine the relevant indicators, and arrive at a certain recommendation. Whether those recommendations are then made public or not—and whether the analysts have *misled* the public—has become the core of the debate. In December 2002 Spitzer reached a US$1.4 billion settlement with ten of the largest global investment banks that involved the creation of an independent research body. This research body will be funded by the banks, while making its stock analyses freely available to the investing public. According to Spitzer (2002b, 2, 14) the independent research body will "restore investor confidence in the marketplace" and ensure that "research recommendations are based upon sound, objective analysis." "The days of the celebrity analyst are decidedly over," concluded *New York Times* correspondent Gretchen Morgenson (2002) when the settlement was announced. "The job of brokerage firm analyst may very well revert to what it had been before the bubble: number-crunching for pay far less than investment bankers make" (see also Morgenson and McGeehan 2002; Thomas and Morgenson 2003).

The image of financial analysis as disinterested number crunching is not a historical constant, as Morgenson implies, but one carefully cultivated and precariously maintained throughout political debate and legal challenge to stock market practices in modern history. In this book, I discussed some of those debates and challenges to recall the "subjugated knowledges"—the questions, protests, and insecurities—that the image of calculative rationality in modern financial practices depends on (Foucault 1980, 81). Rather than being accepted as a rational and disinterested exercise, we have seen that financial analysis, speculation, and investment practice more generally have been attacked, denounced, and forbidden as fraud, gambling, greedy manipulation, effortless profiting from the work of others, and driven by loss of (sexual) self-restraint. These critiques are more than temporary and superficial complaints by those who lost their money speculating: these critiques, and their defenses, have directly influenced the institutional and regulatory structures of modern finance, just as Spitzer's settlement will influence the way in which investment analysis is organized in the future. The debates analyzed in this book moreover show that finance itself—not just its rules of personal engagement, but also its statistics, formulas, instruments, and institutions—is profoundly cultural: the history of finance is one of colonial conquest, gambling, sexual imagination, understandings of time, predictability and ownership of the future, and discourses of moral obligation and (il)legitimate profit making. By recalling these cultural discussions, I have tried to challenge and disturb the expert and depoliticized knowledge of modern financial practices.

My point has not been to deny that financial truth *exists*, nor to claim that the rituals of financial truth are fictional, nor that all financial discourses are false and misleading. On the contrary, the point of this argument is to demonstrate that the institutional and regulatory frameworks of modern finance, which are very *real* in terms of access to wealth and credit have been shaped and produced through the political discourses examined in these chapters. Debates pertaining to speculation, gambling, the meaning of free market, and the legitimate bases for profit making underpin the institutional structure of modern international finance. It is in this sense that financial structures and institutions are not natural or evolutionary developments but are always implicated in politics. While claims about the "natural" and "undeniable" operation of free markets are among the most powerful arguments in modern politics, this historical enquiry demonstrates that the free market has never existed as a natural and undistorted system, but has, on the contrary, been given meaning and legal and moral operative space through political debate and decision. Such a genealogical reading of financial history, I have argued, demonstrates "lines of fragility in the present" and thus contributes to imaging alternative financial futures (Foucault 1988a, 36).

The image of disinterested analysis of financial performance stands in sharp contrast with the understanding, advanced here, of financial discourse as performatively constructing the reality it is supposed to measure and analyze. The Dow Jones illustrates the tension between performance and performativity poignantly. It is commonly seen as, and was historically constructed as, an aggregate and objective measure of the performance of the financial market, the New York Stock Exchange in particular. But it is better understood as a performative: rather than passively reflecting the truth about the financial market, the Dow can be seen to *create* the financial market as a unified and observable phenomenon, and the Dow's historical longevity is at the heart of its performative power.

Thus a different logic of responsibility emerges in finance. While the identification of the objective conditions of the market naturalizes financial discourse and implies that initiated participants can read and understand these conditions, the understanding of financial truth as performatively constituted means that financial participants bear (collective) responsibility for the conditions in which they operate and cannot appeal to god or (human) nature for the inequalities of income generated by contemporary market practices. In the work of Foucault, responsibility emerges at the site of enunciation and rearticulation as an unpredictable "stumbling block" in the operations of financial power (Keenan 1997, 152–53). Responsibility, like power, becomes not something statically owned or possessed, but a possibility always present in relations of power and emerging at the sites in which daily social relations are reproduced and in which new conceptual horizons are being opened (Butler 2000, 14).

FORTUNE FAVORS THE BOLD

At the time of writing, it is too early to tell whether public faith in stock investing will be easily restored. But it is clear that Spitzer's ambitions to restore objectivity to financial practices have the potential to rescue the legitimacy of the markets in the eyes of the investing public. Messages that the turning point of the recession had been reached became widely, albeit carefully, broadcast in the summer of 2003. Indeed, Fidelity Investments, one of the world's biggest mutual funds, advised investors to take a Machiavellian approach to the markets in the wake of the dot-com "bust" with advertisements such as the one from the front page of the *Financial Times* in March 2003 (Figure 8). "Fortune Favours the Bold," the advertisement reads, "The bold investor, who is prepared to go against the herd, knows that the best time to buy is often when it feels most uncomfortable. Nobody can predict when markets have reached their bottom and they may fall further before they rise, but with prices now at their lowest for several years, today's world markets may present real buying opportunities for investors looking for long-term returns." Unwittingly, Fidelity draws upon a long cultural history of conquest, rationality, and manliness in investment practice. Once again, financial men are called on to act boldly, coolly, and with singular determination in the face of the uncertain future, for potentially unprecedented financial rewards.

However, maybe the truly bold are people like Jonathan Franzen, whose 2001 novel *The Corrections* entails a scathing critique of U.S. society in the era of the dot-com boom. In the novel, Gitanas Misevicius, former official of Lithuania's ruling party and post-Communist entrepreneur, laments the sale of Lithuania's national assets to private American investors, under guidance of the World Bank: "So OK, we sold the port. We sold the airline, sold the phonesystem. The highest bidder was usually American, sometimes Western European. This wasn't supposed to happen but it did. Nobody in Vilnius had cash" (Franzen 2001, 128). Since the default of Russia and the global "flight to quality," Gitanas continues, U.S. investors such as Iowa-based investor Dale Meyers, who owns 64 percent of Lithuania's national airline, have been liquidating Lithuania's services: "Dale Meyers says he didn't mean to acquire a controlling stake in our national airline. Dale says it was program trading. . . . Dale says he understands the importance of an airline to a country's economy and self-esteem. But because of the crisis in Russia and the Baltics, nobody wants tickets on Lithuanian airlines. . . . Dale's only way to meet his obligations is liquidate Lithuanian Airlines' biggest asset. Which is its fleet" (128–29).

In response to the dire economic situation in his country, and out of a mix of desperation and irony, Gitanas and his American accomplice and the novel's protagonist, Chip, develop Lithuania.com, which offers global investment opportunities under the banner "DEMOCRACY PAYS HANDSOME DIVIDENDS." Lithuania.com offers investors, "according to the level of financial commitment":

- time shares in ministerial beachside villas at Palanga!
- pro rata mineral rights and logging rights to all national parklands!
- appointment of selected local magistrates and judges!
- blanket 24-hour-a-day parking privileges in perpetuity in the Old City of Vilnius!

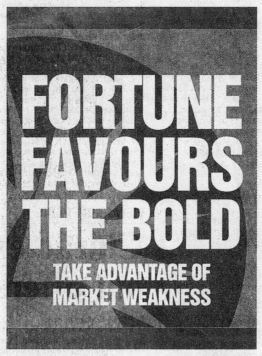

Figure 8. Fidelity Investments, "Fortune Favours the Bold," Financial Times, March 21, 2003.

- fifty-percent discount in selected rentals of Lithuanian national troops and armaments on a sign-up basis, except during wartime!
- no-hassle adoptions of Lithuanian girl babies! . . .
- inclusion of the investor's likeness on commemorative stamps, collector's-item coins, microbrewery beer labels . . .
- honorary doctorate of Humane Letters from Vilnius University, founded in 1578!
- "no-questions-asked" access to wiretaps and other state-security apparatus! (504–5).

Franzen's characters participate in fora of financial knowledge production—answering questions in financial chatrooms, producing creative but *not* entirely fictional press releases, writing tracts on the morality and inevitability of free markets in human history in order to promote Lithuania.com. In the story, the money comes pouring in and in return investors acquire sumptuously printed stock certificates and brochures saying: "Congratulations—You Are Now a Free-Market Patriot of Lithuania." In answer to a query from *USA Today,* Chip writes: "It's for real. The for-profit nation-state, with a globally dispersed citizenry of shareholders, is the next stage in the evolution of political economy" (506).

Franzen's story, of course, is fictional and ironic. But it provides a sharp critique of practices of investment and ownership in the dot-com era, and the problem of financial knowledge is at heart of this critique. The story conjured by Franzen's characters of Lithuania's unique assets and free market future is not so much fraudulent and fictional as a particular representation of actual events and circumstances, just as the stories conjured by analysts during the dot-com boom were not entirely fictional and their scapegoating now functions to rescue the legitimacy of the larger discourse. Lithuania.com, in other words, acquires its satirical force because it mimics so well the logic of the new economy itself (Thrift 2001b). Franzen (2001, 132) provokes his readers to reflect on the accepted knowledge and rules of financial practices to a greater degree than Spitzer does: "The collective fungible assets of my country disappeared in yours without a ripple," Gitanas says in *The Corrections,* "A rich powerful country made the rules we Lithuanians are dying by. Why should we respect these rules?"

Notes

INTRODUCTION

1. Nast was one of the most influential cartoonists of his time and is remembered for creating the images that associate the Republican party with an elephant and the Democrats with a donkey. Many of his images arguably still influence the way we imagine politics today. Jim Zwick, *Political Cartoons and Cartoonists*: http://www.boondocksnet.com/gallery/nast_intro.html.

2. For an explanation of the symbolism on the U.S. Currency, see also U.S. Department of the Treasury, *Frequently Asked Questions about the Currency*: http://www.treas.gov/education/faq/currency/portraits.html.

3. This body of literature is associated with the journal *Accounting, Organizations and Society*. Good examples are Boland (1989), Hopwood and Miller (1994), Miller (1998), Miller and Napier (1993), Montagna (1990), and Power (1997). Compare also Underhill (1997) and Wade and Veneroso (1998a).

4. Secondary sources on Simmel's work and the sociology of money more broadly include Dodd (1994, 24–58), Frisby (1990), Smelt (1980), Leyshon and Thrift (1997, 35–38), Turner (1986), and Zelizer (1994).

5. The argument that money requires social, geographical, and discursive nodal points of trust and authority is made in a number of recent works, including, for instance, Corbridge, Martin, and Thrift (1994); Germain (1997); Gilbert and Helleiner (1999); Helleiner (1999a); Leyshon and Thrift (1997); Leyshon, Thrift, and Pratt (1998); and Sassen (1991, 1994).

6. The Bank of England was not successful in its prosecution of Boggs.

Although the judge was openly sympathetic to the bank's case, instructing the jury that the question of reproduction of banknotes was straightforward and would clearly include the transcription of, for instance, bills' serial numbers, the jury returned a unanimous "not guilty" verdict (Wenschler 1999, 112–16). More recently however, the U.S. Secret Service has intensified prosecution of Boggs by intensively monitoring him and confiscating his work. A court case (without jury), which was started by Boggs in order to have his work returned, was lost by Boggs in December 1993. That decision is currently being appealed in the U.S. Circuit Courts of Appeals in Washington, D.C.

It should be pointed out that Boggs's work benefits from these legal battles, as they underline the legal contestability of banknotes and their value. As Wenschler puts it: "Boggs's rising worth in the market is clearly a direct function of his transgressive approach and the persecution it invariably provokes. Boggs has often said he'd have stopped by himself a long time ago if only the government hadn't been so insistent on trying to stop him" (140).

1. A GENEALOGY OF FINANCE

1. OECD 2000. See also *Financial Times* 2000.

2. Although the Blair government has publicly made the issue of child poverty in Britain a priority in its policies, it has recently come under severe criticism for the remedies it has offered to poor families with children. In April 2001 a committee of members of parliament published a report severely attacking the emergency loans scheme, which is "intended as a lifeline for the poorest in society." Instead of helping financially excluded groups, the report argues, the social fund is "adding to the poverty and social exclusion of families with children by plunging them further into debt and denying them access to basic necessities" (Ward 2001, 10). The government's emphasis on loan funds instead of benefits in its policies toward socially and financially excluded constituencies remains part of the concepts of economic performance and priorities being criticized here.

3. These terms are from Helleiner (1993). Other sources offering a similar argument include Cerny (1993, 1994, 1995), Murphy (1994), Ruggie (1998, chapter 2), Strange (1986, 1998), and the 1994 special edition of *Policy Sciences* 27 (4). For a representation of finance as powerful agent, see, for example, Laffey (2000). For a critical perspective on the representation of finance as structure, see the contributions to Sinclair and Thomas (2001).

4. For discussions of the importance of information, knowledge, and interpretation for finance, see also Boden (2000), Brügger (2000), Germain

(1997), Knorr Cetina and Preda (2001), Porter (1999), and Preda (2000, 2001, 2002).

5. There is a small but growing literature that discusses the performative effects of financial theory and knowledge, including Callon (1998), MacKenzie (2001, 2003a, 2003b), and Muniesa (2000). On capitalism and performativity see also Thrift (2001a). However, none of these sources use Butler's appropriation of the performative, and their reading of performativity thus differs slightly from the one developed here.

6. It needs to be emphasized here that a focus on financial discourse does not imply a neglect of "real" material circumstances, because it draws into question the very dichotomy between the spheres of the "real" and the "ideal." Criticisms of the study of discourse and representation in political practices on the grounds that it ignores material circumstances and resources can be found in Gills (2001), Krasner (1996, 2000), Laffey (2000), Patomäki and Wight (2000), and Wight (1999). As Krasner puts it, for example, "In an environment where normative constraints are weak, and where violent death, big time violent death, is always a possibility, actors ignore material resources at their peril" (2000, 134). Campbell provides a reply to such critiques: "The body lying on the ground, the bullet in the head, and the shell casing lying not far away—tells us nothing itself about the meaning and significance of those elements. . . . For example, did the body and the bullet get to be as they are because of suicide, manslaughter, murder, ethnic cleansing, tribal war, genocide, a war of inter-state rivalry, or . . . ? Each of those terms signifies a larger discursive formation through which a whole set of identities, social relations, political possibilities and ethical outcomes are made more or less possible" (2001, 444). On the politics of discourse and representation, see also, for example, Ashley and Walker (1990), Butler (1992), Campbell (1998a, 5–8), George and Campbell (1990), Peterson (1992), and Shapiro and Alker (1996). I discuss these issues at length in de Goede (2003).

7. Sources that apply Foucault's notions of power to the economic domain include Burchell, Gordon, and Miller (1991); Dean (1995); Hopwood and Miller (1994); Miller and Rose (1990); and Rose (1993).

8. Cohen does discuss the difficult emergence of national currencies and notes that these are a much more recent phenomenon than is often assumed. However, he assumes the unproblematic existence of international currencies for centuries: "The first genuinely international currency, the silver drachma of Athens, established its predominance as early as the fifth century B.C.E." (1998, 29).

9. For a Braudelian view of history within political economy, see, for example, Amoore et al. (2000), Germain (1997, 1999), and Langley (2002).

2. MASTERING LADY CREDIT

1. This is not to say that financial networks did not exist before the seventeenth-century emergence of the British national debt. On the contrary, relatively sophisticated banking networks existed as early as fifteenth-century Florence, at which time Italian bankers gave their name to Lombard Street, the main street in London's financial district (Kindleberger 1993, 43–46). Moreover, from the sixteenth century onward it becomes possible to observe a steady and consistent growth in the mobility of funds between European cities (Germain 1997, 34–44). However, I accept Strange's argument here that it was the unique combination of the institutionalization of credit and the national state that inaugurated modern finance.

2. It is generally agreed that the bubble originated when the South Sea Company's directors proposed to take over the British national debt (which was in the form of illiquid annuities) by transforming it into stock of the South Sea Company (in the form of tradable paper shares). Thus, the national debt would become privatized as well as tradable. The British Court and Parliament were heavily involved in the South Sea Scheme, accepting bribes and purchasing South Sea shares. The price of the South Sea shares surged and reached a peak in 1720, before collapsing as a result of loss of public confidence in the South Sea Scheme.

Secondary sources on the scheme have debated whether the bubble was "rational" (Carswell 1960, Garber 1990, Neal 1990) or whether the bubble was an early manifestation of financial exuberance and irrationality (Chancellor 1999, Mackay 1995 [1841]). A detailed debate of the South Sea Bubble is beyond the scope of this chapter (see Dickson 1967, 90–156), but the point to be stressed is how interpretations of the history of the South Sea Company have advanced their own political agendas (rational, efficient markets versus cycles of irrational exuberance), thus demonstrating that we are all "historians of the present."

3. *Fortune, Volume One, Number One,* University of Brighton School of Design "Visual Telling of Stories Archive," http://cccw.adh.bton.ac.uk/schoolofdesign/MA.COURSE/LInfF29.html.

4. This debate takes place especially within the emerging "discipline" of behavioral finance, including, for example, Posner (1998), Shiller (2000), Thaler (1997), and Thaler, Jolls, and Sunstein (1998).

5. I would like to emphasize that I make no claim concerning the *essential* being of women and men, but rather wish to comment upon the manner in which the essential being of women and men is constructed in modern discourses. Thus it is possible for a woman to be praised for the masculine practice of self-assertion while surrounded by hysterical males in a financial panic. This recently happened in *The Independent* when one fund manager commented as follows on financial advisor Abby Cohen's

behavior during the Asian Crisis: "She was a voice of reason in a sea of panic" (quoted in Usborne 1999).

6. The crash of the Thai *Baht* sparked currency crashes as well as stock market panics in Asian countries such as Indonesia, South Korea, and Hong Kong. The Asian crisis has stimulated intense debates on the nature of the present global financial system. Some see this crisis as symptomatic of systemic instability that jeopardizes the entire financial system; others have identified serious but localized flaws in the "international financial architecture" that can be fixed (Goldstein 1998, 67). The view that the Asian crisis is indicative of inherent systemic weaknesses can be found in, for instance, Wade and Veneroso 1998a and 1998b. The view that flaws in the financial architecture can be fixed is to be found in, for instance, Goldstein 1998 and Rosenberger 1997.

The precise debate on the causes of the crisis are outside the scope of this chapter. Suffice it to say that observers from opposite ends of the political spectrum agree that what all the crisis countries had in common was an overvalued currency and a history of over-hasty financial deregulation. The overvalued currencies are argued to have led to large inflows of money from foreign investors in search of quick and easy profits. Rapid financial deregulation is said to have led to inadequately monitored and controlled banking systems in the Asian countries themselves (this debate is summarized in Strange 1998, 78–96; for a discussion of the cultural politics in the Asian crisis see Higgot 1998; for a discussion of the metaphors of crisis see Kelly 2001).

3. FINANCE, GAMBLING, AND SPECULATION

1. Today, the difference between futures and forward contracts is that futures are standardized and sold on exchanges, while forwards are customized and sold outside exchanges. The introduction of trading rules and standardized contracts on the CBoT can thus be seen to have inaugurated futures trading as currently defined. Earlier "to-arrive" contracts, as used in London and Amsterdam, were created individually and were thus more similar to current forward contracts.

2. The opposition of farmers in general and the U.S. Populist movement in particular to business interests is well documented, and more detailed accounts of these political debates can be found in Cowing (1965), Fabian (1999), and Hofstadter (1955).

3. Short selling is the practice of "selling a borrowed security" (Karpoff 1992, 445). Short sellers sell a security or commodity that that they do not own for delivery at a later date, thus profiting from price declines. Short selling has been a controversial practice throughout financial history and

has been criticized in the aftermath of the 1929 and 1987 stock market crashes.

4. In 1892, Congressman Hatch of Missouri proposed a national bill to levy a tax rate of 10 percent, which he considered to be prohibitive, on all nondeliverable futures contracts. Hatch's proposal led to congressional hearings on what was termed "Fictitious Dealings in Agricultural Products," but the Hatch bill never made it into law (Cowing 1965, 5–24).

5. This argument carried a strong element of anti-Semitism, as many Western arguments against usury had done earlier. Despite the fact that the critique of usury has Judaic roots (Visser and MacIntosh 1998, 178), Jews were often associated with the exploitative practice of money lending in the Western imagination. More generally, the opposition to capital and big business in the United States in the nineteenth century, which was led by the Populists, was coupled to anti-Semitism (Hofstadter 1955, 77–81).

6. These cases are documented in, for instance, Dewey (1886, 1905), Goldman (1923), *Harvard Law Review* (1927, 1932), and MacDougall (1936).

7. U.S. Supreme Court, *Dickson v. Uhlmann Grain Co.*, 288 U.S. 188 (1933). Full text of the decision is available at http://laws.findlaw.com/us/288/188.html.

8. U.S. Supreme Court, *Board of Trade of City of Chicago v. Christie Grain & Stock Co.*, 198 U.S. 236, (1905). Full text of the decision is available at http://laws.findlaw.com/us/198/236.html.

9. U.S. Supreme Court, *Hunt v. New York Cotton Exchange*, 205 U.S. 322 (1907). Full text of the decision is available at http://laws.findlaw.com/us/205/322.html.

10. Moody is known as the founder of Moody's Investors Service, which is still a powerful credit rating agency (Sinclair 1994).

11. U.S. Supreme Court, *Board of Trade of City of Chicago v. Olsen*, 262 U.S. 1 (1923). Full text of the decision is available at http://laws.findlaw.com/us/262/1.html.

12. Information taken from IG Index's Web site, http://igindex.co.uk/. IG Index also accepts bets on the weather (http://igindex.co.uk/content/ne_weather.html) and on major sporting events (http://www.igsport.com/). See also *USA Today* MoneyExchange, at http://money.usatoday.newsfutures.com/. *USA Today* also accepts bets on political and sporting events.

4. THE DOW JONES AVERAGE AND THE BIRTH OF THE FINANCIAL MARKET

1. The connections between census and colonial administration have been well-documented. As Hannah puts it: "Modern nations have only

existed and been governable as nations to the extent that the people, activities, and resources that make them up have been gathered together in the form of statistics and other surveys" (2001, 517). See also Anderson (1991) and Hacking (1990).

2. The history of statistics is well documented, and the tension between the enumeration of contingent events on one hand and the discovery of the laws of society on the other is discussed in, for instance, Daston (1988), David (1998), Hacking (1975, 1990, 1991), Porter (1986), Starr (1987), Stigler (1986).

3. Another contemporary of Jevons and Marshall who sought to make economics an exact science was British mathematician Francis Ysidro Edgeworth, who conceived of the economy as a grand mechanical structure, measurable like the physical world, but still divinely ordered. "Mécanique Sociale may one day take her place along with Mécanique Celeste," Edgeworth wrote, "as the movements of each particle, constrained or loose, in a material cosmos are continually subordinated to one maximum of sum-total of accumulated energy, so the movements of each soul, whether selfishly isolated or linked sympathetically, may continually be realising the maximum energy of pleasure, the Divine love of the universe" (1881, 12). On the connections between Jevons, Marshall, and Edgeworth, see Schabas (1989), who argues that these three figures pioneered the mathematization of economics.

4. Life insurance, however, remained morally and religiously condemned until the end of the nineteenth century (Zelizer 1983, 73–79). As late as 1870, life insurance was prohibited by religious leaders in the United States who perceived the work of Satan in this speculation on human lives. Instead, these preachers taught that God would replace a lost husband and take special care of widows and orphans. Consequently, life insurance companies were careful to emphasize the moral rather than economic functions of their policies and solicited the aid of clergymen to construct their legitimacy. Slowly, a religious worldview was articulated that encouraged active participation of man in managing his future and that constructed reliance on providence as outdated superstition. One preacher particularly in favor of life insurance put it in 1869: "We have no right to trust God for anything which he has enabled us to obtain by our own skill and industry" (quoted in Zelizer 1983, 78).

5. U.S. Supreme Court, *U.S. v. New York Coffee and Sugar Exchange,* 263 U.S. 611 (1924). Full text of the decision is available at http://laws .findlaw.com/us/263/611.html.

6. U.S. Supreme Court, *Board of Trade of City of Chicago v. Olsen,* 262 U.S. 1 (1923). Full text of the decision is available at http://laws.findlaw.com/ us/262/1.html.

7. The tension discussed in Taft's decision was not just a problem for

speculators, but more generally for the emerging professions in the late nineteenth century. The development of rule-governed and numerical knowledge entailed a political tension between professional judgment and rule-based objectivity. If professional knowledge was to be produced merely by internalizing a set of predetermined rules, how could speculators, stock analysts, or accountants justify their expertise and unique knowledge to larger society? As a result, many accountants and auditors were opposed to the push for professionalisation of their field. For example, in 1871 the British *Journal of the Institute of Actuaries* published a paper critical of the benefits of mechanized calculation. "On the whole, arithmeticians have not much to expect from the aid of calculating machines," this author concluded, "and we must fall back upon the wholesome truth that we cannot delegate our intellectual functions, and say to a machine, to a formula, to a rule, or to a dogma, I am too lazy to think, do please think for me" (quoted in Warwick 1995, 330; see also Porter 1995a, 1995b).

8. The twelve industrial stocks included in the initial DJIA were American Cotton Oil, American Sugar, American Tobacco, Chicago Gas, Distilling and Cattle Feeding, General Electric, Laclede Gas, National Lead, North American, Tennessee Coal and Iron, U.S. Leather, and U.S. Rubber (Stillman 1986, 41). Of these, General Electric is the only company still included in today's measurement of the DJIA. For an overview of all the changes in the DJIA see *Dow Jones Industrial Average History*, http://www.djindexes.com/downloads/DJIA_Hist_Comp.pdf.

9. The railroad average consisted of the average price of twenty railroad stocks. In 1970, this average was changed to include air and other transport companies and was renamed the Dow Jones Transportation Average. It still consists of 20 stocks today.

5. REGULATION AND RISK IN CONTEMPORARY MARKETS

1. For other contemporary critiques in the *Atlantic Monthly* see, for example, Carver (1930) and Smith (1930).

2. *The Investor's Advocate: How the SEC Protects Investors and Maintains Market Integrity*, "Introduction," http://www.sec.gov/about/whatwedo.shtml.

3. *The Investor's Advocate: How the SEC Protects Investors and Maintains Market Integrity*, "The Laws that Govern the Securities Industry," http://www.sec.gov/about/whatwedo.shtml.

4. LTCM was set up, most notably, by two Nobel prize winners in economics (Robert Merton and Myron Scholes), a former Federal Reserve vice chairman (David Mullins), and a former top Salomon Brothers bond

trader (John Meriwether). Indeed, as LTCM founder Professor Robert C. Merton proudly asserted at the acceptance of his 1997 Nobel Prize in the Economic Sciences, "the remarkable collection of people at LTCM" was widely considered to be "the best finance faculty in the world" (1997, 7). Good sources on the history and fall of LTCM include Dunbar (2000), MacKenzie (2000, 2003a), Lowenstein (2001), Stonham (1999a, 1999b), and Horizon (1999). For a discussion of LTCM from an international political economy perspective, see de Goede (2001).

5. A recent experiment in the context of National Science Week in the United Kingdom reminds of these experiments with random computer forecasting and drawing cards in order to assess whether stock price movements are statistically predictable or whether speculative investment requires professional study and experience in order to be successful. In April 2001, a psychology lecturer conducted an experiment in which an experienced investor, an astrologer, and a four-year old girl were given a fictional £5,000 to invest in the stock market for one week. While the experienced investor looked at past performance of companies to pick his preferred stock and the astrologer studied star constellations to decide, the child chose her investments randomly. In the declining market, all participants lost money during the experiment, but the child was proclaimed the winner because she preserved most of the £5,000 initially invested. *The Guardian* (2001) noted that the experiment had come under critique by "experts" who "insisted that investments can only properly be judged over at least 12 months."

6. An option gives the right but not the obligation to buy a particular stock for a determined price at a set time in the future. Futures, in contrast, entail the obligation to buy or sell a particular stock or commodity for a certain price in the future. Futures contracts could thus claim to always "contemplate" delivery, but this argument did not hold for options that do not have to be exercised.

7. Meriwether's claim to fame was his appearance in a 1989 sensationalist account of Wall Street practices as "the best bond trader on Wall Street" as well as the "King of the Game" of *Liar's Poker,* which was played on the Salomon bond trading floor (Lewis 1989, 15). Meriwether was forced to leave Salomon Brothers in connection with a scandal around U.S. government bond auctions (Dunbar 2000, 112).

8. This was not their first attempt to test their theories in the financial markets. In the mid-1970s, Black, Scholes, and Merton had attempted, unsuccessfully, to profit from their models by purchasing options that were underpriced according to their calculations. Moreover, in 1976 Scholes and Merton set up an options-based mutual fund called Money Market/Options Investment, which would provide, according to Merton,

"downside protection to the investor while at the same time affording significant exposure to upside movements in the stock market" (1997, 6). However, the fund found few investors and was not a commercial success (Dunbar 2000, 78).

LTCM was a hedge fund, which are speculation vehicles for very wealthy investors; qualified eligible participants (QEPs) must have at least US$5 million to their name. Hedge funds are defined by their unregulated and secretive nature: they are not allowed to advertise and they are exempt from restrictions on leverage and short selling that apply to large investment funds such as mutual funds (Edwards 1999, 190–91). Hedge funds were made possible through an exemption in the 1940 Investment Company Act, which regulates speculative funds in the wake of the 1929 crash. This exemption stipulates that small funds with less than one hundred very wealthy and sophisticated investors need no governmental oversight. As a result of the secretive nature of hedge funds very few data about their activities are available, but since the LTCM debacle their number has been guessed to be around 3000 (Edwards 1999, 192).

9. Greenspan and McDonough moreover argued that the Fed did not really do anything except provide advice, offices, and coffee. Greenspan insisted that "the Federal Reserve Bank of New York's efforts were designed solely to enhance the probability of an orderly private sector adjustment, not to dictate the path that adjustment would take" (HBC 1998, 40). These remarks led Massachusetts Congressman Frank to comment: "You both deserve an award even by the standards of the Fed. The extent to which you have understated this is impressive" (HBC 1998, 80).

10. *Baker to Introduce Hedge Fund Bill,* press release, Subcommittee on Capital Markets, Securities and Government Sponsored Enterprises, September 22, 1999, http://www.house.gov/financialservices/92299bak.htm, accessed in January 2001.

The full text of the Hedge Fund Disclosure Act (HR 2924) is online at http://financialservices.house.gov/banking/hedfunss.htm.

11. This list was obtained from Enron's Web site (http://www.enron.com/corp/products/) in January 2002.

6. REPOLITICIZING FINANCIAL PRACTICES

1. A similar argument is made by Stephen Gill, who notes that security technology and economic ideology converge in what he calls "disciplinary neo-liberalism" (1995, 1; see also Gill 1997a, 21). The continuity and differences between Gill's work and my arguments are discussed below.

2. Strange does go on to explore alternatives to Bretton Woods style

reregulation, such as the institution of an international bankruptcy court which would curb the power of international creditors. However, she calls this idea "naïve" and writes that "utopian ideas are apt to hinder more than they help. By encouraging people to dream about the ideal world, they distract them from doing what can be done in the real world" (1998, 172–73).

3. Keenan, here, criticizes the concept of power offered by Charles Taylor. However, Keenan's statement offers an apt description of the way power is conceptualized in the work of Gramscian political economy, which assumes class identity to be a prepolitical asset and which conceptualizes hegemony as the process by which agents come to believe in political propositions that oppose their "genuine" class interests (de Goede 2003).

4. A recent article by Gill places more emphasis on the multiple sources from which resistance might stem and advocates an "inclusive politics of diversity" (2000, 136). However, within these plural and diverse resistances, Gill seeks to identify "the realisation of a collective will," which he sees emerging through broad-based protests such as in Seattle in 1999 (138).

5. *The HIPC Debt Initiative: Debt Relief for Sustainable Development,* the World Bank Group, http://www.worldbank.org/hipc/about/hipcbr/hipcbr.htm.

6. *The HIPC Debt Initiative: Debt Relief for Sustainable Development,* the World Bank Group, emphasis added. http://www.worldbank.org/hipc/about/hipcbr/hipcbr.htm.

7. In its December 2000 report, Jubilee explains the significance of the symbol of the chain that has accompanied its campaigning as follows: "The chain represents the enslaving nature of the debt burden which undermines development, dignity and even people's sovereignty. It is a sobering fact that in the last four years the debt crisis has led to the deaths of more people than the brutal Atlantic slave trade carried out over decades. Yet the stark imagery of the chain has always had a double meaning. When people form a human chain, alongside anger there is an immense sense of the power of people linked for a common cause. We remember that a popular international movement in the 19th century, after a long struggle, brought about the end of the slave trade. The chains of debt are not yet broken, but they have been loosened; and as people continue to join hands against debt bondage, we will prise the chains of debt apart" (Barrett 2000).

8. Criticizing GDP as a measure of economic activity has earlier been undertaken by feminist economists, who argue that traditional women's activities, including household work, child-rearing, and social care are not included in measurements of GDP because they are not financially rewarded (see, for instance, Bakker 1994 and Nelson 1996). These criticisms are taken up buy Rowe's "Redefining Progress" coalition (see http://www.rprogress.org/).

9. The Dow Jones Sustainability Indexes, "Corporate Sustainability," http://www.sustainability-index.com/htmle/sustainability/corpsustain ability.html.

10. New Economics Foundation, *New Ways of Measuring,* http://www .neweconomics.org/gen/new_ways_top.aspx.

11. For the Inner City 100, see http://www.theinnercity100.org/. For ethical accounting, see also the Institute for Social and Ethical Account-ability, http://www.accountability.org.uk.

12. *Project Description,* Black Shoals/Stock Market Planetarium, http:// www.stain.org/shoals/indexNS.html.

13. All references to possible meanings of "security" in this paragraph are from the online *Oxford English Dictionary,* unless indicated otherwise.

14. In *The New Republic,* Nobel-prize winning economist Robert M. Solow dismisses Soros's arguments as unscientific and ill-informed. An ex-change between Solow and Soros can be found in "Global Capital Markets: An Exchange," *The New Republic,* April 1999, p. 24, http://www.soros .org/textfiles/writings/041299_Exchange.txt. Soros (1994) has repeatedly expressed his "frustration" at the situation "where I am taken so seriously but my theory is not. . . . It is treated as the self-indulgence of a man who made a lot of money in the stock market."

Bibliography

All URL addresses, including the ones mentioned in the notes to the individual chapters, were accessible in August 2003, unless noted otherwise.

Abolafia, Mitchel Y. 1996. "Hyper-Rational Gaming." *Journal of Contemporary Ethnography* 25 (2): 226–50.

Adam, Barbara 1995. *TimeWatch: The Social Analysis of Time*. Cambridge, UK: Polity Press.

Adler, Patricia A., and Peter Adler. 1984. Introduction to *The Social Dynamics of Financial Markets*, ed. Patricia A. Adler and Peter Adler. Greenwich: JAI Press.

Agnew, Jean-Christophe. 1986. *Worlds Apart: The Market and the Theatre in Anglo-American Thought, 1550–1750*. Cambridge: Cambridge University Press.

Ahmed, Kamal. 2000. "Britain Shamed by Child Poverty." *Observer,* June 11, 1–2, 12.

Amoore, Louise. 2002. *Globalisation Contested: An International Political Economy of Work*. Manchester: Manchester University Press.

———. 2004. "Risk, Reward and Discipline at Work." *Economy and Society* 33 (2): 174–96.

Amoore, Louise, Richard Dodgson, Randall D. Germain, Barry K. Gills, Paul Langley, and Iain Watson. 2000. "Paths to a Historicised International Political Economy." *Review of International Political Economy* 7 (1): 53–71.

Anderson, Benedict. 1991. *Imagined Communities*. Rev. ed. London: Verso.

Ashley, Richard K., and R. B. J. Walker. 1990. "Speaking the Language of

Exile: Dissident Thought in International Studies." *International Studies Quarterly* 34: 259–68.

Auster, Paul. 1997. *Hand to Mouth: A Chronicle of Early Failure*. New York: Henry Holt.

Austin, J. L. 1962. *How to Do Things with Words*. Cambridge, MA: Harvard University Press.

Bachelier, Louis. 1964 [1900]. "Theory of Speculation." In *The Random Character of Stock Prices,* ed. Paul H. Cootner. Cambridge, MA: MIT Press.

Backscheider, Paula. 1981. "Defoe's Lady Credit." *Huntington Library Quarterly* 44 (2): 89–100.

Bagehot, Walter. 1991 [1873]. *Lombard Street: A Description of the Money Market*. Philadelphia: Orion.

Bakker, Isabella, ed. 1994. *The Strategic Silence: Gender and Economic Policy*. London: Zed Books.

Banker's Magazine. 1929. "Editorial Comment: Our Orgy of Speculation." 119 (6): 907–14.

Barrett, Marlene, ed. 2000. *The World Will Never Be the Same Again*. Jubilee 2000 Coalition, December. http://www.jubilee2000uk.org/analysis/reports/world_never_same_again/contents.htm.

Bartky, Ian R. 1989. "The Adoption of Standard Time." *Technology and Culture* 30: 25–56.

Barty-King, Hugh. 1991. *The Worst Poverty: A History of Debt and Debtors*. Gloucestershire: Alan Sutton.

Beck, Ulrich. 1992. *Risk Society: Towards a New Modernity*. London: Sage.

Bello, Walden, Nicola Bullard, and Kamal Malhotra, eds. 2000. *Global Finance: New Thinking on Regulating Speculative Markets*. London: Zed Books.

Bellos, Alex. 2001. "Monopoly Money Gives You Credit in the Land of the Bourgeois Poor." *Guardian,* August 23.

Benjamin, Walter. 1978. "Tax Advice." In *One Way Street and Other Writings*. Trans. Edmund Jephcott and Kingsley Shorter. London: NLB.

Bernstein, Peter L. 1992. *Capital Ideas: The Improbable Origins of Modern Wall Street*. New York: Free Press.

———. 1996. *Against the Gods: The Remarkable Story of Risk*. New York: Wiley.

Black, Fischer. 1989. "How We Came Up with the Option Formula." *Journal of Portfolio Management* 15 (2): 4–8.

Black, Fischer, and Myron Scholes. 1973. "The Pricing of Options and Corporate Liabilities." *Journal of Political Economy* 81 (May/June): 637–54.

Bleiker, Roland. 2000. *Popular Dissent, Human Agency and Global Politics*. Cambridge: Cambridge University Press.

Bloss, James O. 1892. "Address Delivered before the Committee on Agriculture of the House of Representatives, February 9, 1892, in Opposition to H.R. 2699, Taxing Dealings in 'Options' and 'Futures.'" In *Dealings in "Options" and "Futures": Protests, Memorials and Arguments against Bills Introduced in the 52nd Congress.* New York: L. H. Biglow.

Boden, Deidre. 2000. "Worlds in Action: Information, Instantaneity and Global Futures Trading." In *The Risk Society and Beyond: Critical Issues for Social Theory,* ed. Barbara Adam, Ulrich Beck, and Joost van Loon. London: Sage.

Boland, Richard J. 1989. "Beyond the Objectivist and the Subjectivist: Learning to Read Accounting as Text." *Accounting, Organizations and Society* 14 (5/6): 591–604.

Bond, Patrick. 2000. "Their Reforms and Ours: Balance of Forces and Economic Analysis in a New Global Financial Architecture." In *Global Finance: New Thinking on Regulating Speculative Markets,* ed. Walden Bello, Nicola Bullard, and Kamal Malhotra. London: Zed Books.

Booth, Garry. 1999. "Towards the Virtual Catastrophe: Computer Modelling." *Financial Times,* June 25.

Bowen, H. V. 1995. "The Bank of England During the Long Eighteenth Century." In *The Bank of England: Money, Power and Influence, 1694–1994,* ed. Richard Roberts and David Kynaston. Oxford: Oxford University Press.

Boyle, David. 1999. *Funny Money: In Search of Alternative Cash.* London: Flamingo.

Boyle, James E. 1920. *Speculation and the Chicago Board of Trade.* New York: Macmillan.

Braudel, Fernand. 1981. *Civilization and Capitalism.* Volume 1, *The Structures of Everyday Life.* London: Collins.

Brenner, Reuven, and Gabrielle A. Brenner. 1990. *Gambling and Speculation: A Theory, History, and a Future of Some Human Decisions.* Cambridge: Cambridge University Press.

Brown, A. E. 1910. "Concerning Attempt to Prohibit Time Dealings in Grain." In *The Functions of the Legitimate Exchanges.* Chicago: Hartzell–Lord.

Brown, Wendy. 1988. *Manhood and Politics: A Feminist Reading in Political Theory.* New Jersey: Rowman and Littlefield.

———. 1998. "Genealogical Politics." In *The Later Foucault: Politics and Philosophy,* ed. Jeremy Moss. London: Sage.

Brügger, Urs. 2000. "Speculating: Work in Financial Markets." In *Ökonomie und Gesellschaft Jahrbuch 16: Facts and Figures: Economic Representations and Practices,* ed. Herbert Kalthoff, Richard Rottenburg, and Hans–Jürgen Wagener. Marburg: Metropolis Verlag.

Burch, Kurt. 1994. "The 'Properties' of the State System and Global Capitalism." In *The Global Economy as Political Space*, ed. Stephen J. Rosow, Naeem Inayatullah, and Mark Rupert. London: Lynne Rienner.

———. 1998. *"Property" and the Making of the International System*. London: Lynne Rienner.

Burchell, Graham, Colin Gordon, and Peter Miller, eds. 1991. *The Foucault Effect: Studies in Governmentality*. Chicago: University of Chicago Press.

Butler, Judith. 1992. "Contingent Foundations: Feminism and the Question of 'Postmodernism.'" In *Feminists Theorize the Political*, ed. Judith Butler and Joan W. Scott. London: Routledge.

———. 1993. *Bodies That Matter: On the Discursive Limits of "Sex."* London: Routledge.

———. 1997. *Excitable Speech: Contemporary Scenes of Politics*. London: Routledge.

———. 1998. "Merely Cultural." *New Left Review* 228: 33–45.

———. 2000. "Restaging the Universal: Hegemony and the Limits of Formalism." In *Contingency, Hegemony, Universality*, ed. Judith Butler, Ernesto Laclau, and Slavoj Zizek. London: Verso.

Callon, Michel. 1998. "The Embeddedness of Economic Markets in Economics." In *The Laws of the Markets*, ed. Michel Callon. Oxford: Blackwell.

Campbell, David. 1992. *Writing Security: United States Foreign Policy and the Politics of Identity*. Minneapolis: University of Minnesota Press.

———. 1993. *Politics without Principle: Sovereignty, Ethics, and the Narratives of the Gulf War*. Boulder, CO: Lynne Rienner.

———. 1996. "Political Prosaics, Transversal Politics, and the Anarchical World." In *Challenging Boundaries: Global Flows, Territorial Identities*, ed. Michael J. Shapiro and Hayward R. Alker. Minneapolis: University of Minnesota Press.

———. 1998a. *National Deconstruction: Violence, Identity, and Justice in Bosnia*. Minneapolis: University of Minnesota Press.

———. 1998b. "Why Fight: Humanitarianism, Principles, and Post-Structuralism." *Millennium* 27 (3): 497–521.

———. 2001. "International Engagements: The Politics of North American International Relations Theory." *Political Theory* 29 (3): 432–48.

Campbell, David, and Michael Dillon. 1993. "The End of Philosophy and the End of International Relations." In *The Political Subject of Violence*, ed. David Campbell and Michael Dillon. Manchester: Manchester University Press.

Carruthers, Bruce G., and Sarah Babb. 1996. "The Color of Money and the Nature of Value: Greenbacks and Gold in Postbellum America." *American Journal of Sociology* 101 (6): 1556–91.

Carswell, John. 1960. *The South Sea Bubble*. London: Cresset Press.

Carver, Thomas Nixon. 1930. "Selling Short: The Morals and Economics of Margins." *Atlantic Monthly* 145 (February): 247–58.

CBoT (Chicago Board of Trade). 1892. "Memorial of the Board of Trade of the City of Chicago against the Passage of Senate Bill 1757 and House Bill 2699, Known as the 'Washburn' and 'Hatch' Bills Respectively." In *Dealings in "Options" and "Futures": Protests, Memorials and Arguments against Bills Introduced in the 52nd Congress*. New York: L. H. Biglow.

Cerny, Philip G. 1993. "The Political Economy of International Finance." In *Finance and World Politics: Markets, Regimes and States in the Post-Hegemonic Era*, ed. Philip G. Cerny. London: Edward Elgar.

———. 1994. "The Dynamics of Financial Globalization: Technology, Market Structure and Policy Response." *Policy Sciences* 27: 319–42.

———. 1995. "The Infrastructure of the Infrastructure? Toward 'Embedded Financial Orthodoxy' in the International Political Economy." In *Transcending the State-Global Divide: A Neostructuralist Agenda in International Relations*, ed. Ronen P. Palan and Barry Gills. London: Lynne Rienner.

Chalmers, Thomas. 1832. *On Political Economy, in Connection with the Moral State and Moral Aspects of Society*. Glasgow: William Collins.

Chancellor, Edward. 1999. *Devil Take the Hindmost: A History of Financial Speculation*. London: Macmillan.

Cioffari, Vincenzo. 1947. "The Function of Fortune in Dante, Boccaccio, and Machiavelli." *Italica* 24 (1): 1–13.

Citizen of Saratoga Springs. 1840. *Humbugs of Speculation: A Satirical Poem Embracing Several Historical Sketches of Speculative Operations, National and Individual During the Last Four Years. Saratoga Springs: printed at the Whig Office*. Archives of the New York Historical Society.

Clark, Geoffrey Wilson. 1999. *Betting on Lives: The Culture of Life Insurance in England, 1695–1775*. Manchester: Manchester University Press.

———. 2002. "Embracing Fatality through Life Insurance in Eighteenth-Century England." In *Embracing Risk: The Changing Culture of Insurance and Responsibility*, ed. Tom Baker and Jonathan Simon. Chicago: University of Chicago Press.

Cobb, Clifford, Ted Halstead, and Jonathan Rowe. 1995. "If the GDP Is Up, Why Is America Down?" *Atlantic Monthly*, October. http://www.theatlantic.com/politics/ecbig/gdp.htm.

Coggan, Philip. 2000a. "The Tyranny of Indices." *Financial Times*, June 11.

———. 2000b. "The Weighting Game." *Financial Times*, June 7.

Cohen, Benjamin. 1977. *Organizing the World's Money*. New York: Basic Books.

———. 1996. "Phoenix Risen: The Resurrection of Global Finance." *World Politics* 48: 268–96.

———. 1998. *The Geography of Money*. Ithaca: Cornell University Press.

———. 2000. "Taming the Phoenix? Monetary Governance after the Crisis." In *The Asian Financial Crisis and the Architecture of Global Finance*, ed. Gregory W. Noble and John Ravenhill. Cambridge: Cambridge University Press.

Cohen, Patricia Cline. 1982. *A Calculating People: The Spread of Numeracy in Early America*. Chicago: University of Chicago Press.

Collier, Jeremy, and Edmund Goldsmid. 1885. *An Essay upon Gaming: in a Dialogue between Callimachus and Dolomedes*. Edinburgh: Privately printed.

Committee on Banking and Currency. 1974 [1870]. *Gold Panic Investigation*. New York: Arno Press.

Connolly, William E. 1995. *The Ethos of Pluralization*. Minneapolis: University of Minnesota Press.

Constantinou, Costas M. 2000. "Poetics of Security." *Alternatives* 25 (3): 287–306.

Corbridge, Stuart, Ron Martin, and Nigel Thrift, eds. 1994. *Money, Power, Space*. Oxford: Basil Blackwell.

Cothran, G. W. 1880. *The Revised Statutes of the State of Illinois, as altered by subsequent legislation, together with the unrepealed statutory provisions of a general nature, passed from the time of the revision in 1874 to the year 1880*. Chicago: E. B. Meyers.

Cowe, Roger. 2000. "Ethical Index Sees UK Entrants." *Guardian*, October 2, 22.

Cowing, Cedric B. 1965. *Populists, Plungers, and Progressives: A Social History of Stock and Commodity Speculation, 1890–1936*. Princeton: Princeton University Press.

Cox, Robert W. 1999. "Civil Society at the Turn of the Millennium: Prospects for an Alternative World Order." *Review of International Studies* 25 (1): 3–28.

Crace, John. 2001. "How Bada Made £6,950." *Guardian*, education section, November 13, 11.

Cronon, William. 1991. *Nature's Metropolis: Chicago and the Great West*. New York: Norton.

Cummings, Neil, and Marysia Lewandowska. 2001. "It's the Thought that Counts." In *Capital: A Project by Neil Cummings and Marysia Lewandowska*. London: Tate Publishing.

Daly, Glyn. 2002. "Globalisation and the Constitution of Political Economy."

In *Politics and Post-structuralism: An Introduction,* ed. Alan Finlayson and Jeremy Valentine. Edinburgh: Edinburgh University Press.

Daston, Lorraine. 1988. *Classical Probability in the Enlightenment.* Princeton: Princeton University Press.

———. 1994. "Baconian Facts, Academic Civility, and the Prehistory of Objectivity." In *Rethinking Objectivity,* ed. Allan Megill. London: Duke University Press.

———. 1998. "Fear and Loathing of the Imagination in Science." *Daedalus: Science in Culture* 127 (1): 73–95.

Daston, Lorraine, and Peter Galison. 1992. "The Image of Objectivity." *Representations* 40: 81–128.

David, F. N. 1998. *Games, Gods and Gambling: A History of Probability and Statistical Ideas.* New York: Dover.

Davis, Mike. 1990. *City of Quartz: Excavating the Future in Los Angeles.* London: Verso.

Dean, Mitchell. 1995. "Governing the Unemployed Self in an Active Society." *Economy and Society* 24 (4): 559–83.

Defoe, Daniel. 1706a. *Review of the State of the English Nation,* no. 5, January 10. Repr. Arthur Wellesley Secord, volume 3, book 6. New York: AMS Press, 1965.

———. 1706b. *Review of the State of the English Nation,* no. 6, January 12. Repr. Arthur Wellesley Secord, volume 3, book 6. New York: AMS Press, 1965.

———. 1706c. *Review of the State of the English Nation,* no. 7, January 15. Repr. Arthur Wellesley Secord, volume 3, book 6. New York: AMS Press, 1965.

———. 1709a. *Review of the State of the British Nation,* no. 31, June 14. Repr. Arthur Wellesley Secord, volume 6, book 14. New York: AMS Press, 1965.

———. 1709b. *Review of the State of the British Nation,* no. 32, June 16. Repr. Arthur Wellesley Secord, volume 6, book 14. New York: AMS Press, 1965.

———. 1710a. *Review of the State of the British Nation,* no. 57, August 5. Repr. Arthur Wellesley Secord, volume 7, book 17. New York: AMS Press, 1965.

———. 1710b. *Review of the State of the British Nation,* no. 105, November 25. Repr. Arthur Wellesley Secord, volume 7, book 18. New York: AMS Press, 1965.

———. 1890 [1729]. *The Compleat English Gentleman,* ed. Karl D. Bülbring. London: David Nutt.

———. 1987 [1726]. *The Complete English Tradesman.* Gloucester: Alan Sutton.

de Goede, Marieke. 2000. "Mastering Lady Credit: Discourses of Financial Crisis in Historical Perspective." *International Feminist Journal of
Politics* 2 (1): 58–81.

———. 2001. "Discourses of Scientific Finance and the Failure of Long-
Term Capital Management." *New Political Economy* 6 (2): 149–70.

———. 2003. "Beyond Economism in International Political Economy."
Review of International Studies 29 (1): 79–97.

———. 2004. "Repoliticizing Financial Risk." *Economy and Society* 33
(2): 197–217.

De la Vega, Joseph. 1996 [1688]. "Confusión de Confusiones." In *Extraordinary Popular Delusions and the Madness of Crowds and Confusión de Confusiones,* ed. Martin S. Fridson. New York: Wiley.

De Marchi, Neil, and Paul Harrison. 1994. "Trading in the Wind and with
Guile: The Troublesome Matter of Short Selling of Shares in Seventeenth-
Century Holland." *History of Political Economy* 26 (supplement): 47–65.

Dent, Martin, and Bill Peters. 1999. *The Crisis of Poverty and Debt in the
Third World.* Aldershot: Ashgate.

Der Derian, James. 1992. *Antidiplomacy: Spies, Terror, Speed and War.*
Cambridge, UK: Blackwell.

Dewey, T. Henry. 1886. *A Treatise on Contracts for Future Delivery and
Commercial Wagers including "Options," "Futures" and "Short Sales."*
New York: Baker, Voorhis and Company.

———. 1905. *Legislation against Speculation and Gambling in the Forms
of Trade.* New York: Baker, Voorhis and Company.

Dickson, P. G. M. 1967. *The Financial Revolution in England: A Study in
the Development of Public Credit, 1688–1756.* London: Macmillan.

Dillon, Michael. 1996. *Politics of Security: Towards a Political Philosophy
of Continental Thought.* London: Routledge.

Dodd, Nigel. 1994. *The Sociology of Money: Economics, Reason and Contemporary Society.* New York: Continuum.

Douthwaite, Richard. 1996. *Short Circuit: Strengthening Local Economies for Security in an Unstable World.* Totnes: Green Books.

Dow, Charles H. 1899. "Review and Outlook." *Wall Street Journal,*
April 21, 1.

———. 1920. *Scientific Stock Speculation: A Condensed Statement of the
Principles upon which Successful Stock Speculation Must Be Based,* ed.
G. C. Selden. New York: The Magazine of Wall Street.

Dunbar, Nicholas. 2000. *Inventing Money: The Story of Long-Term Capital Management and the Legends behind It.* New York: Wiley.

Economist. 1976. "A Flutter on Interest Rates." January 17, 104–6.

———. 1997. "The Nobel Prize for Economics: The Right Option." October 18.

———. 1998. "Long-Term Sickness." October 3, 127–31.

———. 2001. "A Matter of Principals." June 30, 89–90.

———. 2002a. "Investment Banks: The Price of Atonement." November 14.

———. 2002b. "The Real Scandal." January 19, 9.

Edgeworth, Francis Ysidro. 1881. *Mathematical Psychics: An Essay on the Application of Mathematics to the Moral Sciences.* London: Kegan Paul.

Edkins, Jenny. 1999. *Poststructuralism and International Relations: Bringing the Political Back In.* London: Lynne Rienner.

———. 2002. "After the Subject of International Security." In *Politics and Post-structuralism: An Introduction,* ed. Alan Finlayson and Jeremy Valentine. Edinburgh: Edinburgh University Press.

Edwards, Franklin R. 1999. "Hedge Funds and the Collapse of Long-Term Capital Management." *Journal of Economic Perspectives* 13 (2): 189–210.

Eichengreen, Barry. 1996. *Globalizing Capital: A History of the International Monetary System.* Princeton: Princeton University Press.

Emery, Henry Crosby. 1895. "Legislation against Futures." *Political Science Quarterly* 10 (18): 62–86.

———. 1896. *Speculation on the Stock and Produce Exchanges of the United States.* New York: Columbia University Press.

———. 1908. "Ten Years Regulation of the Stock Exchange in Germany." *Yale Review,* May, 5–23.

———. 1915. "Speculation on the Stock Exchanges and Public Regulation of the Exchanges." *American Economic Review,* 5 (1): 69–85.

Ewald, François. 1991. "Insurance and Risk." In *The Foucault Effect: Studies in Governmentality,* ed. Graham Burchell, Colin Gordon, and Peter Miller. Chicago: University of Chicago Press.

Fabian, Ann Vincent. 1999. *Card Sharps and Bucket Shops: Gambling in Nineteenth-Century America.* New York: Routledge.

Fama, Eugene. 1965. "Random Walks in Stock Market Prices." *Financial Analysts Journal,* September/October, 55–59.

Fayant, Frank. 1913. *Short-Sales and Manipulation of Securities.* New York: Privately printed.

Felix, David. 1994. "International Capital Mobility and Third World Development: Compatible Marriage or Troubled Relationship?" *Policy Sciences* 27: 365–94.

Feng, Hengyi, Julie Froud, Sukhdev Johal, Colin Haslam, and Karel Williams. 2001. "A New Business Model? The Capital Market and the New Economy." *Economy and Society* 30 (4): 467–503.

Ferris, William G. 1988. *The Grain Traders: The Story of the Chicago Board of Trade.* Michigan: Michigan State University Press.

Financial Times. 2000. "OECD's Favourable Marks for the Economy." June 11.

Fischer, Stanley. 1998. *The Asian Crisis: A View from the IMF.* Address at the Midwinter Conference of the Bankers' Association for Foreign Trade, Washington, DC, January 22. http://www.imf.org/external/np/speeches/1998/012298.htm.

Foucault, Michel. 1979. *Discipline and Punish: The Birth of the Prison.* New York: Vintage.

———. 1980. "Two Lectures." In *Power/Knowledge: Selected Interviews and Other Writings,* ed. Colin Gordon. New York: Pantheon.

———. 1982. "Afterword: The Subject and Power." In *Michel Foucault: Beyond Structuralism and Hermeneutics,* ed. Hubert L. Dreyfus and Paul Rabinow. Chicago: University of Chicago Press.

———. 1984a. "Nietzsche, Genealogy, History." In *The Foucault Reader,* ed. Paul Rabinow. New York: Pantheon.

———. 1984b. *The Use of Pleasure: The History of Sexuality,* volume 2. London: Penguin.

———. 1988a. "Critical Theory/Intellectual History." In *Michel Foucault: Politics, Philosophy, Culture, Interviews and Other Writings, 1977–1984,* ed. Lawrence D. Kritzman. New York: Routledge.

———. 1988b. "Technologies of the Self." In *Technologies of the Self: A Seminar with Michel Foucault,* ed. Luther H. Martin, Huck Gutman, and Patrick H. Hutton. Amherst: University of Massachusetts Press.

———. 1989a. "The End of the Monarchy of Sex." In *Foucault Live: Collected Interviews 1961–1984,* ed. Sylvère Lotringer. New York: Semiotexte.

———. 1989b. "Ethics of the Concern for Self as a Practice of Freedom." In *Foucault Live: Collected Interviews 1961–1984,* ed. Sylvère Lotringer. New York: Semiotexte.

———. 1991a. "Governmentality." In *The Foucault Effect: Studies in Governmentality,* ed. Graham Burchell, Colin Gordon, and Peter Miller. Chicago: University of Chicago Press.

———. 1991b. "Politics and the Study of Discourse." In *The Foucault Effect: Studies in Governmentality,* ed. Graham Burchell, Colin Gordon, and Peter Miller. Chicago: University of Chicago Press.

———. 1994. *The Order of Things: An Archaeology of the Human Sciences.* New York: Vintage.

———. 1998. *The Will to Knowledge: The History of Sexuality,* volume 1. London: Penguin.

———. 1999. *Madness and Civilisation: A History of Insanity in the Age of Reason.* London: Routledge.

Foucault, Michel, and Richard Sennett. 1982. "Sexuality and Solitude."

In *Humanities in Review,* volume 1, ed. David Rieff. New York: New York Institute for the Humanities.

Franzen, Jonathan. 2001. *The Corrections.* London: Fourth Estate.

Frieden, Jeffry A. 1997. "The Dynamics of International Monetary Systems: International and Domestic Factors in the Rise, Reign and Demise of the Classical Gold Standard." In *The Gold Standard in Theory and History,* ed. Barry Eichengreen and Marc Flandreau. London: Routledge.

Frisby, David. 1990. Preface to the second edition of Georg Simmel, *The Philosophy of Money,* ed. David Frisby. London: Routledge.

Functions of the Legitimate Exchanges. 1910. Chicago: Hartzell-Lord.

GAO (U.S. General Accounting Office). 1999. *Long-Term Capital Management: Regulators Need to Focus Greater Attention on Systemic Risk.* GAO/GGD-00-3.

Garber, Peter M. 1990. "Famous First Bubbles." *Journal of Economic Perspectives* 4 (2): 19–33.

Garrett, Garet. 1911. *Where the Money Grows.* New York: Harper and Brothers.

General Laws of the State of Texas Passed at the Regular Session of the 30 Legislature. 1907. Austin: von Boeckman-Jones Company.

George, Jim, and David Campbell. 1990. "Patterns of Dissent and the Celebration of Difference: Critical Social Theory and International Relations." *International Studies Quarterly* 34: 269–94.

Germain, Randall D. 1997. *The International Organization of Credit: States and Global Finance in the World-Economy.* Cambridge: Cambridge University Press.

———. 1999. "Globalization in Historical Perspective." In *Globalization and Its Critics: Perspectives from Political Economy,* ed. Randall D. Germain. London: MacMillan.

Germain, Randall D., and Michael Kenny. 1998. "Engaging Gramsci: International Relations Theory and the New Gramscians." *Review of International Studies* 24 (1): 3–21.

Gibson, George Rutledge. 1891. *The Utilities and Ethics of Speculation: The Stock Exchange as an Economic Factor.* Address held before the Convention of American Bankers, New Orleans, November 12. Archives of the New York Historical Society.

Gibson, Thomas. 1923. *The Facts about Speculation.* New York: Thomas Gibson.

Gibson-Graham, J. K. 1996. *The End of Capitalism (As We Knew It).* Oxford: Blackwell.

Gilbert, Allan, ed. 1965. *Machiavelli: The Chief Works and Others,* volume 2. Durham, NC: Duke University Press.

Gilbert, Emily. 1998. "Ornamenting the Façade of Hell: Iconographies of 19th-Century Canadian Paper Money." *Environment and Planning D: Society and Space* 16 (1): 57–80.

Gilbert, Emily, and Eric Helleiner. 1999. "Nation-States and Money: Historical Contexts, Interdisciplinary Perspectives." In *Nation-States and Money: The Past, Present and Future of National Currencies*, ed. Emily Gilbert and Eric Helleiner. London: Routledge.

———, eds. 1999. *Nation-States and Money: The Past, Present and Future of National Currencies*. London: Routledge.

Gill, Stephen. 1990. *American Hegemony and the Trilateral Commission*. Cambridge: Cambridge University Press.

———. 1995. "The Global Panopticon? The Neoliberal State, Economic Life, and Democratic Surveillance." *Alternatives* 20 (1): 1–49.

———. 1997a. "Transformation and Innovation in the Study of World Order." In *Innovation and Transformation in International Studies*, ed. Stephen Gill and James H. Mittelman. Cambridge: Cambridge University Press.

———. 1997b. "Finance, Production, and Panopticism: Inequality, Risk and Resistance in an Era of Disciplinary Neo-Liberalism." In *Globalization, Democratization, and Multilateralism*, ed. Stephen Gill. London: Macmillan.

———. 2000. "Toward a Postmodern Prince? The Battle of Seattle as a Moment in the New Politics of Globalisation." *Millennium* 29 (1): 131–40.

Gill, Stephen, and David Law. 1988. *The Global Political Economy*. Baltimore: Johns Hopkins University Press.

———. 1993. "Global Hegemony and the Structural Power of Capital." In *Gramsci, Historical Materialism and International Relations*, ed. Stephen Gill. Cambridge: Cambridge University Press.

Gills, Barry K. 2001. "Re-Orienting the New (International) Political Economy." *New Political Economy* 6 (2): 233–45.

Glass. 1791. *The Glass, or, Speculation: A Poem. Containing an Account of the Ancient, and Genius of the Modern, Speculators*. New York: Printed for the author. Archives of the New York Historical Society.

Goldman, Samuel P. 1923. *Stock Exchange Law, with Special Reference to the New York Stock Exchange and New York Law*. New York: Ronald Press.

Goldstein, Morris. 1998. *The Asian Financial Crisis: Causes, Cures, and Systemic Implications*. Washington, DC: Institute for International Economics.

Gordon, Scott. 1972. "Two Monetary Inquiries in Great Britain: The MacMillan Committee of 1931 and the Radcliffe Committee of 1959." *Journal of Money, Credit and Banking* 4 (4): 957–77.

Goux, Jean-Joseph. 1997. "Values and Speculations: The Stock Exchange Paradigm." *Cultural Values* 1 (2): 159–77.

———. 1999. "Cash, Check, or Charge?" In *The New Economic Criticism: Studies at the Intersection of Literature and Economics*, ed. Mark Osteen and Martha Woodmansee. London: Routledge.

Green, Stephen. 2000. "Negotiating with the Future: The Culture of Modern Risk in Global Financial Markets." *Environment and Planning D: Society and Space* 18 (1): 77–89.

Greenhouse, Linda. 1999. "In Blow to Democrats, Court Says Census Must Be by Actual Count." *New York Times,* January 26.

Greenspan, Alan. 1996. *Remarks at the Annual Dinner and Francis Boyer Lecture of the American Enterprise Institute for Public Policy Research,* Washington, DC, December 5. http://www.federalreserve.gov/boarddocs/speeches/1996/19961205.htm.

———. 1998. *Statement before the Committee on Banking and Financial Services.* Hearing on Hedge Fund Operations, U.S. House of Representatives, October 1. http://financialservices.house.gov/banking/10198gre.htm.

Guardian. 2001. "Girl, 4, Wins Share Tipping Contest." March 24.

Gunning, Tom. 1999. "A Corner in Wheat." In *The Griffith Project,* volume 3, ed. Paolo Cherchi Usai. London: British Film Institute Publishing.

Hacking, Ian. 1975. *The Emergence of Probability.* Cambridge: Cambridge University Press.

———. 1990. *The Taming of Chance.* Cambridge: Cambridge University Press.

———. 1991. "How Should We Do the History of Statistics?" In *The Foucault Effect: Studies in Governmentality,* ed. Graham Burchell, Colin Gordon, and Peter Miller. Chicago: University of Chicago Press.

Hamill, Chas D. 1892. "Argument of Mr. Chas D. Hamill, President of the Chicago Board of Trade, before the Judiciary Committee of the United States Senate." In *Dealings in "Options" and "Futures": Protests, Memorials and Arguments against Bills Introduced in the 52nd Congress.* New York : L. H. Biglow.

Hamilton, William Peter. 1922. *The Stock Market Barometer: A Study of Its Forecast Value Based on Charles H. Dow's Theory of the Price Movement.* New York: Harper and Brothers.

Hamon, Henry. 1970 [1865]. *New York Stock Exchange Manual, Containing Its Principles, Rules, and Its Different Modes of Speculation, etc.* Connecticut: Greenwood Press.

Han, Jongwoo, and L. H. M. Ling. 1998. "Authoritarianism in the Hypermasculinised State: Hybridity, Patriarchy, and Capitalism in Korea." *International Studies Quarterly* 42 (1): 53–78.

Hannah, Matthew G. 2001. "Sampling and the Politics of Representation in US Census 2000." *Environment and Planning D: Society and Space* 19 (5): 515–34.

Hardy, Charles O. 1923. *Risk and Risk-Bearing.* Chicago: University of Chicago Press.

Harmes, Adam. 1998. "Institutional Investors and the Reproduction of Neo-liberalism." *Review of International Political Economy* 5 (1): 92–121.

———. 2001. "Mass Investment Culture." *New Left Review* May/June 9: 103–24.

Harvard Law Review. 1927. "Dealings in Futures." 40 (4): 638–42.

———. 1932. "Legislation Affecting Commodity and Stock Exchanges." 45 (5): 912–25.

Harvey, David. 1989. *The Condition of Postmodernity: An Enquiry into the Origins of Cultural Change.* London: Blackwell.

HBC (House Banking Committee). 1998. *Hearing on Hedge Fund Operations.* Full Committee, Committee on Banking and Financial Services, Washington, DC, October 1. http://commdocs.house.gov/committees/bank/hba51526.000/hba51526_of.htm.

———. 1999. *Hearing on Hedge Funds.* Subcommittee on Capital Markets, Securities, and Government Sponsored Enterprises of the Committee on Banking and Financial Services, U.S. House of Representatives, Washington, DC, March 3. http://commdocs.house.gov/committees/bank/hba55533.000/hba55533_of.htm.

Helleiner, Eric. 1993. "When Finance Was the Servant: International Capital Movements in the Bretton Woods Era." In *Finance and World Politics: Markets, Regimes and States in the Post-Hegemonic Era,* ed. Philip G. Cerny. London: Edward Elgar.

———. 1994. *States and the Reemergence of Global Finance: From Bretton Woods to the 1990s.* Ithaca: Cornell University Press.

———. 1999a. "Historicizing Territorial Currencies: Monetary Space and the Nation-State in North America." *Political Geography* 18: 309–39.

———. 1999b. "Denationalising Money? Economic Liberalism and the 'National Question' in Currency Affairs." In *Nation-States and Money: The Past, Present, and Future of National Currencies,* ed. Emily Gilbert and Eric Helleiner. London: Routledge.

Henwood, Doug. 1997. *Wall Street: How It Works and for Whom.* London: Verso.

Hieronymus, Thomas A. 1971. *Economics of Futures Trading: For Commercial and Personal Profit.* New York: Commodity Research Bureau.

Higgot, Richard. 1998. "The Asian Economic Crisis: A Study in the Politics of Resentment." *New Political Economy* 3 (3): 333–56.

Hilton, Boyd. 1988. *The Age of Atonement: The Influence of Evangelicalism on Social and Economic Thought, 1785–1865.* Oxford: Clarendon Press.

Hirschman, Albert O. 1997. *The Passions and the Interests: Political Arguments for Capitalism before Its Triumph*. 20th anniv. ed. Princeton: Princeton University Press.

Hobbes, Thomas. 1962 [1651]. *Leviathan: Or the Matter, Forme, and Power of a Commonwealth Ecclesiasticall and Civil*, ed. Michael Oakeshott. London: Collier Macmillan.

Hofstadter, Richard. 1955. *The Age of Reform*. New York: Vintage.

Holmes, Steven A. 2000. "Partisan Fight Flares Anew over Handling of the Census." *New York Times*, March 9.

Hooper, Charlotte. 1999. "Masculinities, IR, and the 'Gender Variable': A Cost-Benefit Analysis for (Sympathetic) Gender Sceptics." *Review of International Studies* 25 (3): 475–91.

———. 2001. *Manly States: Masculinities, International Relations, and Gender Politics*. New York: Columbia University Press.

Hopwood, Anthony G., and Peter Miller, eds. 1994. *Accounting as Social and Institutional Practice*. Cambridge: Cambridge University Press.

Horizon BBC Online. 1999. *The Midas Formula*. Transcript, December 2. http://www.bbc.co.uk/science/horizon/1999/midas_script.shtml.

Howe, James Hamilton. 1916 [1882]. *The Dragon and Juggernaut of Speculation, as Exemplified in Gambling in Prices of Our Food Products*. Seattle: Dragon Publishing Company.

Hubbard, George H. 1888. "The Economics of Speculation." *New Englander and Yale Review* 49 (220): 1–10.

Hutchinson, Frances, Mary Mellor, and Wendy Olsen. 2002. *The Politics of Money: Towards Sustainability and Economic Democracy*. London: Pluto Press.

Ingham, Geoffrey. 1999. "Capitalism, Money, and Banking: A Critique of Recent Historical Sociology." *British Journal of Sociology* 50 (1): 76–96.

———. 2001. "Fundamentals of a Theory of Money: Untangling Fine, Lapavitsas, and Zelizer." *Economy and Society* 30 (3): 304–23.

Ingrassia, Catherine. 1998. *Authorship, Commerce and Gender in Early Eighteenth-Century England*. Cambridge: Cambridge University Press.

Izquierdo, A. Javier. 2001. "Reliability at Risk: The Supervision of Financial Models as a Case Study for Reflexive Economic Sociology." *European Societies* 3 (1): 69–90.

Jessop, Bob, and Ngai-Ling Sum. 2001. "Pre-Disciplinary and Post-Disciplinary Perspectives." *New Political Economy* 6 (1): 89–101.

Jevons, William Stanley. 1865. "On the Variations of Prices and the Value of the Currency since 1782." *Journal of the Statistical Society of London* 28 (2): 294–320.

———. 1878. "Commercial Crises and Sun-Spots." *Nature* 19 (November 14): 33–36.

——. 1879. "Sun-Spots and Commercial Crises." *Nature* 19 (April 24): 588–90.

——. 1911 [1871]. *The Theory of Political Economy.* London: MacMillan.

——. 1995 [1862]. "On the Study of Periodic Commercial Fluctuations." In *The Foundations of Econometric Analysis,* ed. Mary S. Morgan and David F. Hendry. Cambridge: Cambridge University Press.

John, Peter. 2000. "MSCI Index Change to Alter Valuations and Portfolios." *Financial Times,* December 10.

Jorion, Philippe. 1999. "Risk Management Lessons from Long-Term Capital Management." *Social Science Research Network Working Paper Series,* June. http://papers2.ssrn.com/paper.taf?ABSTRACT_ID=169449.

Kahler, Miles. 2000. "The New International Financial Architecture and Its Limits." In *The Asian Financial Crisis and the Architecture of Global Finance,* ed. Gregory W. Noble and John Ravenhill. Cambridge: Cambridge University Press.

Kamp, Jurriaan. 2000. *Omdat Mensen er toe Doen: Naar een Economie voor Iedereen (Because People Matter: Toward an Economics for Everyone).* Rotterdam: Lemniscaat.

Kapstein, Ethan B. 1989. "Resolving the Regulator's Dilemma: International Coordination of Banking Regulations." *International Organization* 43 (2): 323–47.

Karpoff, Jonathan M. 1992. "Short Selling." In *New Palgrave Dictionary of Money and Finance,* volume 3, ed. Peter Newman, Murray Milgate, and John Eatwell. London: Macmillan.

Keenan, Thomas. 1997. *Fables of Responsibility: Aberrations and Predicaments in Ethics and Politics.* Stanford: Stanford University Press.

Keller, Evelyn Fox. 1985. *Reflections on Gender and Science.* New Haven: Yale University Press.

——. 1994. "The Paradox of Scientific Subjectivity." In *Rethinking Objectivity,* ed. Allan Megill. London: Duke University Press.

Kelly, Philip F. 2001. "Metaphors of Meltdown: Political Representations of Economic Space in the Asian Financial Crisis." *Environment and Planning D: Society and Space* 19 (6): 719–42.

Kennedy, Margrit. 1995. *Interest and Inflation Free Money.* Michigan: Seva International.

Kern, Stephen. 1983. *The Culture of Time and Space, 1880–1918.* Cambridge, MA: Harvard University Press.

Kindleberger, Charles P. 1993. *A Financial History of Western Europe.* 2nd ed. New York: Oxford University Press.

——. 1978. *Manias, Panics, and Crashes: A History of Financial Crises.* London: Macmillan.

Knorr Cetina, Karin, and Alex Preda. 2001. "The Epistemization of Economic Transactions." *Current Sociology* 49 (4): 27–44.

Kolman, Joe. 1997. "The World According to Nassim Taleb." *Derivatives Strategy*, December/January. http://www.derivativesstrategy.com/magazine/archive/1997/1296qa.asp.

Krasner, Stephen D. 1996. "The Accomplishments of International Political Economy." In *International Theory: Positivism and Beyond,* ed. Steve Smith, Ken Booth, and Marysia Zalewski. Cambridge: Cambridge University Press.

———. 2000. "Wars, Hotel Fires, and Plane Crashes." *Review of International Studies* 26 (1): 131–36.

Krugman, Paul. 1998. *What Happened to Asia?* Conference Address in Japan, January 22. http://web.mit.edu/krugman/www/DISINTER.html.

Kula, Witold. 1986. *Measures and Men,* trans. R. Szreter. Princeton: Princeton University Press.

Kynaston, David. 1988. *The Financial Times: A Centenary History.* London: Viking.

———. 1994. *The City of London.* Volume 1, *A World of Its Own, 1815–1890.* London: Chatto and Windus.

Laclau, Ernesto. 1990. *New Reflections on the Revolution of Our Time.* London: Verso.

Laffey, Mark. 2000. "Locating Identity: Performativity, Foreign Policy and State Action." *Review of International Studies* 26 (3): 429–44.

Langley, Paul. 2002. *World Financial Orders: An Historical International Political Economy.* London: Routledge.

———. 2004. "(Re)politicizing Global Financial Governance: What's 'New' About the 'New International Financial Architecture'"? *Global Networks: A Journal of Transnational Affairs* 4 (1): 69–87.

Langley, Paul, and Mary Mellor. 2002. "'Economy,' Sustainability and Sites of Transformative Space." *New Political Economy* 7 (1): 49–65.

Le Goff, Jacques. 1980. *Time, Work, and Culture in the Middle Ages.* Chicago: University of Chicago Press.

Levitt, Arthur. 2002. *Opening Statement.* Hearing on the Fall of Enron. Committee on Governmental Affairs, U.S. Senate, January 24. http://www.govt-aff.senate.gov/012402levitt.htm.

Lewis, Michael. 1989. *Liar's Poker: Rising through the Wreckage on Wall Street.* New York: Penguin.

———. 1999. "How the Eggheads Cracked." *New York Times Magazine,* January 24.

Leyshon, Andrew, and Nigel Thrift. 1997. *Money/Space: Geographies of Monetary Transformation.* London: Routledge.

———. 1999a. "Lists Come Alive: Electronic Systems of Knowledge and the Rise of Credit-Scoring in Retail Banking." *Economy and Society* 28 (3): 434–66.

———. 1999b. "Moral Geographies of Money." In *Nation-States and*

Money: The Past, Present and Future of National Currencies, ed. Eric Helleiner and Emily Gilbert. London: Routledge.

Leyshon, Andrew, Nigel Thrift, and Jonathan Pratt. 1998. "Reading Financial Services: Texts, Consumers and Financial Literacy." *Environment and Planning D: Society and Space* 16 (1): 29–55.

Ling, L. H. M. 2002. "Cultural Chauvinism and the Liberal International Order: 'West' versus 'Rest' in Asia's Financial Crisis." In *Power, Postcolonialism and International Relations,* ed. Geeta Chowdhry and Sheila Nair. London: Routledge.

Livingston, James. 1986. *Origins of the Federal Reserve System: Money, Class, and Corporate Capitalism, 1890–1913.* Ithaca: Cornell University Press.

Lloyd, Genevieve. 1984. *The Man of Reason: "Male" and "Female" in Western Philosophy.* London: Methuen.

Lowenstein, Roger. 2001. *When Genius Failed: The Rise and Fall of Long-Term Capital Management.* London: Fourth Estate.

Loy, David R. 2001. "Saving Time: A Buddhist Perspective on the End." In *TimeSpace: Geographies of Temporality,* ed. Jon May and Nigel Thrift. London: Routledge.

Luhmann, Niklas. 1993. *Risk: A Sociological Theory.* Berlin: Walter de Gruyter.

MacDougall, Ernest D. 1936. *Speculation and Gambling.* Boston: Stratford Company.

Machiavelli, Niccolò. 1997 [1532]. *The Prince,* trans. and ed. Angelo M. Codevilla. New Haven: Yale University Press.

Mackay, Charles. 1995 [1841]. *Extraordinary Popular Delusions and the Madness of Crowds.* Hertfordshire: Wordsworth Reference.

MacKenzie, Donald. 2000. "Fear in the Markets." *London Review of Books* 22 (8).

———. 2001. "Physics and Finance: S-Terms and Modern Finance as a Topic for Science Studies." *Science, Technology and Human Values* 26 (2): 115–44.

———. 2002. *Opening the Black Boxes of Global Finance.* Paper presented to the workshop "Approaches to Global Finance." University of Warwick, December 6–7.

———. 2003a. "An Equation and Its Worlds: Bricolage, Exemplars, Disunity and Performativity in Financial Economics." *Social Studies of Science* 33 (6): 831–68.

———. 2003b. "Long-Term Capital Management and the Sociology of Arbitrage." *Economy and Society* 32 (3): 349–80.

MacKenzie, Donald, and Yuval Millo. 2003. "Constructing a Market, Performing Theory: The Historical Sociology of a Financial Derivatives Exchange." *American Journal of Sociology* 109 (1): 107–45.

MacKenzie, W. Douglass. 1896. *The Ethics of Gambling.* Philadelphia: Henry Altemus.

Mackie, Charles. 1819. *The History of the Abbey, Palace and Chapel-Royal of Holyroodhouse.* Edinburgh: J. Hay.

Mackintosh, James, and Sathnam Sanghera. 1999. "All in a Day's Trade for Gambling Pharmacists." *Financial Times,* May 25.

Malkiel, Burton G. 1990. *A Random Walk Down Wall Street.* 5th ed. New York: Norton.

Marchand, Marianne, and Anne Sisson Runyan. 2000. "Feminist Sightings of Global Restructuring." In *Gender and Global Restructuring: Sightings, Sites and Resistances,* ed. Marianne Marchand and Anne Sisson Runyan. London: Routledge.

Marshall, Alfred. 1961 [1890]. *Principles of Economics,* ed. C. W. Guillebaud. London: Macmillan.

———. 1966 [1885]. "The Graphic Method of Statistics." In *Memorials of Alfred Marshall,* ed. A. C. Pigou. New York: Augustus M. Kelley.

Martin, H. S. 1919. *The New York Stock Exchange.* New York: Francis Emery Fitch.

Martin, Peter. 2000. "The Internet Enigma." *Financial Times,* June 2.

Martin, Ron. 1994. "Stateless Monies, Global Financial Integration and National Economic Autonomy: The End of Geography?" In *Money, Power, Space,* ed. Stuart Corbridge, Nigel Thrift, and Andrew Leyshon. London: Basil Blackwell.

Maurer, Bill. 1999. "Forget Locke? From Proprietor to Risk-Bearer in New Logics of Finance." *Public Culture* 11 (2): 365–85.

———. 2001a. "Engineering and Islamic Future: Speculation on Islamic Financial Alternatives." *Anthropology Today* 17 (1): 8–29.

———. 2001b. "Islands in the Net: Rewiring Technological and Financial Circuits in the 'Offshore' Caribbean." *Comparative Studies in Society and History* 43 (3): 467–501.

———. 2002. "Repressed Futures: Financial Derivatives' Theological Unconscious." *Economy and Society* 31 (1): 15–36.

———. 2003. "Uncanny Exchanges: The Possibilities and Failures of 'Making Change' with Alternative Monetary Forms." *Environment and Planning D: Society and Space* 21 (3): 317–40.

May, A. Wilfred. 1939. "Financial Regulation Abroad: The Contrasts with American Technique." *Journal of Political Economy* 47 (4): 457–96.

May, Jon, and Nigel Thrift. 2001. Introduction to *TimeSpace: Geographies of Temporality,* ed. Jon May and Nigel Thrift. London: Routledge.

McCusker, John J., and Cora Gravesteijn. 1991. *The Beginnings of Commercial and Financial Journalism.* Amsterdam: NEHA.

McDowell, Linda. 1997. *Capital Culture: Gender at Work in the City.* London: Blackwell.

McNay, Lois. 1994. *Foucault: A Critical Introduction*. Cambridge, UK: Polity Press.

McWilliam, G. H. 1995. Translator's introduction to *The Decameron*, by Giovanni Boccaccio. 2nd ed. London: Penguin.

Meeker, J. Edward. 1930. *Measuring the Stock Market*. An Address before the American Statistical Association, Cleveland, Ohio, December 30.

Melamed, Leo. 1972. *A Futures Market in Currency*. Presented to the New York Society of Security Analysts, New York, April 19. http://www.leomelamed.com/Speeches/72-fut.htm.

———. 1974a. *H.R. 13113I and the Birth of the CFTC*. Testimony before the United States Senate Committee on Agriculture, Nutrition and Forestry, May 14. http://www.leomelamed.com/Speeches/74-cftc.htm.

———. 1974b. *The Sleazy Speculator*. Presented at the University of Chicago Law School, November 27. http://www.leomelamed.com/Speeches/74-spec.htm.

Merton, Robert C. 1994. "Influence of Mathematical Models in Finance on Practice: Past, Present and Future." *Philosophical Transactions of the Royal Society London A* 347: 451–52.

———. 1997. *Autobiography of Robert C. Merton*. http://www.nobel.se/economics/laureates/1997/merton-autobio.html.

———. 1998. "Application of Option-Pricing Theory: Twenty-Five Years Later." *American Economic Review* 88 (3): 323–49.

Miller, Peter. 1998. "The Margins of Accounting." In *The Laws of the Markets*, ed. Michel Callon. Oxford: Blackwell.

Miller, Peter, and Christopher Napier. 1993. "Genealogies of Calculation." *Accounting, Organizations and Society* 18 (7/8): 631–47.

Miller, Peter, and Nikolas Rose. 1990. "Governing Economic Life." *Economy and Society* 19 (1): 1–31.

Mirowski, Philip. 1991. "The When, the How and the Why of Mathematical Expression in the History of Economic Analysis." *Journal of Economic Perspectives* 5 (1): 145–57.

Mishkin, Frederic S. 1992. *The Economics of Money, Banking and Financial Markets*. New York: Harper Collins.

Montagna, Paul. 1990. "Accounting Rationality and Financial Legitimation." In *The Social Organization of the Economy*, ed. Sharon Zukin and Paul DiMaggio. Cambridge: Cambridge University Press.

Moody, John. 1906. *The Art of Wall Street Investing*. New York: Moody Corporation.

Moore, Charles. 1790. *A Full Inquiry into the Subject of Suicide: to which are added (as being closely connected with the subject) two Treatises on Duelling and Gaming*. London: Printed for J. F. and C. Rivington.

Moreau, Dan. 1999. "Money: How Now the Dow." *Modern Maturity* May/June. http://www.aarp.org/mmaturity/may_jun99/dow.html.

Morgan, E. Victor, and W. A. Thomas. 1962. *The Stock Exchange: Its History and Functions*. London: Elek Books.

Morgan, Mary S. 1990. *The History of Econometric Ideas*. Cambridge: Cambridge University Press.

Morgenson, Gretchen. 2002. "Accord Highlights Wall St. Failures." *New York Times,* December 20.

Morgenson, Gretchen, and Patrick McGeehan. 2002. "Wall Street Firms are Ready to Pay $1 Billion in Fines." *New York Times,* December 20.

Muldrew, Craig. 1998. *The Economy of Obligation: The Culture of Credit and Social Relations in Early Modern England*. London: Macmillan.

Muniesa, Fabian. 2000. "Performing Prices: The Case of Price Discovery Automation in the Financial Markets." In *Ökonomie und Gesellschaft Jahrbuch 16: Facts and Figures: Economic Representations and Practices,* ed. Herbert Kalthoff, Richard Rottenburg, and Hans-Jürgen Wagener. Marburg: Metropolis Verlag.

Munting, Roger. 1996. *An Economic and Social History of Gambling in Britain and the USA*. Manchester: Manchester University Press.

Murphy, Craig. 1994. *International Organization and Industrial Change: Global Governance since 1850*. Cambridge, UK: Polity Press.

Neal, Larry. 1990. *The Rise of Financial Capitalism: International Capital Markets in the Age of Reason*. Cambridge: Cambridge University Press.

Neild, James. 1802. *An Account of the Rise, Progress and the Present State of the Society for the Discharge and Relief of Persons Imprisoned for Small Debts throughout England and Wales*. London: Nichols and Son.

Nelson, Julie A. 1996. *Feminism, Objectivity and Economics*. London: Routledge.

Nelson, S. A. 1964 [1903]. *The ABC of Stock Speculation*. Vermont: Fraser Publishing.

New York Cotton Exchange. 1892. "Protest of the New York Cotton Exchange Against the Following Bills: H.R. 2699, S. 685, and S. 1268." In *Dealings in "Options" and "Futures": Protests, Memorials and Arguments against Bills Introduced in the 52nd Congress*. New York: L. H. Biglow.

Nicholson, Colin. 1994. *Writing and the Rise of Finance: Capital Satires of the Early Eighteenth Century*. Cambridge: Cambridge University Press.

Nietzsche, Friedrich. 1990 [1886]. *Beyond Good and Evil,* trans. R. J. Hollingdale. London: Penguin Books.

———. 1996 [1887]. *On the Genealogy of Morals,* trans. Douglas Smith. Oxford: Oxford University Press.

Nitzan, Jonathan. 1998. "Differential Accumulation: Towards a New Political Economy of Capital." *Review of International Political Economy* 5 (2): 169–216.

Noble, Gregory W., and John Ravenhill, eds. 2000. *The Asian Financial*

Crisis and the Architecture of Global Finance. Cambridge: Cambridge University Press.

Norris, Frank. 1936 [1902]. "A Deal in Wheat." In *An Anthology of Famous American Stories,* ed. Angus Burrell and Bennet Cerf. New York: Modern Library.

North, Peter. 1999. "Explorations in Heterotopia: Local Exchange Trading Schemes (LETS) and the Micropolitics of Money and Livelihood." *Environment and Planning D: Society and Space* 17 (1): 69–86.

O'Brien, Timothy, and Laura M. Holson. 1998. "A Hedge Fund's Stars Didn't Tell, and Savvy Financiers Didn't Ask." *New York Times,* October 23, C22.

OECD. 2000. *Economic Survey of the United Kingdom, Assessment and Recommendations.* Paris, 31 May. http://www.oecd.org/dataoecd/50/49/1827210.pdf.

O'Malley, Michael. 1994. "Specie and Species: Race and the Money Question in Nineteenth-Century America." *American Historical Review* 99 (2): 369–95.

———. 1996. *Keeping Watch: A History of American Time.* Washington, DC: Smithsonian Institution Press.

Osteen, Mark, and Martha Woodmansee. 1999. "Taking Account of the New Economic Criticism: An Historical Introduction." In *The New Economic Criticism: Studies at the Intersection of Literature and Economics,* ed. Mark Osteen and Martha Woodmansee. London: Routledge.

Palmer, Colin. 1981. *Human Cargoes: The British Slave Trade to Spanish America, 1700–1739.* Urbana: University of Illinois Press.

Parks, Lawrence. 1999. *Written Testimony Submitted for the Record.* Subcommittee on Capital Markets, House Committee on Banking, Hearing on Hedge Funds, March 3. http://financialservices.house.gov/banking/3399park.pdf.

Partnoy, Frank. 2002. *Testimony before the United States Senate Committee on Governmental Affairs.* Hearing on the Fall of Enron, the Committee on Governmental Affairs, U.S. Senate, January 24. http://www.senate.gov/~gov_affairs/012402partnoy.htm.

Patch, Howard R. 1967 [1927]. *The Goddess Fortuna in Mediaeval Literature.* London: Frank Cass.

Patomäki, Heikki, and Colin Wight. 2000. "After Postpositivism? The Promises of Critical Realism." *International Studies Quarterly* 44 (2): 213–37.

Pauly, Louis. 1997. *Who Elected the Bankers?* Ithaca: Cornell University Press.

Pearson, Ruth. 2003. "Argentina's Barter Network: New Currency for New Times?" *Bulletin of Latin American Research* 22 (2): 214–30.

Peterson, V. Spike. 1992. "Transgressing Boundaries: Theories of Knowledge, Gender and International Relations." *Millennium* 21 (2): 183–206.

Pettifor, Ann. 1998. "The Economic Bondage of Debt—and the Birth of a New Movement." *New Left Review* 230: 115–22.

———. 2001. "Concordats for Debt Cancellation: Making Relief Work Twice." June. http://www.jubilee2000uk.org/analysis/articles/Ann_concordats_debt_cancellation.htm.

Pitkin, Hanna Fenichel. 1984. *Fortune Is a Woman: Gender and Politics in the Thought of Niccolò Machiavelli.* Berkeley: University of California Press.

Pocock, J. G. A. 1975. *The Machiavellian Moment: Florentine Political Thought and the Atlantic Republican Tradition.* Princeton: Princeton University Press.

———. 1985. *Virtue, Commerce, and History.* Cambridge: Cambridge University Press.

Poovey, Mary. 1988. *Uneven Developments: The Ideological Work of Gender in Mid-Victorian England.* London: Virago.

———. 1991. "Figures of Arithmetic, Figures of Speech: The Discourse of Statistics in the 1830s." In *Questions of Evidence: Proof, Practice, and Persuasion across the Disciplines,* ed. James Chandler, Arnold I. Davidson, and Harry Harootunian. Chicago: University of Chicago Press.

———. 1998. *A History of the Modern Fact: Problems of Knowledge in the Sciences of Wealth and Society.* Chicago: University of Chicago Press.

Popke, E. Jeffrey. 1994. "Recasting Geopolitics: The Discursive Scripting of the International Monetary Fund." *Political Geography* 13 (3): 255–69.

Porter, Theodore M. 1986. *The Rise of Statistical Thinking, 1820–1900.* Princeton: Princeton University Press.

———. 1994. "Objectivity as Standardization: The Rhetoric of Impersonality in Measurement, Statistics, and Cost-Benefit Analysis." In *Rethinking Objectivity,* ed. Allan Megill. London: Duke University Press.

———. 1995a. "Precision and Trust: Early Victorian Insurance and the Politics of Calculation." In *The Values of Precision,* ed. M. Norton Wise. Princeton: Princeton University Press.

———. 1995b. *Trust in Numbers: The Pursuit of Objectivity in Science and Public Life.* Princeton: Princeton University Press.

Porter, Tony. 1999. "The Late-Modern Knowledge Structure and World Politics." In *Approaches to Global Governance Theory,* ed. Martin Hewson and Timothy J. Sinclair. New York: State University of New York Press.

Posner, Richard A. 1998. "Rational Choice, Behavioral Economics, and the Law." *Stanford Law Review* 50 (May): 1551–76.

Power, Michael. 1997. *The Audit Society: Rituals of Verification.* Oxford: Oxford University Press.

Preda, Alex. 2000. "Financial Knowledge and the 'Science of the Market' in England and France in the Nineteenth Century." In *Ökonomie und Gesellschaft Jahrbuch 16: Facts and Figures: Economic Representations and Practices,* ed. Herbert Kalthoff, Richard Rottenburg, and Hans-Jürgen Wagener. Marburg: Metropolis Verlag.

———. 2001. "The Rise of the Popular Investor: Financial Knowledge and Investing in England and France, 1840–1880." *Sociological Quarterly* 42 (2): 205–32.

———. 2002. "Financial Knowledge, Documents, and the Structures of Financial Activities." *Journal of Contemporary Ethnography* 31 (2): 207–239.

———. Forthcoming. "On Ticks and Tapes: Financial Knowledge, Communicative Practices, and Information Technologies in Nineteenth-Century Financial Markets." *American Journal of Sociology.*

Pujo Committee. 1912. *Money Trust Investigation: Investigation of Financial and Monetary Conditions in the United States under House Resolutions Nos. 429 and 504, before the Subcommittee on Banking and Currency.* Washington, DC: Government Printing Office.

Reddy, Sanjay G. 1996. "Claims to Expert Knowledge and the Subversion of Democracy: The Triumph of Risk over Uncertainty." *Economy and Society* 25 (2): 222–54.

Richards, R. D. 1934. "The Lottery in the History of English Government Finance." *Economic History* 3 (9): 57–76. Supplement to *Economic Journal.*

Robinson, Gwen. 1997a. "Backward in Coming Forward." *Financial Times Derivatives Survey,* June 27, iv.

———. 1997b. "Japan to Lift Derivatives Ban." *Financial Times,* January 29, 34.

Rose, Nikolas. 1993. "Government, Authority, and Expertise in Advanced Liberalism." *Economy and Society* 22 (3): 283–29.

———. 1999. *Powers of Freedom: Reframing Political Thought.* Cambridge: Cambridge University Press.

Rosenberg, Jerry M. 1982. *Inside the Wall Street Journal: The History and the Power of Dow Jones and Company and America's Most Influential Newspaper.* New York: MacMillan.

Rosenberger, Leif Roderick. 1997. "Southeast Asia's Currency Crisis: A Diagnosis and Prescription." *Contemporary Southeast Asia* 19 (3): 223–51.

Ross, Stephen A. 1992. "Stock Market Indices." In *The New Palgrave Dictionary of Money and Finance,* volume 3, ed. Peter Newman, Murray Milgate, and John Eatwell. London: Macmillan.

Rotman, Brian. 1987. *Signifying Nothing: The Semiotics of Zero*. London: Macmillan.

Rowe, Jonathan. 1999. "The Growth Consensus Unravels." *Dollars and Sense Magazine*, July/August. http://www.dollarsandsense.org/archives/1999/0799rowe.html.

Royal Swedish Academy of Sciences. 1997. *Additional Background Material on the Bank of Sweden Prize in Economic Sciences in Memory of Alfred Nobel 1997*. http://www.nobel.se/economics/laureates/1997/back.html.

Ruggie, John Gerard. 1998. *Constructing the World Polity: Essays on International Institutionalization*. London: Routledge.

Sachs, Jeffrey. 1997. "Lessons from the Thais." *Financial Times*, July 30.

Said, Edward. 1994. *Orientalism*. New York: Vintage.

Sassen, Saskia. 1991. *The Global City: London, New York, Tokyo*. Princeton: Princeton University Press.

———. 1994. *Cities in a World Economy*. London: Pine Forge Press.

Schabacker, R. W. 1967 [1934]. *Stock Market Profits*. Vermont: Fraser Publishing.

Schabas, Margaret. 1989. "Alfred Marshall, W. Stanley Jevons, and the Mathematisation of Economics." *Isis* 80 (301): 60–73.

Scholes, Myron S. 2000. "Crisis and Risk Management." *American Economic Review* 90 (2): 17–21.

Scott, Walter. 1822. *The Fortunes of Nigel*, volume 2. Edinburgh: Arthur Constable.

Seyfang, Gill. 2000. "The Euro, the Pound, and the Shell in our Pockets: Rationales for Complementary Currencies in a Global Economy." *New Political Economy* 5 (2): 227–46.

Shapin, Steven. 1994. *A Social History of Truth: Civility and Science in Seventeenth-Century England*. Chicago: University of Chicago Press.

Shapiro, Michael J. 1993. *Reading "Adam Smith": Desire, History, and Value*. London: Sage.

———. 1997. "Value Eruptions and Modalities: White Male Rage in the '80s and '90s." *Cultural Values* 1 (1): 58–80.

Shapiro, Michael J., and Hayward R. Alker, eds. 1996. *Challenging Boundaries: Global Flows, Territorial Identities*. Minneapolis: University of Minnesota Press.

Shell, Marc. 1982. *Money, Language, and Thought: Literary and Philosophical Economies from the Medieval to the Modern Era*. Los Angeles: University of California Press.

———. 1995. *Art and Money*. Chicago: University of Chicago Press.

———. 1999. "The Issue of Representation." In *The New Economic Criticism: Studies at the Intersection of Literature and Economics*, ed. Mark Osteen and Martha Woodmansee. London: Routledge.

Sherman, Sandra. 1996. *Finance and Fictionality in the Early Eighteenth Century: Accounting for Defoe.* Cambridge: Cambridge University Press.

Shiller, Robert. 2000. *Irrational Exuberance.* Princeton: Princeton University Press.

Showalter, Elaine. 1997. *Hystories: Hysterical Epidemics and Modern Culture.* London: Picador.

Silverman, Gary, and Joshua Chaffin. 2000. "Hedge Fund Guru Back in the Game." *Financial Times,* August 21, 9.

Simmel, Georg. 1990 [1900]. *The Philosophy of Money,* ed. David Frisby, trans. Tom Bottomore and David Frisby. London: Routledge and Kegan Paul.

Simmons, E. H. H. 1930. *The Principal Causes of the Stock Market Crisis of Nineteen Twenty Nine.* Address at the Thirty-First Annual Dinner of the Transportation Club, the Pennsylvania Railroad. Archives of the New York Stock Exchange.

Sinclair, Timothy J. 1994. "Between State and Market: Hegemony and Institutions of Collective Action under Conditions of International Capital Mobility." *Policy Sciences* 27: 447–66.

———. 1999a. "Bond-Rating Agencies and Coordination in the Global Political Economy." In *Private Authority in International Affairs,* ed. A. Claire Cutler, Virginia Haufler, and Tony Porter. New York: State University of New York Press.

———. 1999b. "Synchronic Global Governance and the International Political Economy of the Commonplace." In *Approaches to Global Governance Theory,* ed. Martin Hewson and Timothy J. Sinclair. New York: State University of New York Press.

Sinclair, Timothy J., and Kenneth P. Thomas, eds. 2001. *Structure and Agency in International Capital Mobility.* London: Palgrave.

Smelt, Simon. 1980. "Money's Place in Society." *British Journal of Sociology* 31 (2): 204–23.

Smith, Charles William. 1906. *International Commercial and Financial Gambling in "Options" and "Futures": The Economic Ruin of the World.* London: P. S. King and Son.

Smith, Edgar Lawrence. 1930. "The Break in the Credit Chain." *Atlantic Monthly* 145 (January): 108–13.

Soederberg, Susanne. 2002. "The New International Financial Architecture: Imposed Leadership and 'Emerging Markets.'" In *Socialist Register 2002: A World of Contradictions,* ed. Leo Panitch and Colin Leys. London: Merlin Press.

Soros, George. 1994. *The Theory of Reflexivity.* Speech delivered to the Massachusetts Institute of Technology Department of Economics World

Economy Laboratory Conference, Washington, DC, April 26. http://
www.soros.org/textfiles/speeches/042694_Theory_of_Reflexivity.txt.

———. 1997. "The Capitalist Threat." *Atlantic Monthly,* February, 45–58.

———. 1998. *The Crisis of Global Capitalism: Open Society Endangered.*
New York: Public Affairs.

———. 1999. "Global Capital Markets: An Exchange." *New Republic,*
April 12. http://www.soros.org/textfiles/writings/041299_Exchange.txt.

———. 2001. "The New Global Financial Architecture." In *On the Edge:
Living with Global Capitalism,* ed. Will Hutton and Anthony Giddens.
London: Vintage.

Spitzer, Eliot. 2002a. "Merrill Lynch Stock Rating System Found Biased
by Undisclosed Conflicts of Interest." Press release, Office of New York
State Attorney General, New York, April 8. http://www.oag.state.ny.us/
press/2002/apr/apr08b_02.html.

———. 2002b. *Testimony.* Hearing on Corporate Governance, U.S. Senate, Committee on Commerce, Science and Technology, June 26. http://
www.oag.state.ny.us/press/reports/testimony7.pdf.

Spring, Samuel. 1931. "Whirlwinds of Speculation." *Atlantic Monthly* 147
(April): 477–86.

Stäheli, Urs. 2002. "Fatal Attraction? Popular Modes of Inclusion in the
Economic System." *Soziale Systeme* 8 (1): 110–23.

Stallabrass, Julian. 2001. *Art Now: Art and Money Online.* Introduction to the Art and Money Online Symposium, Tate Modern, London,
May 4.

Starr, Paul. 1987. "The Sociology of Official Statistics." In *The Politics of
Numbers,* ed. William Alonso and Paul Starr. New York: Russell Sage
Foundation.

Stein, Jeremy. 2001. "Reflections on Time, Time-Space Compression and
Technology in the Nineteenth Century." In *TimeSpace: Geographies of
Temporality,* ed. Jon May and Nigel Thrift. London: Routledge.

Stevens, Albert Clark. 1892. "The Utility of Speculation in Modern Commerce." *Political Science Quarterly* 7 (3): 419–30.

Stigler, Stephen M. 1986. *The History of Statistics: The Measurement of
Uncertainty Before 1900.* Cambridge, MA: Belknap Press.

Stillman, Richard J. 1986. *Dow Jones Industrial Average: History and
Role in an Investment Strategy.* Homewood, IL: Dow Jones-Irwin.

Stix, Gary. 1998. "A Calculus of Risk." *Scientific American.* http://www
.sciam.com/1998/0598issue/0598stix.html, accessed May 2002.

Stonham, Paul. 1999a. "Too Close to the Hedge: The Case of Long Term
Capital Management LP. Part One: Hedge Fund Analytics." *European
Management Journal* 17 (1): 282–89.

———. 1999b. "Too Close to the Hedge: The Case of Long Term Capital

Management LP. Part Two: Near Collapse and Rescue." *European Management Journal* 17 (4): 382–90.

Strange, Susan. 1986. *Casino Capitalism*. London: Basil Blackwell.

———. 1988. *States and Markets*. London: Pinter.

———. 1998. *Mad Money*. Manchester: Manchester University Press.

———. 1999. "The Westfailure System." *Review of International Studies* 25 (3): 345–54.

Targett, Simon. 2000. "Old Economy versus New Economy: Where P/E Fails Try Eye-Whites." *Financial Times*, March 18.

Taylor, Telford. 1933. "Trading in Commodity Futures: A New Standard of Legality?" *Yale Law Journal* 48 (1): 63–106.

Tett, Gillian. 1998. "Japan: Traders Gamble on an Anomaly." *Financial Times Derivatives Survey*, July 17, 6.

Teweles, Richard J., Edward S. Bradley, and Ted M. Teweles. 1992. *The Stock Market*. New York: Wiley.

Thaler, Richard. 1997. "Giving Markets a Human Dimension." *Financial Times: Mastering Finance*, June 16, 6: 2–5.

Thaler, Richard, Christine Jolls, and Cass R. Sunstein. 1998. "A Behavioral Approach to Law and Economics." *Stanford Law Review* 50 (May): 1471–1550.

Thomas, Landon, and Gretchen Morgenson. 2003. "Analysts to Pay Millions in Fines." *New York Times*, April 28.

Thomson, Adam. 1998. "Colombia's Municipalities Look to Lotteries to Fill Finance Gap." *Financial Times*, September 17, 4.

Thornhill, John. 1998. "Russia Seeks to Demystify Derivatives." *Financial Times*, July 6, 2.

Thrift, Nigel. 1994. "On the Social and Cultural Determinants of International Financial Centres: The Case of the City of London." In *Money, Power, Space*, ed. Stuart Corbridge, Ron Martin, and Nigel Thrift. Oxford: Basil Blackwell.

———. 1996. "Shut Up and Dance, or, Is the World Economy Knowable?" In *The Global Economy in Transition*, ed. P. W. Daniels and W. F. Lever. London: Longman.

———. 1998. "The Rise of Soft Capitalism." In *An Unruly World? Globalization, Governance and Geography*, ed. Andrew Herod, Gearóid Ó Tuathail, and Susan M. Roberts. London: Routledge.

———. 2001a. "Chasing Capitalism." *New Political Economy* 6 (3): 375–80.

———. 2001b. "It's the Romance, Not the Finance, That Makes the Business Worth Pursuing." *Economy and Society* 30 (4): 412–32.

———. 2002. "Performing Cultures in the New Economy." In *Cultural Economy*, ed. Paul du Gay and Michael Pryke. London: Sage.

Tickell, Adam. 1996. "Making a Melodrama Out of a Crisis: Reinterpreting the Collapse of Barings Bank." *Environment and Planning D: Society and Space* 14 (1): 5–33.

———. 1998. "Creative Finance and the Local State: The Hammersmith and Fulham Swaps Affair." *Political Geography* 17 (7): 865–81.

———. 2000. "Unstable Futures: Creating Risk in International Finance." *Geoforum* 31 (1): 87–99.

———. 2003. "Cultures of Money." In *Handbook of Cultural Geography*, ed. Kay Anderson, Mona Domosh, Steve Pile, and Nigel Thrift. London: Sage.

Truong, Thanh-Dam. 1999. "The Underbelly of the Tiger: Gender and the Demystification of the Asian Miracle." *Review of International Political Economy* 6 (2): 133–65.

Tsing, Anna. 2001. "Inside the Economy of Appearances." In *Globalization*, ed. Arjun Appadurai. Durham, NC: Duke University Press.

Turner, Brian. 1986. "Simmel, Rationalisation, and the Sociology of Money." *Sociological Review* 34: 93–114.

Underhill, Geoffrey R. D. 1997. "Private Markets and Public Responsibility in a Global System: Conflict and Co-operation in Transnational Banking and Securities Regulation." In *The New World Order in International Finance*, ed. Geoffrey Underhill. New York: St. Martin's Press.

UNICEF. 2000. "A League Table of Child Poverty in Rich Nations." *Innocenti Report Card*, no. 1, June. Innocenti Research Centre, Florence, Italy. http://www.unicef-icdc.org/cgi-bin/unicef/Lunga.sql?ProductID=226.

United States Magazine and Democratic Review. 1846. "Stock Gambling." 18 (92): 83–90.

Untermyer, Samuel. 1915. "Speculation on the Stock Exchanges and Public Regulation of the Exchanges." *American Economic Review* 5 (1): 24–68.

Ulman, Erik. 2001. "A Corner in Wheat: An Analysis." *Senses of Cinema* 14. http://www.sensesofcinema.com/contents/01/14/cornerwheat.html.

Usborne, David. 1999. "She's Got It Made." *Independent On Sunday*, March 21.

Valentine, Jeremy. 2001. "I.O.U. Nothing." In *Capital: A Project by Neil Cummings and Marysia Lewandowska*. London: Tate Publishing.

Velthuis, Olav. 2002. "In Boggs We Trust." *Tout-Fait: The Marcel Duchamp Studies Online Journal* 2 (4). http://www.toutfait.com/issues/volume2/issue_4/articles/velthuis/velthuis1.html.

Visser, Wayne A. M., and Alastair MacIntosh. 1998. "A Short Review of the Historical Critique of Usury." *Accounting, Business and Financial History* 8 (2): 175–89.

Wade, Robert, and Frank Veneroso. 1998a. "The Asian Crisis: The High Debt Model Versus the Wall Street-Treasury-IMF Complex." *New Left Review* 228: 3–24.

———. 1998b. "The Gathering World Slump and the Battle over Capital Controls." *New Left Review* 231: 13–42.

Walker, R. B. J. 1989. "The Prince and 'The Pauper': Tradition, Modernity, and Practice in the Theory of International Relations." In *International/ Intertextual Relations: Postmodern Readings of World Politics,* ed. James DerDerian and Michael J. Shapiro. Lexington, MA: Lexington Books.

Ward, Lucy. 2001. "MPs Attack Emergency Loans to Poor." *Guardian,* April 4, 10.

Warner, John DeWitt. 1894. *Anti-Option Legislation—Paternal Interference with Business.* Speech in the House of Representatives, Washington, DC, June 18. Archives of the New York Public Library.

Warwick, Andrew. 1995. "The Laboratory of Theory or What's Exact about the Exact Sciences?" In *The Values of Precision,* ed. M. Norton Wise. Princeton: Princeton University Press.

Wasendorf, Russell. 2003. "Innovation Deserves More Than 15 Minutes of Fame." *SFO Magazine,* June. http://www.sfomagazine.com/featurestory_print.asp?ID=17, accessed June 2003.

Wendt, Lloyd. 1982. *The Wall Street Journal: The Story of Dow Jones and the Nation's Business Newspaper.* Chicago: Rand McNally.

Wenschler, Lawrence. 1999. *Boggs: A Comedy of Values.* Chicago: University of Chicago Press.

Werner, Walter. 1975. "Adventure in Social Control of Finance: The National Market System for Securities." *Columbia Law Review* 75 (7): 1233–90.

White, Horace. 1909. "The Hughes Investigation." *Journal of Political Economy* 17 (8): 528–40.

Whitney, Richard. 1930. *The Work of the New York Stock Exchange in the Panic of 1929.* Address delivered before the Boston Association of Stock Exchange Firms, Algonquin Club, Boston, Massachusetts, June 10. Archives of the New York Stock Exchange.

Wight, Colin. 1999. "MetaCampbell: Epistemological Problematics of Perspectivism." *Review of International Studies* (25) 2: 311–16.

Williams, David. 1999. "Constructing the Economic Space: The World Bank and the Making of *Homo oeconomicus.*" *Millennium* 28 (1): 79–99.

Williams, Eric. 1944. *Capitalism and Slavery.* Chapel Hill: University of North Carolina Press.

Winjum, James Ole. 1972. *The Role of Accounting in the Economic Development of England, 1500–1750.* Urbana, IL: Center for International Education and Research in Accounting.

World Bank. 2001. *Financial Impact of the HIPC Initiative: First 22 Country Cases.* HIPC Unit, March 1. http://www.worldbank.org/hipc/Financial_Impact.pdf.

Young, Kung. 1999. "Risky Business." *The Banker* 149 (876): 70–71.

Zelizer, Viviana A. Rotman. 1983. *Morals and Markets: The Development of Life Insurance in the United States*. New Brunswick: Transaction Books.

———. 1994. *The Social Meaning of Money: Pin Money, Paychecks and Other Currencies*. Princeton: Princeton University Press.

———. 1999. "Official Standardisation Versus Social Differentiation in Americans' Uses of Money." In *Nation-States and Money: The Past, Present and Future of National Currencies*, ed. Emily Gilbert and Eric Helleiner. London: Routledge.

Index

Fabian, Ann, 69, 80
faith, xviii–xix, xxiv, 6, 114–15, 137
Fama, Eugene, 126–27
farmers, 60–61, 65, 111–13
fictitious commodities, 60–61, 73
finance: depoliticization of, x, 2–3,
    123–24, 135, 147–48, 173; and
    information, 6, 9, 77–79, 89,
    126; linear history of, 15–17;
    repoliticization of, xxv–xxvi,
    3, 14, 152–53, 161, 171; as
    science, 125–32; as system,
    3–5, 22–23, 41, 101, 104–5,
    116–19, 146–50, 162. See also
    speculation
Financial Revolution, 25
Financial Times, 102
foresight, 32, 35, 71, 78–79, 83, 95,
    108, 119, 173
Fortuna, 29–31, 38, 41, 171–75
fortune, x, 21, 30, 40, 58, 180, 182;
    wheel of, 32, 41–42
Foucault, Michel: on power, 110,
    162; on discourse, 9; on gene-
    alogy, 1, 3, 13–14, 19–20, 151;
    on governmentality, 91–92; on
    hysteria, 40; on moral problema-
    tization, 53–54, 81; on normali-
    zation, 121, 124; on resistance,
    145, 152, 178; on responsibility,
    180; on self-government, 35–36;
    on truth production, 9, 124
Franzen, Jonathan, 177, 181–83
freedom. *See* resistance
free market, 95–96, 100, 148, 179
futures, 59–60, 65–67, 71–75,
    99–100, 129–32, 162, 189, 193

gambling, ix, 65–68, 99, 111,
    129–30, 134, 155, 172–73,
    179; moral problematization
    of, 50–57, 80, 84; by women,

56, 80–81. *See also* lotteries;
    speculation
Gaming Act, 57, 64
Garrett, Garet, 62
GDP, 163, 195
gender, 6, 26–45, 56, 80, 115, 129,
    147, 155, 168, 173, 188–89, 195.
    See also masculinity
genealogy, 13–20, 150–51, 179
gentleman, 6, 27, 38, 116
Germain, Randall, xvi, 151
Gibson, George Rutledge, 76–77,
    173
Gibson, Thomas, 78
Gibson-Graham, J. K., 150
gift, 169–70
Gill, Stephen, 10, 149–50, 176,
    194–95
global finance, 3, 141, 146–50
globalization, 48–50, 129, 147
governmentality, 9, 91–92
Goux, Jean-Joseph, xix, 95
Grain Futures Act, 99–100
Green, Hetty, 84–85
greenback debate, xvii–xix
Greenspan, Alan, 39, 117, 133–35,
    194
Griffith, D. W., 111–12

Hacking, Ian, 50, 90–91, 94, 139
Hardy, Charles O., 83–84
Harvey, David, xxiii
Hatch bill, 61, 75, 190
hearing on hedge funds. *See* U.S.
    Congress
Hedge Fund Disclosure Act,
    135–36
hedge funds, 135–36, 194. *See also*
    Long-Term Capital Management
hegemony, 150–51, 153, 195
Helleiner, Eric, xxiv, 123, 125, 147
Henwood, Doug, 120

U.S. Congress, 133–36, 190
U.S. Supreme Court, 67–68,
71–73, 88, 98–100
usury, 108, 190

value, xiii–xvi, 169–70
value-at-risk (VaR), 138–39
virtue, x, 28, 31–34, 37–39, 43, 58,
79, 89, 95, 121

Wall Street, 85, 177. *See also* New
York Stock Exchange
Wall Street Journal, 89, 102–5, 116
White, Horace, 97
World Bank, 158–61, 181

Zelizer, Viviana, xvii, 11, 53, 90,
167–68, 191

Marieke de Goede is lecturer in political history and international relations at the Faculty of Humanities of the University of Amsterdam. Her work has appeared in *Economy and Society, Environment and Planning D, New Political Economy,* and *Review of International Studies.* She is currently working on a book about the politics of the war on terrorist finance.